T0354561

No cure for the TRAVEL BUG

Michael SN Godfrey

For book orders, email orders@traffordpublishing.com.sg

Most Trafford Singapore titles are also available at major online book retailers.

Printed in Singapore.

ISBN: 978-1-4669-3140-4 (sc)
ISBN: 978-1-4669-3141-1 (hc)
ISBN: 978-1-4669-3142-8 (e)

Trafford rev. 11/17/2012

 www.traffordpublishing.com.sg

Singapore
toll-free: 800 101 2656 (Singapore)
Fax: 800 101 2656 (Singapore)

PREFACE

Michael Stephen Newton Godfrey was born in London, England in 1939, and enjoyed an English 'Public School' education after winning a scholarship to Dulwich College in south London.

Trained and qualified as a Quantity Surveyor with a British construction company before spending much of his working life in Nigeria, Afghanistan, Oman, the UAE, Malaysia and Mauritius.

He is a Fellow of the Royal Institute of Chartered Surveyors and an Associate of the Chartered Institute of Arbitrators

The adage "My home is where my toothbrush is", continues to be one that Michael believes in.

He retired in Malaysia in 1999, and enjoys traveling to interesting but out of the way destinations with Lian, his Malaysian wife. It is Lian who does most of the research for the trips.

It is preferable to have a companion when travelling, but the choice can be critical to one's enjoyment of the trip. Lian has made a wonderful travelling companion for me. If Walt Disney made a cartoon of our trips, she would be the lively and fit little Jack Russell, whilst I would be cast as the laid-back Labrador. We thus trade on our strengths, and this reduces the overall stress that can so easily spoil a trip when things do not go to plan.

We continue to be budget conscious on our travels. If we can get a small clean hotel in a good location at half the price of a hotel full of facilities that we are unlikely to use, then we can stay twice as long for the same cost. However, after a few rough days traveling, then a better hotel with crisp white sheets makes a very welcome change, and one appreciates it so much more.

This is Michael's second book in the TRAVEL BUG series, following 'Catch the Travel Bug', and is based on his extensive notes and comments outlining the trials and tribulations of independent travel to places normally thought to be off the beaten track. His goal is to let a reader feel that they have shared the experience of the trip being described, but all from the safety of their armchair.

Each chapter is self-contained and covers a different trip and is not meant to be guidebook.

CONTENTS

CHAPTER 1

Himachal Pradesh—Northern India

Ki Monastery—Spiti Valley.

One person who seems to get respect around the world is the Dalai Lama. We all remember his smile and his glasses.

So when we had the opportunity of attending some lessons he was giving in northern India, we took it.

Lian had been in contact with his office over the Internet, but then heard that a Buddhist group based in Singapore had already arranged for three days of lessons in September. We decided to go with them, but to make our own travel and accommodation arrangements.

So flights were booked and visas obtained, making allowance for a few days to get from Delhi to Dharamsala, and then having a week or more afterwards for further sightseeing.

But for a week or so prior to our departure, there were horrific floods in the areas to the west and the northeast of our destination, and we wondered whether this trip should be aborted.

Delhi.

The 5-hour flight to Delhi went without incident, and despite a speedy immigration procedure, my bag took ages to reach the carousel.

We had no choice but to hire an old Ambassador taxi to take us to the old railway station, but soon found ourselves in a bad traffic jam. All the cars, taxis and buses continue to push and shove, and no one will give way. Their horns never cease.

It was drizzling, but the window wipers only worked once. The driver asked if I smoked, as he wanted to light up. We both shouted "No!"

If only the new overhead railway system had started, but we were told we would have to wait another month for this to happen.

Then the traffic seemed to ease a little, and some progress was being made, so we would not miss our pre-booked train.

The station was a seething mass of people: standing, walking, or sprawled sleeping on the platforms. We struggled up some stairs as our train was waiting at a platform on the other side.

We had booked a 1st class sleeper (two lower berths) with air-conditioning. We inspected a printed sheet of paper stuck to the outside of the carriage, adjacent to a door, and found our names and berth numbers. I crammed our bags under the seats, and Lian set off down the platform to buy some bottled water.

The carriage had seen better days, but we were supplied with two white sheets and blanket.

Two Sikh gentlemen joined us. The elder one owns a factory making nuts and bolts of different types, and his nephew works for him. They were returning home after a business trip.

They both took off their turbans with extreme care in order not to mess up their shape, and laid them side-by-side on a top bunk. The elder then allowed his nephew to roll off his socks and place them in his shoes, whereupon he sat crossed legged like a Maharajah at one end of Lian's bunk.

At 10:30pm the train slowly leaves the station, only twenty minutes late.

We chatted for a while, before Kuldeep gives us his card and says we can call him night or day if we need anything. He then enquired as to whether we wanted to go to sleep. As our answer was in the affirmative, our new friends climbed up onto their own bunks.

The train was to take us to Pathankot, and from there we would continue our journey by road. The train may have been called the Dauladhar Express, but it stopped every few miles to let goods and other trains pass in the other direction, as most of the line is single track.

Our companions left us at dawn, so I did not get to see whether the nephew had the job of putting on his uncle's socks. But I was awake in time to see how they slowly lowered and adjusted the turbans onto their heads, and used the topknot to anchor it. The Sikhs are a very proud people.

So we had a few hours on our own before the train reached Pathankot.

Lian used our heating coil to boil some water to make us some coffee to go with the fruitcake we had brought. The power outlet is only 110volt, so it took a while to boil.

At 9:10am we pulled into Pathankot station, and ten minutes later we were in a taxi on our way to the small village of McLoed

Ganj, where the Dalai Lama has his residence and temple. The village is about 5 miles (8 km) above the town of Dharamsala.

McLoed Ganj and Dharamsala.

The road is narrow and in poor condition. Our driver stops for a rest and a smoke, and Lian buys some freshly fried samosa from a village stall.

We passed through Dharamsala, and arrived in McLoed Ganj in just over 3 hours, before checking into a room at the Akash Hotel. This is run by a German woman and her Kashmiri husband.

The room was comfortable despite the orange walls. From our small balcony we had views across the valley, and when the clouds and mist part, one has great views up a valley. As they recede into the distance, the colour of the mountains become a lighter and lighter grey.

The bathroom has a hot water shower, which we try out. The rain starts, so we rest until it stops, before walking up the steep road into the main town. When we reached the monastery we were frisked and our bags were searched before they let us enter. Even the monks in their dark maroon clothes were searched.

As the sun went down we open our duty free drinks and enjoyed some nuts on our balcony. We looked at the houses clinging to the sides of the steep hills. Most are flat roofed, as in this part of the world owners have the habit of adding another storey as soon as they can afford it. The older pitched roofs are finished with large slate tiles that are laid without the usual horizontal stagger, and the newer ones have corrugated iron sheeting, much of which is rusted.

McLoed Ganj is a very Tibetan oriented village, with the majority of the occupants from Tibetan stock with features quite different from the Indians. Shops sell Tibetan clothes, souvenirs and food. Many Kashmiris have also opened shops here following the troubles they are having in their own state to the north.

It would certainly be fair to say that without the Dalai Lama's presence in Dharamsala and McLoed Ganj, these towns would be mere backwaters.

In the evening we wandered up the road deciding what to eat. In deference to our health, the order of the day seemed to be something vegetarian, and hot in temperature. A pizza seemed a good compromise, and it was.

When we got back to the hotel, a group of musicians were beating tom-toms and playing what looked like an Australian didgeridoo. There was also a guitar in there somewhere.

Would we be able to sleep through this sound barrier? Certainly it was too early to complain.

Our hotel's bedding comprised a highly patterned bottom bed-sheet, and a thick fleece blanket. So we brought out our own cotton sleeping bags to go under the blankets, and were soon in the land of nod.

We had found on the Internet that one of the hotels was said to have a resident bird-watching guide. So we thought we would go and find the 'Eagles Nest', doing some bird-watching on the way.

It was a pleasant stroll up the hill through a pine forest, and an hour later we reached the Himalayan Tea-House on the outskirts of Dharamkot. We pass a worker using a long branch of a tree like a broom, clearing the road of pebbles.

Asked directions from a local, who pointed us to a track to the west. Walked for a long way along the track, that kept to the same contour. We were just about to give up when we met someone who said there was a turn off around the next bend. We found the turning, and the track that started climbing again. Steep and rocky in places, we saw several pieces of broken mud flaps and number plates. Vehicles have been using the route. Soon after passing a small Hindu shrine, we were surprised to come upon another small coffee house, named the 'Rest a While'. A car was there and a couple of motor bikes. A group were sitting in the open and enjoying the surrounding clouds. A dog waggled over to be patted, with it's tail flailing.

Given our new directions, we followed the path to our destination. The dog came with us and led the way. This was strictly a non-vehicular path, but we did see a few hoof prints. A ten-minute walk later and we reached the 'Eagles Nest', comprising a few two-storey buildings set around a lawn.

The owner was kind enough to show us round and give us a cup of tea. The guide we had come to find was not around.

We had come up on the new jeep track as far as the 'Rest a While', and from there we were advised to take a short cut down, using the old mule track.

We set off, this time accompanied by another dog. Met an American couple that are staying at the 'Eagles Nest', and had a chat with them. They advised us to take care, as some of the rocks on the short cut are very slippery.

Just passed the Hindu shrine, when we saw the rocky path. This certainly saved a lot of time, but it was indeed at times slippery.

As we reached the Himalayan Tea-House it started a gentle drizzle and this kept up all the way back to the hotel. Our return journey took us just two hours.

When the rain stopped, we explored a short cut to take us to the main temple, which is located on the other side of a hill. It is a real 'rat run', up a number of sets of steps and alleyways until we reach the summit, and then drops down to the main entrance of the complex. It took us several trips before we could complete the route in either direction without getting lost on the way.

That evening we had a different pizza in a different restaurant. Tried the Kingfisher Strong beer, which turns out to be very palatable, and Lian could share some to make a shandy.

Next morning we decided to visit the Norbulinka Institute, a 9-mile (15km) public bus ride away.

One bus took us down to Dharamsala, and another from there along to within about a kilometre of the Institute.

The road down to Dharamsala passes through a number of army encampments with side roads to army barracks, quarters and messes.

The Norbulinka Institute was set up to keep alive the traditional Tibetan art and skills needed to adorn the monasteries and holy places. Here young Tibetans can learn to paint the holy 'tankas' using natural hand ground pigments, or make them with silk and needlework. The thread is made of horsehair wrapped with coloured fine silk thread.

They also have rooms teaching carving, and a metal-shop making large and complicated Buddha figures from brass and copper sheets. The buildings are set out in a beautifully landscaped area, all designed by a Japanese architect, but in a Tibetan style.

One exhibit not to be missed here is the doll museum. The dolls are dressed in the various ethnic costumes of the many tribes making up Tibet. And there are a surprisingly large number of different tribes.

On the way back to McLoed Ganj, the bus horn was not working, so the driver pulled into the side of the road, and his conductor reached through the bus window and broke off a small twig of a similar diameter to a normal fuse. He then stripped a piece of wire with his bare teeth and wrapped it along the piece of wood, and pushed it into the fuse board. And "voila"— the horn worked again.

In the evening we went to the Carpe Diem restaurant to try their pizza. We took a table on the first floor near the window. Then Lian noticed a big tan coloured dog lying under our table, with his head against the wall. She said he smelt, and asked a waiter to move him or her. But the dog did not want to go, and resisted until it had no more options, when it walked across the room and down the stairs. Then to every ones surprise and laughter, a different black dog appeared and made a beeline for the vacated spot. He too was persuaded to move in the end

We awoke to blue skies and clear views of the mountains. Today is the day we are to meet up with the Singaporean group at 2pm and collect our registration papers etc.

After breakfast we decided to walk the kilometre down the road through the pine forest to have a look at the church 'St.

John's in the Wilderness'. This Anglican church was built in 1852, when the British had a garrison nearby.

There is a memorial to Lord Elgin (James Bruce), who died in 1863 of a heart attack whilst crossing a bridge in the Spiti Valley at the young age of 52. He had already been Ambassador to China, Governor General of Canada, Governor of Jamaica, and finally Viceroy and Governor General of India.

We saw a man sweeping, and he asked if we wanted to go into the church. It turns out that he is the resident priest, but only has one service a week.

They still have some very impressive stained glass windows, and many fascinating plaques on the wall commemorating soldiers. There are so many stories to be told here:

> 'Lieutenant R.D. Angelo, who died in Waziristan, 30th November 1894. Killed in action against the Mahsuds . . . .'

> 'Lieutenant S.R. Master who died in Sima, Upper Burma, 6th January 1893, of wounds received in action against the Kachins . . . .'

> 'Captain J.L. Barry, MBE . . . . who died at Moffat on 21st January 1924, aged 25 years on the eve of his marriage . . . .'

We then strolled along to the graveyard with its 499 graves, and sat and did some contemplation, together with some bird-watching, as the sun warmed our backs. A few cows wandered around and acted as grass cutters. Many of the graves had been vandalised or broken over the years.

We met the priest again, who said he had been there over twenty years. Before that time the place had been abandoned. He stays and sleeps in the church. At first he was kept awake by strange noises and things walking about outside, until they held an exorcism, and from then on the place was quiet and no more damage was done to the graves.

Lessons with His Holiness the Dalai Lama.

At 1:45pm we set off for the Tsuglagkhang Temple to meet the others. Many people had already registered, and we joined a long queue of independent travellers. At last we received our red-ribboned security passes which had our photos on, together with a plastic folder containing nine pages of instructions and information, together with books entitled 'His Holiness Dalai Lama, Southeast Asia Teaching Prayer Book' and 'Commentary on the Thirty Seven Practices of a Bodhisattva' by HH the XIV Dalai Lama. This would be plenty of homework.

We were then asked to hold on for further instructions.

The Singapore group organiser, then asked us to line up behind the relevant numbered flag corresponding to the number shown on the back of our security pass. Each group comprised about 18 persons, and we were in group number 16 of the 17.

Ours was a multinational group: we had several from Singapore, a Bruneian, a few Malaysians, a Frenchman, a Ukranian, a Mexican, another Mexican who actually was a Brit, and ourselves. We were told that we would be entering the teaching hall in strict order and to follow our flags. The order of entry would be changed at each lesson, so we would all have a chance of sitting close to the Dalai Lama. This sounded very fair.

Once back at the hotel I recharged my iPod battery, as we would be sharing this, using the FM radio attachment, whenever translations were made from Tibetan.

It rained all night, but the mountains were at their clearest this morning. The town was full of people and one could almost taste the excitement.

After coffee and carrot cake in the room we set off at 7:15am, taking the short cut to the temple.

There was a very long queue for the women's security, but a much shorter one for the men. The security check was very thorough, and any cameras and telephones were confiscated. All pockets and bags had to be opened for inspection.

As well as the Singaporean group, there were hundreds of monks, nuns and other Tibetans and foreigners who would fill all the areas surrounding the main prayer hall, and some would watch the instructions on close circuit TV screens.

We chatted with our group until it was time to follow our flag up the stairs to the main hall, took off our shoes, and moved into the hall, which was already packed. The whole floor inside was covered with thin mattresses for us to sit on.

One is supposed to sit cross-legged in the lotus position. But my old European knees, ankles and legs are not telescopic, and I had to move my lower anatomy every fifteen minutes or so. Also one is not supposed to point ones feet at the Dalai Lama, as this is considered rude and disrespectful. At a later session I also found out from a senior monk, that neither could I rest the prayer book on the floor, as this also was disrespectful. He would simply pick up the offending book, touch it to the crown of his head, and pass it back to me with a smile and a nod.

The hall had two wide-open doorways each side and two low windows either side of the door. The people sitting outside do therefore have a chance of looking into the main hall and hear what is spoken, even if they cannot see the Dalai Lama. Senior monks have been allocated the main exterior viewing points.

We were seated by 8:15am and the chanting started. A nun on the main raised dais began with "Ohm made padre hum", repeated over and over again in a beautiful clear melodious voice, and we all slowly followed her.

I look around, and could see a civilian guard in the corridor outside armed with a small machine gun. They are certainly taking security very seriously here.

It was nearly 9:30am when the people outside started to stir and stand. The Dalai Lama was coming, walking along the outside corridor, nodding and greeting participants.

He entered the hall, and sits on a small throne at the front of the dais, and addresses us in English. He said that his office had also included some Christians, non-believers, and about twenty Moslem for the lessons.

He said he had met many Moslem priests, and said that the terrorists were not good Moslems. He then said he admired the Christians, as they had brought education to so many people. However the Christians had spoilt things by trying to convert people. He said that one should not convert, but continue to follow one's own religion.

Then some monks came around with small buckets full of small flat loaves and huge kettles of butter tea. They trod between the people and somehow managed to serve without spilling any. This indeed was a small miracle. We had to wait until the Dalai Lama said a short prayer before starting our breakfast. This wait caught out several of those around us.

Speaking again about Buddhism, he considers Tibetan Buddhism to be the most modern of all the major religions, as it is all about today, and does not include a lot of out-dated customs which are not relevant to the 21st century.

At any time he was not sure of his words or the correct definition, he would look at one of the younger monks sitting at the side, who would whisper a prompt, or explanation

The main theme of the lessons is the so-called 'Heart Sutra', a short ancient text, with a major theme of emptiness i.e. 'Form is empty. Emptiness is Form'.

Pretty deep thoughts, and certainly away above my head.

The end of the morning's lesson reverted to Tibetan, so we all rushed to get our FM radios out and tuned into the translator.

At 11:30am he blessed some nuns, and handed them some blessed white scarves before performing a similar action with a grey clad Vietnamese group.

It was time for the lunch break. Our SEA group had a fenced of area where they served us a vegetarian buffet lunch which was surprisingly tasty. Monks came with buckets of food to keep the various serving dishes full.

There was a lot left over, and some of the outsiders were allowed in to take what was left. Our group were paying for the food for all the attendees over the three days, as well as making a contribution to an orphanage.

We were seated again in the Ghompa by 12:30pm and the Dalai Lama continued his lesson from 1:15pm to 3:30pm with a little of the history of Tibetan Buddhism, and the importance of questioning all the early teaching as there were many contradictions. Buddhist shows you a path, but it is up to you whether or not you follow it. He then went on to discuss 'cause and effect', and the concept of truth, stressing the importance of education and continual reading.

At 4pm the groups reassembled to go through what they had learnt, but our path led back to the hotel for a hot coffee and a fruitcake.

Next day, we were up again early to join Group 16.

We were shocked to learn that the 72-year-old Singaporean in our group had passed away the previous evening with a heart attack in his room. By the time he reached the hospital he was gone. He was there with his son, who was one of the official photographers. I suppose it is a good place to die if you are a Buddhist.

The chant was changed this day to "Tayato o muni mumi aha munier swahaa", which sounded very soothing.

Both the morning and afternoon sessions were in Tibetan.

The Dalai Lama announced that on the 3rd day he would be holding a rarely held service, where he would plant a symbolic seed of Buddhism, and then anyone could take any oaths they felt happy with giving. Everyone seemed to be very excited about this, as it would be an honour for us to be present at such an occasion.

He then proceeded to talk about 'The 37 Practices of Bodhisattva', a list of do's and don'ts for a Buddhist.

Then at 3:10pm, he grinned and said in English, "I have finished—so holiday, holiday".

The next evening we would be leaving, so before setting off for the last day of lessons, we checked out of our hotel, and left our bags in their store.

On the way of the short cut, we surprised a mongoose, but it soon scurried away.

Then, as we arrived, the Dalai Lama walked from his house to the prayer hall, where he sat hidden behind a small screen in prayer and meditation. We were led into the hall, and today we have places in the front. We were told to sit quietly in 'noble silence' whilst a nun chanted the mantra.

We had been each given a disc in which was a seed, together with a red ribbon. After 50 minutes, the screen was taken away and the Dali Lama moved to his throne. He then started a very low chant. We were then each handed a few rice grains.

He then talked about the five main vows of never: killing, telling big lies, stealing and consuming alcohol. He suggested that as alcoholic drinks also had a pleasant smell, then perhaps we could just smell them—then his face broke into a wide grin. We could individually choose to omit any of these from our vows. Lian and I looked at each other, and decided to omit the last one.

After another excellent lunch we reconvened to a question and answer session, to be followed by a photo session.

Once again his sense of humour came through strongly.

He was asked one question about having possessions. "Yes", he said, "I have a watch", pulling on its elasticated strap. "and I have shoes—made in China". He himself led the peals of laughter. He then said "We have 10 fingers, but it would look stupid if we had a number of rings on every finger".

There followed a series of photo sessions where we all had the chance to have large group photos with an ever-smiling His Holiness.

It was mid afternoon by the time we finished and said our goodbyes to the others in our group.

Road to Manali.

That evening we set out on the second sector of this holiday. We would be attempting to do a large circular tour, passing through the Spiti Valley, and hoped to be able to obtain the necessary permits which would take us close to the border with Tibet / China. This route is open for only four months in the year, as the rest of the time the valley is cut off due to snow, ice and rains which close the high passes. We would go as far as we could, without having to backtrack. With any luck we could reach Shimla, and from there the journey back to Delhi should be easy.

So we took a small 9-seater bus from McLoed Ganj at about 9pm and arrived in the town of Manali at 5am as dawn was breaking. During the night we had a stop for the driver to rest for half an hour. No toilet facilities, so we had to find somewhere along the road to relieve oneself. The journey was bumpy and uncomfortable.

On arrival, Lian set off to find some accommodation, whilst I looked after the bags. Whist there I was chatting with a man called Gudu who was trying to persuade me to stay at his place in an orchard in Old Manali. He said he would give us transport back to the bus depot whenever we needed it. So we crammed into his car and set off.

It seemed a long way from the town up narrow roads. Then he parked and asked us to follow him. The bags to stay in the car and would be brought to us later. It was just light enough to see him ahead, and we walked as fast as we could down a very narrow pathway, pass some very old houses with stone slate roofs and cattle peering out from the lower storeys. By now Lian was getting very apprehensive and worried. But at long last he turned into a more modern house and announced that we had arrived.

I must say it was a delightful place and we had a big corner bedroom on the first floor, with an excellent attached bathroom. The balcony was wide and we were surrounded with apple trees all ready for harvesting. The orchard is situated in a valley protected by mountains on either side. We could see cascading waterfalls and some snow on the upper levels of the mountains.

We sat on the balcony and enjoyed a cup of 'marsala chai', a milky tea spiced with cinnamon, ginger and cardamom, before taking nice hot showers.

Soon after 8am we took a walk back to the old village. There were so many photo opportunities: the old tumbled down houses, the orchards, the apple collection point where they were being boxed for the long road journey to Delhi, and women doing their laundry at the village well.

Stopped for breakfast at the 'English Bakery'.

All the tourists here seemed to be Israeli. A couple of girls explained that following the compulsory national service, most Israelis take off for a long holiday. India is a favourite destination, and Himachal Pradesh is especially popular.

We continued down through the old village, crossing a bridge, and then taking a delightful short cut through a pine forest to the new town of Manali.

By the time we got back we were tired, and actually got lost for some time taking the last twisting path down to the 'Orchard House'. We asked directions from men who were picking apples in the many orchards, and also those carrying big baskets of apples on their backs, but they did not understand what we wanted, and kept pointing in conflicting directions.

To Kaza and the Spiti Valley.

Gudu had arranged for us to take a 'shared taxi' on to Kaza the next morning. So after tea in our room, we had our torches out to struggle up the path in order to be at the roadside for 5:45am. Gudu's wife carried Lian's bag, but I was on my own. The taxi was half an hour late. We had booked the front seats, being the only ones with any semblance of legroom. Behind us were two rows of four seats, so space is at a premium. Luggage goes on the top. It was 7am before all the passengers had been picked up from surrounding villages, and we were at last on our way.

The road was rough, and zig-zagged its way via hairpin bends up through grass-covered mountains. We were approaching the Rothang Pass. I thought we were there an hour or so later, but no, we could still see the road snaking up into the clouds above us. A number of landslides made the road muddy in places and strictly single file for some distance. Our driver overtook every thing before us: be they cars, lorries or buses. Just sound the horn, flash the lights, and pray to God as we skid around blind corners.

We all wanted a pee stop, and when at last we reached the summit at about 9:30am, there was a general rush off into the cloud and mist to relieve ourselves. We were at 12,600 feet (3,845m).

From there the rough road had slowly dropped by about 2,000 feet (600m), when we stopped a couple of hours later for a food stop for the driver and ourselves. After crossing a river on a Bailey bridge, some enterprising people had build a dry stonewall waist high, and erected an orange tarpaulin tent over it. Here you could buy tea or soft drinks and eat a hot meal. We had a few chapattis that were freshly cooked and singed over a primus stove.

From here the road followed the river valley down, so was much straighter. But then the switchback started as we climbed again to the 14,650 feet (4,470m) Kumjum Pass. We stopped at a stupa complex draped with Tibetan prayer flags. It was windy, but the sky was clear, and at this height our breathing was certainly laboured.

Once again the road followed along the side of a valley, following the river as it flowed down to the Spiti Valley. At the small outpost of Lossar a barrier was raised, and we had to stop and show our passports at the police post.

The Spiti Valley is wide, but with steep rocky sides. The sun was casting beautiful shadows on the rocks as the taxi followed the river, which was now wide and glistening. We passed a few small villages, with all the houses built in the Tibetan style. In the distance we see a beautiful monastery clinging to a conical hill.

Although today's journey was long, we saw some magnificent scenery, with amazing geological and physical features.

It was 5pm when we at long last drove into Kaza. A notice at the only petrol station claims it to be the worlds highest retail garage outlet at 12,270 feet (3,740m).

It was recommended that we stay at the Mandala Hotel in the old part of the town, as it was close to the bus station. We booked for two nights, as in the morning we would have to get the permits that would be necessary if we were to travel any further. The road south would pass quite close to the China / Tibetan border, and thus the security in the area would be very strict.

The room was adequate and we had good views over the valley and the hills behind.

After a cup of coffee in our room, we set off to the new town to try to find where we had to go to obtain the permit. The guide books said that we would have to have the permits registered at the police station, but when we got there the place was in darkness and we could find no-one, so we gave up. On the way back we saw three men, and asked them what time the police station would open. It appears that they were policemen and were returning after having a meal.

The old town has no paved streets and the road meanders around between houses and shops. Walking back in the dark we had to use our torches. We stopped for a meal at a restaurant where the only light was a candle on the table. I ordered fried rice with eggs. The waiter took the order, but later returned to say they had run out of eggs.

Then, when we got back to the hotel, there was no power. This was why everything had been so dark. Due to the altitude, the packaging of a fruitcake we brought with us has blown up like a balloon.

We were woken at 6am just as the sun touches the tip of the hills across the valley.

The voltage is so low that boiling water takes a long time, and you can clearly read the writing on the bottom of a turned on light bulb. As we enjoyed our early morning tea, we tried to plan how long we should stay at each of our future stopovers, assuming we could get back to Delhi in time for our return flight to Malaysia. We would not have any spare time.

By 8am we were out trying to find somewhere open for breakfast. But everywhere they say they only open at 9am, so had chapattis and an omelette in our hotel dining room.

Walked to New Kaza and found the permit office. A small shop opposite had a copying machine, and they were selling application forms.

Being a Monday, there were a number of applicants, as the office had been closed over the weekend. So it took some while for the clerks to copy out all the passport details onto a form and into an exercise book. Then we had to sit and wait and look at the walls. A hand written notice glued to the wall is addressed 'To all Israelis on how to apply for permit'. Some wag had inserted '(and other countries)'. And yes, half the day's applicants were Israelis. Because there were over a dozen applicants, they arranged for the police countersignatures so we did not have to traipse down to the police station.

Permits in hand, we set off for the bus station to check on departure times.

In the afternoon, we joined an Italian man and a French woman and shared a taxi to take us to the Ki Monastery that we have seen perched on top of a conical hill. From there we went to Klibber, a pretty little Tibetan style village that claims to be the highest in the world at 13,800 feet (4,200m).

Since 9am there had been no power in the town, and it only came on for a short period, so dinner was taken by candlelight again. The hotel dining room, one really could not stretch the word to restaurant, claimed there were no vegetables in the market but they did have chicken curry. This sounded good, but with the power problems they were having, the refrigeration could have been a problem. So we settled for chapattis and omelette.

Still no power when we woke at 6am, but Lian managed to get hot water from the kitchen where they were using gas cylinders.

As we waited, we heard that the road from Manali, where we had just come from, was now closed to traffic due to the weather conditions; so many people in Kaza would now have to travel back in the other direction, making a several day trip around the big circle.

By 6:45am Lian was queuing for the bus ticket office to open at 7am, so we managed to get our preferred seats so maximizing legroom. The old bus was parked, and a mechanic was lying on his back under the engine compartment. It looked like he had a hammer in his hand, so obviously he was very experienced. At 7:30am the bus goes off to fill its diesel tank, so it was past 8am when we rumbled off on our 2-hour trip to the small village of Tabo.

The bus was full, with many standing, and as people flagged down the bus, it became more and more full, and flies were everywhere.

Tabo.

On arrival in Tabo, I guarded our luggage, whilst Lian and the French woman—Caroline, went off in search of accommodation. They did an excellent job, and found The Dewadren Retreat, the best in town. Caroline was impressed with Lian's negotiating skills, as we enjoyed a very reasonable rate. The room was pleasant with great views of the monastery and the valley with the hills behind, and had a small but useable balcony.

Whist we were in McLoed Ganj, Lian had been given the name of one of the monks here, and we were told to contact him. So when we walked to the monastery, we mentioned his name, Geshi Thamo Kalsang, and a monk took us into a courtyard garden area, then scurried off. Geshi came down and asked us into his room, where we were given mango juice to drink. He had just got back from Daramsala himself, and had been at His Holiness's lessons.

Geshi is the 'debating teacher' and we later found he is the number two to the Abbot.

The monastery was founded in 996AD, and is said to be the oldest functioning monastery in the country. It has been made an UNESCO site, and it is said that the Dalai Lama will eventually retire here.

It was time to look around. The old monastery is in a walled area and comprises a number of single storey buildings, stupas and raised areas. It is unlike any we had seen before: the walls have no windows, and the external walls are finished in mud plaster, and are not painted. Small entrance doors are padlocked, but once one is taken in, it is hard to believe what one is seeing. The walls and ceilings are covered with holy paintings and the carved Buddha figures seem to be alive as they protrude into the gloom. We have our own powerful torches, and the place seems alive as we swing the beam across. Most of the colours are still rich. The main temple has seating for the praying monks. Another wonderful room opens from the main prayer hall, and yet another room opens off from this. The only natural light is from small skylights set into the roof, and these cast a magical glow into the rooms.

During history, several invading armies, including the Sikhs, had taken Tabo but somehow these understated buildings had kept their secrets well.

We were taken into a number of other eight small temples, and each was a gem. What a pity that photography is strictly forbidden. Thus we had no option but to purchase a guidebook that contains just some of the magnificent artworks.

In the afternoon, we decided to walk up to some caves just above the town. But the access was steep and rocky, and after the first one we went back down to the monastery.

In the yard were a number of ladies, sitting on a timber platform. Lian went over to ask if she could take some photos. The ladies belonged to a women's union or group, and were holding their elections, as votes were being counted. Soon Lian was communicating with them, and took a number of photos whilst I kept well away. But when I offered to take a group photo of them with Lian, using Lian's camera, there was no objection. I then retreated, only to be called back by the women, who wanted a group photo with me. An elderly one really held on to me tightly, and there was a lot of laughter and giggles. I made a quick count of twenty-two women and a couple of children.

They then insisted I sit with them and partake from the kettles of salty milk tea they were passing around. It was a nice experience. And later that afternoon or the next morning, we would see the same women around the town, and they would laugh and wave to us as if we were long time friends.

At about 5pm we went back to the new monastery, and met Geshi who was supervising six young monks in their 'debating' lesson. It seems that there are seventy monks living at the Tabo monastery.

Back at the hotel we asked Caroline to join us for sun-downers on the balcony. Lian finished off the Bristol Cream, and Caroline and I made do with some of our duty free Johnny Walker Black Label.

We could see over the apple orchards with their branches bowed down with the ripe fruit. These trees belong to the monastery, which benefits from the income.

Once again there was no electricity when we woke up, but we did have a wonderful view. It was 6:15 am by the time we reached the new monastery, and we slipped into the prayer hall. We stayed for about 15-minutes as they continued the rhymic chanting. They read their scriptures, slowly turning over the wide but short single pages written in Tibetan. Geshi nodded his acknowledgement to us. His number two position in the monastery was confirmed by the strict pecking order of the serving of the tea to the monks during their service.

To Shimla.

The hotel manager tells us that the bus would be coming at 9am, even though yesterday it only arrived at 10am. We suspect that this is to give him time to clean up the room prior to other potential guests arriving.

The bus was half empty when it arrived at 9:40am, and the conductor allowed us to stack our bags next to the driver instead of having to put them on the roof. We sat on the back seat, and I had my legs stretched down the corridor. But the road is quite rough and we get bounced about a bit, as we are well aft of the rear axle. As soon as one person got off from one of our 'preferred seats,' I moved down to take it. The conductor realized our intention, and asked the man sitting beside me to move and make way for Lian. It was all a little embarrassing, and the man did not appear to be too put out.

The driver had a half hour break at a small village, and we bought fresh parattas with potato fillings straight off the fire

The bus stopped at a check post, and we joined the queue for our permits to be checked and stamped. The policeman said "Don't you remember me?" It turned out that he was one of the policemen we had met in Kaza a few days before when we tried to find the police station. He certainly had a good memory for faces, as it was quite dark when we had met.

Soon after the bus stopped following the river, and started its switchback way up and over a pass. Made a diversion to one small village in order to deliver and collect sacks of post.

Then back to following a river and through an impressive gorge. The road is narrow, and the bus passes oncoming buses and lorries with only inches to spare. There is a rock face one side and a sheer drop the other.

The bus seems to have a very tight turning circle, and the driver takes hairpin bends with hardly a touch on his brakes. The tyres are literally within inches of a sheer drop. His skill and confidence is very impressive. Bad drivers on these roads soon become dead drivers.

It is past 3pm when we reach the next check post, and soon after the driver has another break at the village of Spillo. We have now left the Spiti Valley and are in Kinnaur. The men all wear a little beige coloured pillbox hat with half the vertical sides covered with green felt. A big pile of flat packed cardboard apple boxes cover half the street. They are being moved into one of the shops.

The bus is now filled to overflowing, and somehow the conductor has managed to keep our two seats for us. A man is asleep on the floor in front of us, quite oblivious of the men and women standing over him. The conductor locks the door so no more passengers can squeeze their way on.

The bus now follows a steep gorge shaped valley. We stop for sometime whilst a rock fall is cleared, and as we get lower the hillsides are forested with pine trees.

It was gone 6pm when the bus arrived at the town of Rekong Peo. The 8.1/2-hour journey had been tiring, but at no time did we nod off, as there was so much to see and try to absorb.

The bus station was at the highest part of the town. I stood under the porch of the post office guarding our things whilst Lian set off in a light drizzle to find some accommodation. When she returned she said she had seen two. One was bad and the other was quite disgusting, and suggested we take a night bus out as it would be leaving within an hour. A night trip on these now wet mountain roads did not appeal, as it would be very dangerous. So we set off for the better of the two. At least we had our own sleeping sheets to protect us.

It was still dark when next morning we left the Sairag Hotel in order to catch the early bus to Shimla. We bought tickets for our favourite seats, and waited for the bus to arrive. The hills around us were covered with fresh snow.

Imagine our surprise to find that the conductor and the driver were the ones we had the previous day, so we were greeted by a lot of handshakes and smiles. As we left at 6am, the conductor explained to the other passenger all he knew about us.

A major dam and hydro powered generating station is under construction, and so the unpaved road has at least been widened a little to enable large loads to be brought in.

After one bumpy patch, a bag of apples falls on my head from the overhead rack. Quite apt, as my third Christian name is Newton.

By mid-day, we are on a tarmac road with a white line down the centre, and a signpost shows that Shimla is only 110km away. The bus is full by now, and does not stop for passengers trying to flag down the bus.

Lorry after lorry is overloaded as they take boxes of apples down to Shimla and onwards for export.

It was past 6pm when at long last we reach the bus station in Shimla.

Shimla.

Shimla is a town cascading down a steep hillside. We were forced to take a taxi to find the hotel that we had been recommended. This cost more than the days bus ride, as the taxi drivers have a strong union. The roads are narrow and zig-zag up and down the hill. It took more than 5 miles (8km) to do what should be a half-mile (1km) journey as the crow flies. The driver got lost a couple of times, but at last we reached the Doegar Hotel, which we found to be very well located if you walk, despite the long taxi journey.

We took a room with a great view over the town. The only problem was that the windows were all covered with mesh grills. Only later did we appreciate that this was to keep the monkeys out. These big macaques have the run of the town and think nothing of a smash and grab raid on any food left around.

The walls of our room were covered with timber panels and the ceiling was mirrored. Quite kinky, but the bathroom was good. At roof level was a big verandah, with a 'to die for' panorama.

We firstly enjoyed a long hot shower, and then went up to the roof verandah to finish off the rest of my whiskey, which had unfortunately leaked a little during the journey.

Next morning we were up at dawn with cameras and binoculars to enjoy tea and then coffee on the rooftop. Watched the sun clip the top of the hills and slowly make its way down over the huddled cascading rooftops. A truly magical time.

Christchurch is at our level, and through our binoculars we spot the bus station and try to trace the taxis route. But to no avail as the road must go around the hill behind us through this sprawling town.

We walk along past Christchurch, and onto a wide paved area on the ridge. We pass very colonially styled government offices left over from the time when Shimla was the summer centre of government for all India.

A part of a notice outside the Railway Office about the history of Shimla is worth quoting:

> . . . . In 1864, under the Viceroyalty of John Lawrence, Simla was officially declared as the 'Summer Capital' of the British Empire in India—a status it retained up to Indian Independence in 1947. Interestingly, the Government of India ended up spending more time in the little town than in the 'real' capitals—Kolkata (earlier Calcutta) and later Delhi . . . . . And during this period, a staggering one-fifth of the human race was ruled from these heights as the jurisdiction of the Indian Empire extended from Aden in the west, to Mynammar (earlier Burma) in the east . . . . .

At the railway office, we bought our rail tickets to Delhi for the next morning. Firstly on the famed 'Toy Train' as far as Kalka, from where we would change to the normal gauged train to Delhi.

That night I had a bit of a scare. I woke in the night with a loose tummy and had a run for the bathroom. But as well as the normal 'squits', there was a lot of blood in the pan, and when I returned to the bed I saw a big pool of blood. I passed blood a number of times, and Lian arranged with reception to get a car to take me to the hospital, which is the main teaching hospital for Himachal Pradesh.

The emergency area was a bit of an eye-opener for me. On the way in I spotted the nearest toilet, and had to make one run there during my fairly short wait. The main room was crammed with beds: many patients were on drips, and a number were being stretchered in following a road accident, and some had nasty head wounds. Someone was crying in pain.

Saw a young intern who took my blood pressure and made a diagnosis. However I had to wait for the senior doctor to come and check this. He was very thorough, and I lay on a bench whilst he pressed and prodded. He said it was bacillary dysentery, and gave me something to close my bowels and some strong antibiotics. He insisted that I also take a lot of electrolytes to replace the salts I had been loosing. He said it would be OK to take the train in about 7 hours time, but at the time I certainly had my doubts. However, by 9am the heavy diarrhoea had stopped.

We considered staying an extra day in Shimla, then flying to Delhi, but heard that there were delays on the flight due to the weather conditions, and if the flight is cancelled, they simply put you on the train anyway.

To Delhi.

So with some apprehension we took a taxi to the station and settled into the 'toy train' carriage. The accommodation is fairly basic, with plastic covered bench seats. And more importantly there is a nearby toilet.

The views were magnificent, and we passed through countless rocky tunnels.

On the train we got talking to a couple of English chaps who were on a motorcycling holiday. One was the leader and guide, and said he did photography for Lonely Planet. They come to India and hire Royal Enfield Bullet motorcycles. This manufacturer has long gone from the UK scene, but the motorcycles have been made in India under licence. Although a 1950's design, the men say it is ideal for touring in India with its dirt roads and potholes. They say the modern Japanese motorcycles are too high revving and are inclined to spin their wheels and so skid too easily. We were able to get a good recommendation for our hotel stay in Delhi. At one small station they got off as they had motorbikes waiting for them for the drive to Kolka where they would join the train.

Arriving at Kolka at after 5.1/4 hours, I saw a train marked for Delhi, and had to wait some time as it was late leaving. We joined the first class, air-conditioned carriage and settled in.

Then, when a conductor came round to check the tickets, he said we were on the wrong train, and said we had to pay again with a 100% surcharge. Or we could get off at the next small station. We could get a refund on our ticket at Delhi.

This just about wiped out our local cash.

Seems there had been another train waiting on another platform at Kolka.

At Delhi they said it would take some time to get the refund, and we had no spare time.

Reached Delhi station after a 4-hour journey. Outside the station it was a madhouse. The taxis literally wanted to 'take us for a ride'. So we crammed into a motorised trishaw, and the driver shot off like a bat out of hell down a series of dark alleys. I was sure we were about to be mugged. "Short-cut" he announced as we skidded into the side of a traffic jam. He then had an argument with a taxi, which nearly came to fisticuffs. The taxi turned and went the wrong way down the one-way street with our driver shouting and chasing after him and trying to ram him. Lian was also shouting, telling the driver not to fight. He must certainly have been on some fairly strong drugs.

He calmed down a little, but was determined to get wherever he was taking us at great speed.

At least this experience was ensuring that my bowels were kept well clenched.

Then to our relief he pulled up in front of the hotel that had been recommended. In rather a squalid part of town, but Billa's Jvoti Mahal Guest House was a very pleasant hotel.

It had an inner courtyard with arches in the Mogul style. Life size carved figures stood or sat around the corridors, with old carved furniture. The room was well decorated in similar style, and the sheets were white and clean. For the first time on our trip we used the hotels sheets instead of those we brought with us.

My tummy problem was still there, but the medicines were certainly doing their duty.

We decided that we would spend the next morning resting in our room rather than doing a lot of sight seeing, although we did later have a walk around the local market once the rain had stopped. This proved to be a sensible decision as some Taiwanese tourist were shot that morning close by the Red Fort.

Early that evening, we took a taxi to the airport and had a pleasant flight back to Kuala Lumpur.

CHAPTER 2

Indonesia: Bali—a tennis tournament and the Bali Starling

Pair of the rare Bali Starlings.

It was over 22 years since Lian and I last visited Bali. That was on our honeymoon, and so perhaps we saw everything then through the proverbial rose-tinted spectacles.

A good golf buddy of mine was running the annual WTA Tour for this part of the world, and so had invited most of the top ladies tennis players for the Wismilak International Tournament being held in Bali. The players that year included both the French and the US Open champions.

He and his wife suggested we might like to join the volunteers helping to run the tournament. They could arrange reasonable hotel rates, and outfits and meals would be provided. It seemed to fit into our plans when we spotted a three-day tour to Bali, with an opportunity to extend the return flight for a further week.

The hotel provided by the tour was located superbly right on Kuta beach next to the Hard Rock Hotel, but was otherwise nothing to shout about. The last time we saw Kuta, it was during the monsoon; the beach was completely covered by rubbish and the place was pretty tacky. Today the streets are lined with hotels, shops, and trendy cafes, with the beach right across the road. Stunning sunsets, and one can watch world-class surfing.

That year the tournament was being held at the Grand Hyatt Hotel in Nusa Dua, an area at the southern tip of the island, which was an area allocated for 5-star hotels. The idea was to have the hotels where they would have the minimum impact on the Balinese.

The hotel was certainly very grand with a sprawling tropical landscape. But it was just too big and spread out for our taste. After our three days in Kuta, we moved into a really nice little hotel just north of Nusa Dua, which was being used by the press and media covering the tournament. It also better suited our budget. We enjoyed a shuttle service to and fro the Hyatt.

We had no idea what our duties might be. We were appointed as 'ushers', and our duty was to man the visitors entrances on the three courts, check tickets, and make sure that people could only enter and exit during the change of ends, and stop smoking. Nothing too onerous and we get to enjoy the games.

Security was very tight at the Hyatt following a recent Jakarta bombing. In spite of having security passes, our bags were carefully searched and we had to pass a metal detector every time we went into the tournament area.

The matches started each afternoon at 3pm and usually went on until about 11pm. So we would have lunch prior to the start, and then took turns to have a dinner break. The food provided was extremely palatable.

Our mornings were free, and we managed to explore the area and visit Tanjung Sari in Sanur, where we had stayed during our honeymoon. Did some bird-watching here and spotted six Lesser Frigate Birds flying high under the scorching sun.

An endangered bird found only in Bali was on our 'must see' list. On the brink of extinction, there are only approximately thirty-five Bali Starlings (*leucopsar rothchildi*) living in the wild. The internationally supported Bali Starling project is attempting to rebuild the population by captive breeding, and then releasing the young birds into the wild.

The Bali Starling The Bali Starling is the size of an English blackbird. It is a snowy white, with an obvious crest, black wing tips and tip of tail and has blue bare skin around the eye. It lives in the dry scrubby forest of the Bali Barat National Park, at the far north west of the island.

Once the tennis tournament finished, we hired a car and driver for three days, and set off for the west end of Bali and the small town of Gilimanuk where the main ferry to West Java is located. One can see Java from the jetty. Initially, we were told that we would have to take a boat and a guide to the northern tip of Teluk Telor in order to have any chance of seeing the bird, or to take a guide and trek five miles (8km) each way.

We stopped at the Park office at about mid-day on the Sunday. The offices were closed, and would also be closed on the Monday for the local elections. A couple of men were sitting talking. One turned out to be a guide and said he could take us to see the bird, but he would have to check and get permission. So we drove to find the Chief Forest Officer, but he was not in. After some negotiation, the guide said he would pick us up at 6am the next morning and we would go in by motorbike, and it would take an hour.

At 6am he arrived, but no second motorbike. Then along came a man in army uniform on a trials type motorbike. He had a big dagger on his belt, and a sub-machine gun strung across his chest. His badges indicated he was a 'forest policeman'. In fact the area where the birds live is guarded against poachers, as the birds are very valuable (US$ 4,000) on the black market.

I was given no safety helmet, and the motorbike had a broken footrest. Off we went. The first couple of miles were on tarmac. Then came a dirt track that became narrower and narrower. My knees stuck out a bit, and were often brushing the bushes. I also had to keep alert whenever we went under a low branch, or I would soon be sitting on my arse on the hard ground. The track was very twisty, and the undergrowth was dry and thorny. A couple of times thorny branches snatched off my hat. Some areas were mangrove, and were pitted with crab holes. We surprised a few Green Jungle Fowl, Button Quails, two Barking Deer, a family group of black Silver-leaf Monkeys/Langurs, and a large Monitor Lizard.

Suddenly we came across a fenced compound with watchtowers. Two layers of high chain link fencing with barbed wire at the top. We could see forms sleeping on raised platforms with thatching to the roof. Then in the middle one had glimpses of fenced cages with white birds in. This must be the guarded captive breeding area for the Bali Starlings. Our two motorcycles did not stop.

At one time out path was blocked with hanging lianas. The Forest Ranger and our guide spent some time looking and feeling around in the leaf litter and the lianas. Checking for booby-traps? If so, who set them? We did not ask.

Another half an hour and we arrived at a hut by the beach. This was the forest guard's sleeping quarters. Time to stretch our legs and have a pee. Lian thought she saw a white bird fly into a tree. But before she had the chance to raise her binoculars it had flown.

We walked inland for some way up the hill to a wooden spotting tower. The ground was rocky and the scrub dry and thorny. There were few tall acacia type trees. The guide then took us back down, as he thought there was a better chance nearer the beach, as the birds tend to go inland only in the wet season.

Then we saw one Bali Starling foraging for food in a large acacia tree. A second bird joined it, and we had reasonable views through our binoculars.

Time to search for Beach Thick-knees along the rocky shoreline. Found three, and watched them feeding before we walked pass the mangroves to search out some other species.

We returned to the ranger station and found a couple of the Bali Starlings even closer in a tree. I very slowly crept nearer and nearer, and then to my delight they both sat side-by-side facing me. They preened, and pushed against each other, and one kept bobbing up and down. The other one had a very fine crest. They certainly gave the appearance of a couple near mating. Yes—I did get a lot on video.

In the meantime Lian had gone for a pee, and found a pair of the birds in a tree right above her. Lian said she did not know whether to use her binoculars before or after zipping up her slacks. At first she thought it was the pair that I had been filming, but then saw that I was still at it. So there were at least four Bali Starlings in the vicinity.

The guard had mended the footrest of his motorcycle, but after the first few bumps it fell apart again. But having had such a successful visit took most of the discomfort away.

That afternoon we enjoyed the pleasure of riding in a car, when we went along the north coast, and then south to the hill town of Ubud. There we found a really delightful cottage in a typical Balinese garden. A Javan Kingfisher came both mornings to sit near the garden wall We took some gentle walks through the terraced padi fields and it was very relaxing. During our visit we saw over fifty species of birds.

In the 80's, we had seen beautiful bare breasted maidens bathing in the roadside streams. On this visit I saw only one, and unfortunately I think it was either the same girl, or her mother.

Previously I had told people that if God lived anywhere in our world, he probably resided in Bali. It is not really surprising that the place has changed and become more materialistic. Religion is still very important to the Balinese, and this is seen especially in the small villages. Everywhere one goes one sees small woven plates filled with flowers and offerings.

However, now I think that God has probably emigrated to Tibet, and only visits Bali for his holidays.

CHAPTER 3

Indonesia: 'Son of Krakatoa'

With Lian on the side of 'Anak Krakatoa'.

As a schoolboy, I had heard of two volcanoes. One was Mount Vesuvius, that had destroyed Pompeii, and the other was the rather mythically named Krakatoa, that had blown itself into smithereens somewhere in the far-east.

So the word Krakatoa joins those other mysterious place names such as Kathmandu, Timbuktu, Mandalay, Galapagos and Easter Island. Places we know exist, but may not immediately be able to pinpoint on the world map.

Between Sumatra and Java in Indonesia are the narrow Sundra Straits, and it is at the mouth of these straits lay the group of volcanoes known as Krakatoa.

The 750 mile (1,200 km) long island of Sumatra in Indonesia, lies approximately north / south, with the adjacent island of Java lying approximately east / west, and continuing for over 1,250 mile (2,000 km) in a string of islands including Bali, Lombok, Sumbawa, Flores and Timor.

And the so called 'rim of fire' runs either offshore or along this string of islands as the Indo-Australian plate slowly moves under them.

Nowadays the majority of shipping uses the Straits of Malacca, which lie between Sumatra and Malaysia. However, in Dutch colonial times the Sundra straits used to be an important shipping route from the Indian Ocean to the Indonesian spice-islands and onwards to China.

Many ships would daily pass close to Krakatoa, so when it started to rumble in early 1883, it was all well documented both by the passing captains and the Dutch administrators. Then, at 10:02am on the 27th of August 1883, it erupted as the largest explosion ever experienced by man, and this was followed by a tsunami that killed thousands.

For further reading, I can only recommend that you read Simon Winchester's, 'Krakatoa'. This extremely well documented book brings to life the whole fascinating history of Krakatoa, when six cubic miles of rock simply disappeared into the air.

So what happened to Krakatoa after it disappeared? Well, it seems that it appeared above the surface a few times, but was soon destroyed by the waves and strong tides. But then, in about 1927, Anak Krakatoa (The Son of Krakatoa) rose again from the seabed and was able to resist the sea's action. It continued to grow and is now approximately 860 feet (263m) high, and growing at a rate of 5 inches (12cm) a week.

So we thought that, if it is safe, it might be worth a visit. The volcano is situated approximately 32 miles (50 km) off shore. So how do we get there, and how long would it take? And would we be allowed on shore, and could we reach the top?

You can read all the guidebooks, but they are not up to date. As usual, there is really only one way to find out.

Go there and 'suck it and see'.

We did find that 'Google Earth' was extremely helpful, as we were able to check out the elevations, and the sizes and distance from the surrounding islands that form the rim of what had been a much larger volcano than Krakatoa.

So in June we took an AirAsia flight from Kuala Lumpur to the Indonesian capital of Jakarta on the island of Java.

After the two-hour flight, we landed at 1am local time, and I paid for my 'visa on arrival'. As a Malaysian, there was no visa requirement for Lian.

Our destination was to be the tourist town of Carita on the western shore of Java. As this would take at least two bus journeys, Lian started some long negotiations with the airport taxi drivers whilst I sat quietly doing some Sudokus. The price steadily dropped and someone phoned an unlicensed taxi whose driver was willing to do the job, as he had family in a nearby village.

So an hour later we set off westwards on a two-lane highway. The road surface was very bad, but at least they were carrying out a lot of repair works. Traffic was very heavy, with many lorries on their way to the port for the ferry crossing over to southern Sumatra. The road then turns southwards along the western shore, and traffic was much quieter.

On the way south the driver stopped for a cigarette, and pointed out the islands of Krakatoa in the distance.

We reached Carlita by 4:45pm, but it took another hour before we found accommodation to suit our budget. One problem we found was that it was the school holidays period, and many people from Jakarta bring their children down for a week by the seaside. So the daily hotel rates are substantially increased from the usual mid-week rates.

Hotel Prameski is a small family run hotel, and we had a room overlooking a Balinese inspired garden, with carved walls lined with gods and 'apsaras'. During our search for a hotel, we had been joined by a colourful tousle-haired man, who said he had a boat, and could get us out to Krakatoa. Usually, I do not like these pushy chaps, but in this case I explained to Lian that rightly or wrongly, "I liked the cut of his jib", and so asked him to come back later.

Once we had settled in and had a shower, we sat down with Saardi and Kapal, his assistant boatman, to see what he could offer. He claimed to have a speedboat with fairly new twin 40HP outboards, and could reach the volcano in one and a quarter hours. The price could be cheaper with only one engine. However, with 30 miles (50km) each way, there was no way I would want to trust a single engine.

Following a lot of negotiation and laughter, we agreed on a lump sum price of 1.9 million Indonesian rupiah (200 US$). He would include packed food, and a thermos of hot water so we could make some coffee. It was dark by now, so an inspection of the boat was too late, so he left on his motorbike to bring back some photographs of his speedboat. We agreed on an early start, as the sea might be calmer, and any climb cooler.

Then Saardi said he would like an advance, enough to buy petrol for the journey, so we agreed on a sum and got him to sign for it. He would pick us up the next morning at 6am.

We were up at 5:30am, and pleasantly surprised to find Saardi ready and waiting for us, as good time keeping is not a common attribute in this part of the world.

We then followed him down the road for a 100 yards (100m) or so, and thence into a small hotel that had it's own small jetty.

As we arrived we saw quite a small speedboat nose it's way into the jetty.

It certainly looked somewhat smaller than the boat in the photo we had been shown the previous evening. Saardi claimed that this was because the boat had just been painted before the photo had been taken. He considered this to be a completely reasonable explanation for the shrinking size of the boat.

A man fishing from the jetty said "Hati hati" which means, 'Be careful'.

Why would he say that? Was this an omen?

It was a fibreglass boat, with a covered cabin area shielding three forward facing seats for two passengers and the captain. A canvas sunshade over the stern area covered benches each side that could each seat 3 passengers. But it did have two 40hp Yamaha engines. We were introduced to captain Samsuri.

So it was 6:15am as we nosed our way around the stone breakwater, and headed N.W. out into the Sundra Staits. Dawn had broken, and the sun was slowly rising over the old volcanic mountains to the east of the town. The sea was calm with just a slight swell. Then, after 3/4 of an hour, we seemed to reach deeper water, and the small boat started to slap into the small waves and the boat shuddered. Does fibreglass suffer from fatigue in the same way as an aluminium aircraft frame? It was too late to worry now.

We could now see the large island of Rakata ahead, with steep conical slopes in typical volcano shape rising to over 2,000 feet (600m) There were low cliffs at sea level, making any landing there difficult. Beyond it we could now clearly see Anak Krakatoa, with the 400 feet (120m) high islands of Pulau Krakatoa Kitjil to it's right, and with Pulau Sertung in the distance behind.

From Google Earth, we had noted that Anak Krakatoa had now grown to about 860 feet (263m) high.

After about an hour and twenty-five minutes, we were in rougher water between the tallest island of Rakata and Pulau Krakatoa Kitjil, and had excellent views of Anak Krakatoa, one and a half miles (2.1/2km) ahead of us.

The whole island was dark brown, apart from a slash of green vegetation at sea level to our right, a large area of white on the volcano's side, and with steam / smoke billowing from the top and a few areas on the side. The white side looked like an area of melting snow, but was made up of salts residue from the evaporating steam.

Our boat turned eastwards and at 7:45am we nosed up onto the black sand beach as we landed on the eastern side. There were trees and bushes in profusion. A concrete signboard reads 'Cagar Alam Krakatoa', and thus announces that we had landed in the Krakatoa National Park, and that this was an UNESCO Work Heritage Park. Another board showed a diagram of Krakatoa pre and after 1883.

Three French-speaking people appeared to have spent the night on the island, but soon packed their hammocks and returned to the mainland.

Saardi set off at a good pace past the rather derelict covered shelter, and we followed him through the woods. It was surprising that so many species of plants had established so well. Soon the path started to rise as we followed the well-worn track.

I had brought my trekking boots on shore with me, but decided to leave them at one of the timber markers, and continue in my sports shoe. I noticed that Saardi was still bare footed.

At the top a long steep slope, we saw what had obviously been a small meteorological station. But most of the wire fencing had been flattened, and the solar panels smashed. My first thought was why would vandals do such a thing? Then I realised that the volcano itself had done this. Rocks still lay on the shattered panels.

We were on a moonscape ridge, which dropped into a shallow valley before rising steeply all the way to the summit. On this ridge were a couple of concreted benchmarks, which I assume are used to record the volcanoes growth. Steam was blowing hard from a crevice below us. We went to inspect the 'snow' on the surface, and found that the surface in these areas was quite hot to the touch. The white sediment has a yellowish hue in places, but did not smell of sulphur. In places there were also some bright coral red stones.

The weather was fine, and we had good views across to the vertical face of Rakata, where over half of the island had disappeared in the Krakatoa explosion.

Even at 475 feet (144m) above sea level, the wind started blowing hard and was flapping my trouser legs.

It was obvious to us that climbing any further might be risky, so we mooched about, taking photos and videos, and picked up a couple of small pieces if rock as souvenirs.

Below us we saw a pair of Wood Swallows swooping around with their distinctive white rumps. Then Lian spotted a small hawk wheeling above us near the volcano's cone. It had a dark cap and a rufous chest and belly. We later identified this as an Oriental Hobby.

We returned to the shoreline, picking up my boots on the way, and sat in the covered shed to enjoy our rice and vegetable breakfast of 'nasi udek', a Sudranese speciality.

Before leaving we took the boat right around the one and a half mile (2.2km) diameter island. The northern and western sides appeared far more active, with the summit steam having a reddish hue. More disturbing was a long line of steam venting from a level about 55 yards (50m) below the summit. This is obviously on a weakened fault line, and we could imagine that the whole area above it could easily be thrown sky high and rain down upon us.

Although the wind had come up, and the first part of the return journey quite choppy, we were both on a bit of a high and enjoyed the sight and sound of the twin engines and the wake with this iconic island in the background. Slowly it was lost from view in the haze and the shoreline came into view again.

I looked at our three companions, and daydreamed that they and their forefathers had been pirates. The daydream finished as we reached our jetty and we settled up with our captain and guide.

Our time on Krakatoa had certainly been a most memorable experience, and one we will not easily forget.

In the afternoon we had a look at what Caritas had to offer. There appeared to be 3 or 4 large car parks catering for local visitors. Some housed busloads of day-trippers from Jakarta.

The visitors all went swimming, with the locals making money by hiring inflated car tyres, or giving 'banana boat' rides, where the day trippers sit on a long inflated tube towed by a speed boat. Then they all crowd into the hired changing rooms.

A big handball competition is in progress. And the people eat and laugh, and eat, and eat, and have a thoroughly good time.

We left Carita the next morning, and after nearly ten hours in buses, arrived for a few days in Bandung, a town up in the hills, to the east of Jakarta.

CHAPTER 4

China: Macau & Southern China

Limestone hills at Yangshuo.

Macau.

It was early January, and having just recovered from the New Year festivities we took the early evening flight to Macau, arriving just before midnight. No problems with immigration, and we took a taxi to the London Hotel, where we had made a booking on the Internet.

The taxi driver said he knew a better place, but I insisted on going to the hotel we had designated. We took out our bags, paid him, and off he went.

A small dingy reception area greeted us, with a staircase opposite the entrance door. The staircase was lined with young ladies sitting on the steps, many wearing thigh length boots.

Should I have listened to the taxi driver? By now it was 1am, and road outside was dark and there was little hope of finding another taxi.

"Lets see the room, and if it's clean, we stay". It was just passable and had plenty of hot water. We stayed.

By 8am we were out and checking other hotels. Found an acceptable one on the waterfront of the inner harbour, and after a rather poor Dim Sum breakfast, checked out, and carried our bags to the Macau Masters Hotel.

In Macau the hotels seem to have different rates for the same room, depending on the day of the week. Friday is more expensive than mid-week, with Saturday topping the expense list.

Macau is really a very small place, and you can walk anywhere. They also have a very good public bus service. The main island is approximately 2.1/2 miles x 1.1/4 miles (4 km x 2km). The bus routes all seem to be circular and thread down small streets, which is quite unlike routes in England where the bus returns by the same route that it took on it's outward journey. Within Macau you pay a set fee whenever you get onto a bus, as distance does not matter. You either drop the exact coins into a box, with no change given, or use a touch card that can be purchased outside.

We started our morning walk along streets lined with traditional Chinese shops, until we came to the Church of St. Paul. Only the front façade of the College of the Mother of God remains, as the rest was burnt down many years before.

Adjacent is the old Monte Fortress, which also houses the Museum of Macau. The museum was very good and shows the history of Macau both pre and after the arrival of the Portuguese, and now its return to China. It also explained the significance of all the statues and carvings on the St. Paul's façade, which meant we had to visit that again. From the battlements of the fort we had good views over Macau. We could clearly see the Chinese coast on the other side of the inner harbour even though it was a little misty.

All the streets have their names displayed on ceramic wall plates. On top is the name in Chinese characters, with Portuguese names below. The vast majority of inhabitants are Chinese, and speak Cantonese and / or Mandarin. Quite a few spoke some English, and we were often stopped so someone could practice his or her English on us.

We continued our walk, seeing the mansion of the Consul General of Portugal. The Macau Cathedral had an impressive nativity scene inside, a flat ceiling, but was spoilt by unpleasant vertical fluorescent lighting. On the other-hand, the Church of St. Dominic had good natural lighting and an impressive altarpiece.

We were now in the main town square, Senate Square, with some impressive old buildings, many brightly painted in the Portuguese style. You could easily imagine oneself in Lisbon.

We spent the rest of the afternoon wending our way through narrow streets. At a supermarket we spotted bottles of good Portuguese plonk at US$6 a bottle.

Next morning we checked out some bus companies in regard to our trip into China, before having our 'dim sum' breakfast in a local coffee shop. As usual the locals were very curious about us. It was here that I found that at yesterdays breakfast, in another restaurant, I had chosen dog meatballs! Very red meat, mixed with onion etc, rather mushy. Yuk! Poor little Fifi!

We walked south to visit the A-Ma Temple. This Chinese temple was dedicated to a Goddess. The story goes that a young girl called Lin Mo watched a storm about to engulf some fishermen, and when she prayed the storm calmed and the fishermen were saved on this beach. They built a temple in thanks, and she became the patron saint of fishermen. It is the same goddess as in the temple where Lian grew up in Malaysia. On a rock outside the temple, they had carved a fishing boat in commemoration.

Macau is famed for its casinos, so we went along to see the old 'Casino Lisboa', which was one of the most famous. Even mid-morning it was full. No James Bonds here. No dress code, just a lot of noise. As well as the usual casino games, there were several others we had not seen before. It seems that some of the Las Vegas casinos operators are about move in, so this may bring up the standards.

To the south of Macau are two islands, which are reached by three spectacular bridges. Taipa also has the airport, and Coloane. Both these islands are now joined together by reclaimed land. We took a local bus to Coloane village and checked out the black sand beach there.

China: Guanzhou.

After three days in Macau, we checked out of the hotel and took a local bus north to the border. We had no problems leaving Macau through their new border terminal, and walked the 100 yards or so to the Chinese immigration. We had arranged our visas in Kuala Lumpur, so found the immigration fast and efficient. Lots of local people were making the crossing, many of them pulling shopping baskets. It seems that many make a living crossing three or four times a day taking various goods in each direction.

We planned to go to Guanzhou (previously known as Canton) and then northwards to a town just south of Guilin. At the bus station below the customs building, we took a luxury bus to Guangzhou.

It was a very comfortable bus, with reclining seats, and the bus left at 9am as soon as we sat down. The landscape was very flat being in the Pearl River delta. Lots of rivers to cross, and much of the route was on elevated highways. Plenty of bananas being grown, and green vegetables. The rice fields were dark brown with stubble. Visibility was poor and misty. Had one pee stop on the way. Two and a half hours later and we were in Guangzhou. A huge and busy place. Even before we reached the terminal at the China Hotel, we had decided that we did not really want to stay here, and would move out as soon as possible.

So we took a taxi to a really busy bus terminal area. Yes, there was a bus leaving for our destination of Yangshuo in an hour. We bought our tickets.

Better have some lunch. Bought two tubs of pot noodles and ripped off the tops. Then added boiling water, waited two minutes and it was ready to eat, and quite tasty. We have found that they supply boiling hot water at a lot of public areas in China. Also bought some really tiny oranges, only 1.1/2 inches in diameter, but very sweet and juicy

The bus pulled out the terminus at 3pm. We passed more vegetable farms, as well as many fish farms.

The bus has reasonably comfortable seats, but has a bad case of the rattles. It starts to get hillier, and bamboo seems to be the most cultivated crop. After 2 hours the bus stops for half an hour and everyone gets out and stuffs themselves with food. We bought some pau (steamed dumpling stuffed with vegetables), and tea eggs, (hard boiled eggs boiled in tea)

Much of the road was being upgraded by putting about 12 inches of crushed stone, and 12 inches of concrete slab onto the existing road surface. This meant that in many places only half the road width was available for the traffic to use. With no traffic lights or men with flags to direct the vehicles, this meant there were numerous hold-ups as every one wanted to claim priority.

By 5:30pm it was dark, and all one could see was the white lime paint on the tree trunks lining the road. The bus stopped for another pee stop, and at a number of tollbooths on the way.

Yanshuo and Guilin.

We finally stopped at Yangshuo 7.3/4 hours after leaving Guangzhou. We were at a roundabout that did not look like anything shown on the map in our 'Rough Guide'. It was 10deg C (50 F), and we were shivering. No alterative but to take a taxi. We had a booking at a hotel—but for the following night. The driver started off down a road, but then turned off into a dark building site. I shouted at him to stop, as I feared a mugging was about to happen. He took no notice and said "Short-cut", and we could see bright lights ahead. Then he stopped the taxi as we had reached a pedestrian street. Lian insisted that the driver go with her to find the hotel, and I stayed with the taxi and our luggage. Then I saw Lian returning with a porter, and we paid the taxi off. The Sinhai Hotel was small, but we had a large room with a sitting area at one end with a TV, and a double bed the other end. So by midnight we were settled in and able to have a hot bath or shower. The room had an air-conditioner that could also be a heater. We wound the thermostat up to 25deg C (75 F) and relaxed.

Woke next morning and looked out to see very old picturesque tiled roofs, and with the fabled limestone of hills all around. Even in the mist it was very impressive. The walkway outside was stone lined, with shops and restaurants either side.

Walked across to the Drifters Café, and I ordered a good English breakfast, with fresh coffee, a large glass of freshly squeezed orange juice, a bowl of fresh fruit, and doorstep sized slices of toast. Lian had coffee and pancakes.

Dressed up now in many layers of warm clothes, and with our thermal gloves in place, we walked along our lane to the riverfront. The view was very impressive, with the hills of limestone jutting out of the flat landscape like huge thumbs. With the mist around, it was just as shown in the Chinese brush paintings.

The water is very clear. It is here that fishermen use trained cormorants to catch fish for them. They put a loop around the bird's neck, and only allow it to keep and eat about 1 in 7 of the fish it catches. An old man was on the waterfront with his 2 birds, so we could take a close look.

We kept walking northwards along the riverbank and took the opportunity of catching up on our bird-watching. A young Chinese student joined us in order to practice her English. She later took us around the back of the town to see a school. We thought she was showing us her own school, but it was not. Still do not know why she wanted us to see it.

We then walked around looking at the shops, and found the roundabout that we had been dropped at the previous evening. Not so far away.

Bought a bottle of Chinese 'Great Wall' Cabernet Sauvignon wine, and took it with us for a pizza dinner.

Went for an evening walk, and the temperature had dropped to 5deg C (42 F).

Our room was on the 2nd floor, and we found they had live music in our hotel ground floor on a Saturday night. It was pretty noisy.

On Sunday morning we repeated the breakfast experience, and went out in a light drizzle to look for some quieter accommodation. But at the best alternative, they started playing about with the prices, so we decided to stay put, as our hotel assured us that it would be quieter.

At mid morning we went along to the bus station and took an express bus for the 1hr 20min journey to Guilin. We walked along the riverside, and were pleased that we had chosen Yangshuo to stay in. Guilin was quite a big town, and they wanted money for every tourist attraction. Also the famed hills were not close to town at all. They have 6-hour river cruises down to Yangshuo.

By mid afternoon we had had enough and took another express bus back. We found that the express bus drivers take the word 'express' very seriously. I do not want to sit in the front row, as my heart rate would certainly increase, and I would wear out the shoe leather on my foot brake side.

We found that they have a night sleeper bus direct from Yanshuo to the border town with Macau. This leaves on alternative days. Not only would we save a night's accommodation, but also we would bypass Guangzhou. So we made reservations.

One day we took a bus to Ximping, a small town further downstream. We had been planning to hire bicycles to go there, but it was a bit cold and damp. What a good job we chose the bus, as it turned out to be a 16-mile (26 km) trip each way.

Had a great walk northwards for several kilometres along the riverbank and through cultivated fields until the track came to a ferry crossing. The hills here are remarkable and seem so close. Their limestone bases rise vertically from the flat fields and the upper sides and tops are covered with shrubs and small trees. You feel you are standing in the midst of a Chinese water colour painting, and realize that the painting is not an exaggeration or stylized, but is very real, and right there before you.

Took the bus back, but got off a couple of miles before Yangshuo, at the main river crossing, and slowly meandered back to the town centre. Once back in town we stopped at a hole in the wall joint for hot noodle soup and pau (steamed buns).

Next morning we tried a different breakfast spot—the Café China was also very good. Light rain, so once again no bikes.

Took a bus south to see Moon Rock. The path up was all granite paths and steps, through groves of bamboo. Very slippery, especially coming down, so we had to be very careful. An old lady followed us up the 600-foot climb, despite our telling her we had our own water and would not be buying any from her. She was a bit grumpy when she found we had not been bluffing. Anyway, the sweaty climb was worth it, with good views to both north and south. It would be spectacular on a clear day, with none of the mist and cloud. Mind you, then it would loose its effect of mystery, and the 'Chinese watercolour' feeling. Near the top of the hill is a large circular hole through the rock, hence the name Moon Rock.

We did see a few European tourists around, but they must have problems with the language as soon as they get off the tourist route, or they want to change any plans. Bargaining becomes very difficult. Luckily Lian knows enough Mandarin now to get by, and can screw down prices to an acceptable figure. Even then she knows that there is I price for locals and another for foreigners. If she spots this we walk out.

We did our packing and took advantage of a 3pm late checkout. Left our luggage at the reception and had a final walk about the town area until we went to the pick up point at 6pm to wait for our night bus. Sat around a small charcoal fire to keep warm.

At 7:15pm the bus arrived and we were hustled aboard. There are three lines of bunk beds each about 20" wide, with 2 narrow corridors for access down the bus. We had lower bunks. Each bunk slopes up from waist level, which allows the person behind to slot their feet down a narrow space below my head. Works very well for average height people, but certainly not designed for myself. It's like jamming yourself in a F1 racing car. And you can't sit up straight as the bunk above gets in the way. The bus made a few 'pee' stops during the night, and we reached the bus depot after a 16-hour journey.

Macau.

The depot was a long way from the border and we shared a taxi with a Chinese woman living in Macau. No problems with immigration between China and Macau, and we were delighted to check back into the Macau Masters Hotel by lunchtime. One big advantage of this hotel is that many buses stop outside.

After a shower and hot coffee, we felt revived enough to start walking again. Commenced with a visit to the Pawn Shop

Museum. The only interesting part was a ten-storey strong room to house the pawned items.

Walked on to see some gardens, and sat on a bench with a packet of chips and listened to a man playing a two string fiddle. I think I know why the neighbours won't let him play in his house.

Hong Kong.

Next morning we took a bus to the ferry terminal and from then the Turbo Jet-foil to Hong Kong. Very smooth and fast, the 40-mile (65km) trip only took an hour and five minutes. Boy, that Hong Kong skyline is certainly something to marvel at from the bay. So many skyscrapers: The HSBC building, Standard Chartered and the Bank of China building are all pretty impressive. Unfortunately we could not see The Peak due to the low cloud, so there was little point in going up there. We walked around, and did not try out the double-decker bus or the trams. Not wearing the dress code for the Hong Kong Club, we took the subway under the bay to Kowloon, where we enjoyed the hospitality of the Kowloon Cricket Club, which is also affiliated to the Kuala Lumpur's Royal Lake Club. It was a chance to have a leisurely meal and read the English language dailies. After a walk around Kowloon, we took a direct ferry back to Macau.

Macau.

Next day we put on our walking boots yet again, visiting Dr. Sun Yat-Sen's house (the founder of Taiwan) and then on to the Guia Fort. Great views over the city, and the place where they display the typhoon warnings. From the battlements we spotted a large cemetery, and so walked down to find St Michaels church.

After a rest we walked northwards alongside the inner harbour. Went onto several of the wharves to see the unloading and the small sampans coming across the harbour from China. I wonder what the authorities think of this. Lots of tough looking guys hanging about, and I reminded myself that this was not the route to take in the dark or the return journey.

Walked as far as Illa Verde, the green island, which due to reclamation work is now part of the main island. Then along passed the Dog Racing Track, aptly named the 'Canodrome', before returning to our base by bus.

Saturday would be our last day. We started with a 'dim sum' breakfast at a real restaurant rather than a typical Chinese coffee shop, and walked down to see the Maritime Museum. Yet another good museum. They had models of the old island, so comparing that with our map we could appreciate how much land had been reclaimed from the sea over the years.

The Zin Zexu was the only museum in town that was very disappointing.

In the afternoon we checked out of the hotel and stored our things at the reception.

Found a fascinating old building which was now a library. The house had belonged to a Sir Robert Ho Tung, who left it in his will as a library. As we showed interest, one of the senior librarians who spoke good English showed us around, and then took us to the main library in Senate Square. There they have a real traditional library, with a balcony all around. Filled with old volumes on dark panelled bookcases.

Hung around the square area listening to some children's orchestras playing on a bandstand, before collecting our bags and making our way to the airport for our return flight to Malaysia.

CHAPTER 5

East Malaysia: A tour of Sabah

Young Orang-utan.

Malaysia comprises Peninsular Malaysia, (with Thailand to the north and Singapore to the south), together with the states of Sarawak and Sabah that together form the northern and western edge of the island of Borneo. Sarawak and Sabah have the independent country of Brunei between them, and the rest of the island is known as Kalimantan and is part of Indonesia.

In late May we arranged a trip to Sabah on the northern side of the island of Borneo, flying into Sandakan from Kuala Lumpur, and then taking a direct flight home from Tawau.

At one time Sandakan had been the capital of Sabah, before it was moved to Jesseltown, which was later renamed as Kota Kinabalu.

An old friend and colleague, Kenneth Tiong, had a development and construction project in Sandakan, and had offered the loan of a 4WD vehicle whilst we were there. We could pick it up in Sandakan on the north coast, and leave it in Tawau on the west coast.

Reaching the airport, we heard that our afternoon flight would be delayed, so phoned Michael Foo, who had arranged to meet us in Sandakan, to inform him of our delay, only to find that he was also still in Kuala Lumpur, but booked on a different flight to Sandakan and this would be via Kota Kinabalu. So even though we were delayed, we would arrive ahead of him.

On our arrival we were met by Matthew Leng, and taken to the golf club for a few drinks until we could meet Michael from his flight. We then all went out for one of Sandakan's famed seafood dinners.

Sandakan.

After breakfast at the Sandakan Hotel, we went for a visit to Kenneth's project. A major one for Sandakan, as the fishing port and main seaside market are being relocated, and a new commercial area, with shops, hotel etc are being provided, thus making a new business hub for Sandakan.

From there we were taken on a sightseeing tour to a Chinese Temple on the hillside, a fishing village, and St Michael's Church.

In the afternoon we visited the memorial to the Australian prisoners of war, that had been provided by the Australian Government. It is situated in the old prisoner of war camp, and a visit is a very moving experience.

Then, to lighten the mood, we visited the English Teahouse for tea and scones. It is still all very colonial.

Sepilok Orang-utan sanctuary.

On a Friday morning we were provided with a Toyota Hilux twin-cab, and started our journey.

Sepilok, is only 15 miles (25km) from town, and here they have an Orang-utan sanctuary. Firstly we checked into the Sepilok Jungle Resort, where we had a pleasant room with a balcony.

We were in time for the 10am feeding time. Walking along the boardwalk to the feeding station we saw a big young male sitting on the hand railing. He let us pass, and then stepped down and followed us. It was all somewhat disconcerting.

At a later visit to the sanctuary we were talking to one of the keepers about this young male. "Ah, that's Karl. We had to move him elsewhere as he could be very naughty. Whilst sitting on that handrail, he snatched a German's camera. He then opened it and pulled the film out, before climbing a tree, and smashing the camera on the tree trunk."

The apes came in slowly, lazily swinging along ropeways. Some females had youngsters grimly hanging on to their mothers. Once at the station, the youngsters seemed to get together and were shyly trying to keep the Long-tailed Macaques from stealing any of the bananas.

The place was full of visitors, mostly from Australia and Europe, and all making a hell of a lot of noise. They were treating it like a zoo, and the Orang-utans sat looking at them as if they were the ones who had been brought on for the Orang-utans pleasure. A bit sad really.

Then right under the boardwalk by the station, we heard a series of long low whistles. It took us some time, but we had great views of a little Garnet Pitta. We tried a bird trail, but it started raining, so we gave up and returned in the afternoon.

The majority of visitors are on conducted tours, and so cannot hang around. So at closing time, we decided to do some bird-watching around the car park area. It was then that we saw the Giant Flying Squirrels. They move from tree to tree by climbing up the main tree trunks and then gliding across to a nearby tree. The distance covered is quite incredible. Some 'flights' of about 50 yards (45m) were seen.

We spent the next day bird-watching around the area.

Sukau and the lower Kinabatangan River.

It was time to move on, so after breakfast we continued our journey and headed for Sukau, a village on the lower Kinabatangan River. Much of the journey was on laterite roads through the palm oil estates. We found a small hotel and checked in. The Temenggong River Lodge is situated right on the riverside, with a large forested cliff on the opposite bank. Later we saw Proboscis Monkeys sitting in the trees. The males have huge noses and big pop-bellies.

It rained after lunch, and as soon as it cleared we took a boat ride down the river. We enjoyed some very rewarding bird-watching, including several species of Hornbill, Oriental Darters, and even the rare Storme's Stork.

Next morning at 6:30am, we took a boat again with Cede Prudence, our guide. Cede is a well-known guide, and a well-published photographer. He managed to show us a Hooded

Pitta as well as a number of other good birds, and we even came upon a Pygmy Elephant swimming across a small stream

At 10:30am we returned to a big breakfast.

Then in the afternoon we all went to the Gomantong Caves. Quite a few longhouses outside, belonging to the men who collect the bird's nests of the Swiftlets who also make their homes in the caves with the bats. We saw the long rolled up rope ladders that they use. After our first sortie into the caves we came out and had tea with the workers. We had great views of a family of real wild Orang-utans above the cave entrance (Rather than the ones being rehabilitated at Sepilok) Then, as twilight approached, we watched as the bats started to stream out of the cave. Not so much from the main entrance, but from small hidden holes high up in the cliff side. It looked just like smoke coming out and swirling and curling up into the sky.

And then the Bat Hawks arrived. Several of them: about the size of a Peregrine Falcon. They dive-bombed the groups, often doing great acrobatics in mid air before catching an unlucky bat in its talons, and taking it straight back to its nest, before returning for another sortie. Just like the Spitfires in the Battle of Britain.

As we walked through the secondary forest on our way to the car, the bats were flying all around us at high speed, and seemed to be missing us by only inches.

Dunum Valley.

Had an early breakfast, and set off for the Dunum Valley. We had to drive to Lahat Datu first, to the Dunum Valley office to obtain a permit to take the car in. Even managed to pick up a parking summons there!

The road to Dunum Valley is entered through laterite palm oil estate roads.

Dunum Valley is a large conservation area of virgin lowland forest. It was gazetted some years ago and has a well-established Field Station for scientific research. As Malaysian Nature Society members, we were fortunate to be able to arrange to stay there rather than the main Borneo Rainforest Lodge, where visitors normally stay.

The field station has four rooms for visitors, and we were the only ones staying there. The foreign scientists have separate chalet accommodation, but do come to the area, as that is where the canteen is.

There is a large verandah around the canteen, and this was an excellent location for bird-watching. From there we also saw 'Boo', a wild Orang-utan who often drops by.

We spent four full days there, and found it delightful exploring the trails and the entrance road.

Visited the Borneo Rainforest Lodge and enjoyed their canopy walk. There we were very close to Whiskered Tree Swifts, who were doing their hunting from the guy ropes, with no fear of us.

Semporna.

We left and proceeded southwards to the seaside town of Semporna. This is famous as the jetty for the diving on the island of Sipadan, and the local dive shops were making very some good offers, but we did have time to take them up. Since then the hotel on the island has been closed, so there are no longer any overnight stays there.

We booked into Semporna's Dragon Inn, a hotel on stilts over the sea. The rooms are accessed along walkways. This is a really delightful and very quaint spot. At night you can hear the water lapping under the cabin, as there are cracks between the wooden floorboards. The shower room is open to the sky.

The town is quite fascinating as most of the locals use very fast narrow boats as their form of transport to visit the colourful market. It seems that in the old days most of the men were pirates, and even now we suspect many make their money smuggling goods in and out of the Philippines.

Went to a supermarket to find some wine. Came away with a bottle labelled 'Chateau de Pratt'. Aptly named and pretty awful, but we enjoyed drinking it whilst sitting on the end of the jetty watching the sun going down and the speed boats streaking their way across the bay, and the occasional sailing boat with the sun shimmering off it's billowing sails.

After breakfast we walked around the market area and as usual we were subject to a lot of curiosity.

Tawau.

It was then time to drive on to Tawau, the principal town in the south west of Sabah.

We checked into the Emas Hotel, and then called up David Lee. He and Kenneth had been in university together, and Kenneth had arranged for us to meet him.

That evening David and his wife took us to a local food stalls where we had a superb selection of seafood.

Next morning David insisted upon giving us a tour of Tawau, and some of the local golf courses that he frequents.

Next day, after a tour round the old timber yards in the industrial area, we left our Toyota at David's house, and went to the airport for our direct flight to back to Kuala Lumpur.

CHAPTER 6
China:—The Provinces of Yunnan & Sichuan

The Dafo or Great Buddha at Leshan.

It was mid May when Lian and I flew on Thai Airways, via Bangkok, to Kunming, the capital of Yunnan Province in southwest China.

We had bought our China visas in Kuala Lumpur, but the immigration office in Kunming did not like mine, and I had to wait some time whilst they took it away to check it. I had the similar trouble when we left the country on our last visit. Perhaps because my name had been inserted as 'Michael S' in the middle of the visa, even though they had it correctly at the bottom.

Kunming

Took a taxi to the Camellia Hotel and got a room with no problem. This is a hotel listed in all the travel guides and the majority of the clients are foreigners.

At 6,000ft (1,850m), Kunming is known as the 'spring city'.

Bought tickets for a bus to Dali for the next day, before taking a walk to see the old quarter of the city. We were disappointed to find that it was being demolished. Took a local bus back to the hotel.

The police had stopped a man on a pavement who was selling bananas from a wheelbarrow. Obviously he did not have the right license. So they simply took off the axle with the two wheels attached, and a policeman carried them away despite the protests from the man. I often wonder how he managed to salvage the rest of the barrow and his bananas.

The public bus services in towns everywhere is very good, and one never seems to have to wait long. In Kunming they even have double-decker buses. One pays 1 Yuan per person (approx. 15 cents US), or occasionally 2 Yuan, and can travel as far as one wants.

Woke early and partook of the hotel's buffet breakfast. Had a choice or mixture of Western and Chinese foods, before enjoying the hotel's courtesy bus to the main bus station.

The bus for Xiaguan took nearly an hour to get out of town, as there is a new overhead highway being constructed. I did note the complete lack of safety barriers for the workmen.

We were on the famed 'Burma Road'; build by allied prisoners in 1938. This is on part of the old Southern Silk Road, and also known as the Tribute Road. We pass through wooded hills and valleys, and a number of tunnels. At one time we were caught in a jam and did not move for an hour. A coal lorry had run into the back of a car, causing a six-vehicle accident, just in front of a tunnel.

Dali

Although we thought we had bought a ticket for 'old Dali', we were dumped at 'new Dali'. So then we had to get a small bus for the half hour journey and arrived late afternoon. Booked into Jim's Place. Went for a walk around Dali and checked out some other alternative hotels.

Dali is a walled city, and very much a tourist spot. The pedestrian tourist area is largely new, but built in the old style. The town is on an agricultural plain, with a long lake to the east, and a range of hills to the west. The height above sea level is about 6,350ft (1,935m).

Some areas in town were experiencing a power cut, but we did have a good hot shower as our accommodation had a solar hot water system.

Our room was at the front overlooking a noisy street. Every bus and car that passed was blasting it's horn. The room was small, with a double bed squashed in one corner, and was decorated in the Tibetan style. A huge prayer table filled another wall, and I soon had bruises on one hip as I tried to squeeze by it.

We did not sleep too well, as all night it continued to be noisy, so after breakfast we checked out and moved into the Koreana Hotel, situated in the pedestrian area. Our room was off a corridor overlooking a small courtyard.

We had planned to spend several days in the Dali area, as we had read of an impressive 'Monday market' that was held in a small town to the north. It was said that all the ethnic tribes come down for this weekly market. However, when we enquired, we were told this was no longer so, but there was a similar market that day at another village. It would not start until after 10am, as the people needed time to reach the market, as many would travel from afar. This sounded just what we wanted, and would allow us to move on a couple of days earlier.

So we walked out through the north gate and got into a mini-bus. These leave as soon as they are full. An interesting journey, passing by fields of rice and vegetables, and with people jumping on and off as we passed through the small villages. The conductor told us we had reached our destination, but we soon found that although this village had a market, it was not the one we wanted. So we had a wait for another bus for a further ride northwards.

The Youshwor market turned out to be all we had anticipated. In fact the nearest thing to the famed Kashgar market that we had seen in China. Huge heaps of onions, garlic and potatoes were piled on the ground. Pigs and chickens ran around, and tanks and basins full of river fish were lined up along a pathway. Men sat having their haircut, and women manned the vegetable stalls in colourful traditional garb. There were stalls full of farming tools, and rows of coal burning stoves. The stoves usually were made from old metal drums and we noted that one poorly painted one had once contained potassium cyanide. I wondered what that had been was used for.

The main ethnic tribe here is the Bai. Anyway, there were lots of photographic and video possibilities.

We returned to Dali by bus, but this one dropped us at the East Gate, and we had a quite long walk back to our hotel, so stopped off at a small place for noodle soup and a plate of mushrooms. Then went for a wander around.

The town is full of Chinese tourists. Some of the older local residents sit in a park, and play cards, dominoes and mah-jong.

On the bus yesterday we had met a Liverpudlian from England, and a South African, and later in the evening saw them in a café so joined them for a chat. Also met a Frenchman with a Madagascan wife, so spent a while practicing our French and talking about the island.

At the hotel there are three young Koreans staying. Both the boys and the woman use sign language to converse with each other. Being deaf /dumb certainly did not seem to stop them having fun and a good time. They insisted that we have some of their bananas, and so Lian reciprocated with some of our 2-in-1 coffee sachets.

Next morning set off for the north end of town, which we found to be far more original. Sat for some time watching Bai women selling small baskets of chicken, duck and goose eggs, as well as joss sticks and other prayer paraphernalia.

It was time to check out of the hotel, and we took a local bus northwards alongside the lake, before starting a long climb through bare and stony hills. At the top of the climb was an army camp at 8,000ft (2,460m) and we could see tanks on training manoeuvres, leaving huge dust trails as they sped along.

Lijiang.

A number of more valleys and passes, and three hours later reached our destination of Lijiang.

This is the main town for the Nexi peoples (Pronounced: 'nessie' as in Loch Ness monster.)

A clear stream comes from the north, and this splits into about five tributaries, which then split into smaller streams. The town is built alongside this web of streams and is thus a complicated place. Quaint stone bridges cross the streams. It's something out of a child's' storybook. The town centre is quite old, but 'mock old' on the outskirts and towards the bus station.

Friends from Mauritius had stayed in a hotel on a hill overlooking the old town and had raved about it. So I crossed a small plank bridge and settled down in a restaurant with a beer and the luggage, whilst Lian went up to find accommodation. The recommended hotel proved to be above our budget, but the Sunshine Zone, next door, seemed more than adequate. So a chap from reception came down and helped us as we struggled up the slippery granite steps, and checked in.

Lijiang is at 7,500ft (2,300m) so the oxygen levels are a little depleted.

There was a light drizzle, so we dressed up in our warm things and sat outside on the balcony and enjoyed the views over the grey-tiled roofs of the town. A ginger cat, which thinks he is a dog, comes sprinting up the wooded stairs and begs for food with loud meows.

Went for a walk, but the weather gets wetter and it is a bit chilly and a little miserable for us at 11deg C (50 F).

The main banks of the streams are lined with restaurants. Many have strings of red lanterns outside, and give striking reflections in the clear streams. Girls in national ethnic costumes stand outside the restaurants enticing customers with their singing and dancing. They seem to be having so much fun themselves, that you can't stop oneself smiling.

Next morning we were out early before the crowds, and had the chance to take a few photos without throngs of people around.

Followed a few women carrying empty baskets and soon found ourselves in the market. Here they had incredible giant vegetables. Any would win a prize at an English village agricultural show. The Nexi women all wear their traditional blue clothing with a white band criss-crossed over the chest, holding up the padding covering their backs. One woman we saw had the traditional back pad of reeds, but most now use plastic.

We watched young pigs oinking as they were being lifted from a pen into the back of van, before meandering over to the chicken section. Here chickens were being taken from cages, killed, and dipped into boiling water before being plucked and finally sold to the public.

We had been following a scruffy looking chap leading an Alsatian sized dog. Then we saw a few dogs crowded together in a wire cage. Only then did it occur to us that the dogs were for the cooking pot. The scruffy man was talking to two others. One produced a pair of giant tongs and held them round the big dogs neck. The second man picked up a 7lb hammer on a long shaft and swung it at the dog's head. It was a glancing blow, and the dog backed and yelped. The man then turned and ran into a shop and came out with a big woodsman's axe. He started to swing this at the dog that in the meantime had been forced to the ground by the other man. It was at this time I stopped videoing the episode, as I really did not want to see what was to happen next. It also occurred to me that the men might not welcome the episode being put on film, and they had already proved themselves to be brutal people. We saw one dead dog in the back of a barrow. It already had had all it's fur burnt off.

Then watched a man skinning live eels and degutting them, with the blood running down to his forearms and dripping off his elbows.

Bought strawberries and pears and went back to the hotel for hot coffee.

As we passed the main square we came across a group of elderly Nexi women (and I mean really elderly) and a lone man, doing a shuffling dance for the public. Music provided from an old cassette player being held by a woman with an umbrella. Hardly the Windmill Girls, but great fun.

Yes, apart from the market incident, Lijian is all about fun.

Walking again along the small lanes, and admiring the crystal clear water and the goldfish holding station in the current.

There are a number of 'triple wells'. The water enters the first open tank, then overflows into the second, and then finally into the third before being diverted back into a stream. The first well is for cooking water, the second for washing vegetables, and the last for washing clothes. They are still being used.

Had lunch in a Nexi restaurant. Proved a bit disastrous. Had Nexi pancake (like a heavy chapatti—not too bad), Nexi liver (these thin slices had been cooked in vinegar, and were cold. An acquired taste and we only nibbled at it), and rice sausage (rice soaked in blood and deep fried was not too bad).

Then I went for a pee in a public toilet nearby—½ Yuan (7cents US)—and was flabbergasted. Each toilet stall had a squat toilet and an individual video screen similar to those found on an aircraft. Showing a tourist film of the area. I can imagine people going in and staying for a long time.

There is a lake just outside town, called Black Dragon Lake. When we got there, they wanted US$10 each as an entrance. Pretty expensive when you compare it with the US$12 we pay for our room. As it was still drizzling, we decided to wander back to the hotel.

Checked at the bus station for our trip out of town, and then booked a trip to Tiger Leaping Gorge for the next day. This had not been on our itinerary, but we had read that the authorities were likely to build a dam here, so it might all disappear.

I find it difficult to pass a camping / outdoors shop, and here was no exception. We came out with two collapsible trekking walking sticks, and two pairs of trousers. And all very good value.

Lian had used up a memory stick on her camera and we took it into a camera shop to have it downloaded onto a CD, so she would have more memory. The man was very amused that the memory stick was so small, and we finished up bargaining for a larger capacity memory stick at a good price, which included a 5 RM Malaysian currency note, as they had not seen plastic notes before.

A side trip to the Tiger Leaping Gorge.

Next morning we were at the travel agents early for our trip, so managed to get a front seat with sufficient legroom for me. On the way we stopped off to see the 'stone drum' at Shigu. This is a stone stele with characters on both sides. We then visited what was said to be the 'first bend in the Yangtze River', before being taken to a jade factory, followed by an excellent lunch.

We had two hours at the gorge, which sounded a long time. However it is a long (1.6 mile-2.6km) walk to the viewing area, so by the time one takes photos, there is not much spare time. There is a big rock in the middle of a raging torrent, and historically a mystical tiger was supposed to have used this rock as a step as it leapt across the ravine. It was all very impressive.

On the way back we stopped at a Wetland Park just outside town. Flat grasslands surround a shallow lake. Here you can go pony trekking. The interesting thing here was the three sets of bride and groom having their wedding photos taken with the lake and hills behind as a backdrop. The photographers were very professional with fill-in flashes and a series of set poses for the couples.

Got dropped off at the bus station and made our bookings for two days ahead to Panzhihua, where we could take a train northwards.

Watched some Dogba singing and dancing, and also visited a shop where they were making paper and selling various paper products that they had made. Dogba is an old religion which is partly animalist, partly Buddhist and partly Shamanistic. The Sharman we saw looks more like an African witchdoctor than a Chinese. They have their own pictogram form of writing, which is said to be the only one in the world that is in daily use.

The weather that night was cold, so we had extra duvets on the bed and slept like babies.

On this morning in mid May we awoke to clear skies and bright sunshine, and we took full advantage with camera and video to revisit old haunts and find new ones. But keeping well away from the dog market!

In the afternoon we went to the old square, the level of which slopes from one end to the other. This paved stone area has a very clever cleaning method. There are gaps between the paving stones at the higher end, so when they dam a stream, the water level rises and bubbles out through the gaps between the upper paving slabs, and then washes any rubbish down across the square. Once clean, they can un-dam the stream and the water stops. Unfortunately they did not do it the day we were there.

We went into the 'Love Bird Bar', and sat at the third level balcony with a beer and watched the world go by. The old Windmill Girls were all sitting around playing card-dominoes and getting quite excited whilst waiting for the next show. Some enterprising men in Mongol dress had a horse, and tourists were virtually fighting for the opportunity of dressing up as the Mongol horde and sitting on the horse, complete with Davy Crocket fur hats. They were encouraged to brandish a flintlock rifle and then a sword whilst having their pictures taken. The horse however looked bored.

The rubbish collection is also worth a mention. A small dust cart the size of an ice cream van, does it's rounds playing a Chinese melody. People come running out from the various restaurants and tip their rubbish into the cart. It's a nice tune, and reminds one of the Pied Piper of Hamelin.

We had to leave our hotel early, and as usual had to wake the staff to come and un-padlock the courtyard door. One helped Lian down the hill with her bag. Lian had negotiated for a front seat on for us on the bus, so I was very comfortable.

The journey had been described as being spectacular, and it certainly lived up to its reputation. The road climbed out of the valley through pine forests to 8,500ft (2,600m) before plunging down into fertile valleys and tree-lined roads. This was repeated several times before reaching and crossing the Yangtze River at 4,000ft (1,240m).

The bus driver had noticed that I had been filming some of the scenery, and stopped at one pass for me to get out and film a panorama of a valley below.

Had several stops to top up the water tank of the bus, as due to the steep gradients the brake system would soon fail without water being sprayed onto the brake drums to cool them. This was also an opportunity to have a pee.

The toilets were extremely basic. One I can remember was a room about 9ft x 6ft (3m by 2m). The floor was of pine logs split in two, with a 6" (15cm) gap between the logs. Beneath the logs was a pit, which in this case was nearly full up with excreta. Lian chickened out of using the ladies, and preferred to go round the back of the mud building.

Knowing whether to use the Ladies or the Gents was a problem as the writing was often only in Chinese. However, the sign for the ladies seemed quite apt, it looks like a box with two legs coming from the bottom. And the legs are crossed at knee level. So I simply use the other entrance.

Some of the drops on this mountain road were huge, and we were caught up in one queue whilst everyone gawked down at what was left of a lorry (or was it a bus?) that had plunged off the edge. With a fall like that there could be no survivors.

A little more on toilets: Those in shopping centres and hotel public areas are usually not too bad, but one must get used to the fact that people are loathe to flush a toilet, and one is expected to put dirty toilet paper into a waste bin rather than flush it away.

Many of the trucks were very large and overloaded with coal. Passing them could be a problem, but our driver simply whacked his horn and slid past. Is it sensible to sit at the front and watch all this? I have bruises on my palm where the fingernails have dug in.

By now we had left Yunnan and were in the province of Sichuan. Our destination, Panzhihua, was not a pretty place. Several coal mines and lots of pollution. Although we were to have gone to the railway station, we were all told to get out and into a small bus. We then had to pay again for the ½ hour trip to the station.

Had trouble getting tickets, as they wanted us to take an afternoon train north to the station at Emei, whilst we wanted the sleeper train which would leave 3 hours later.

We booked what we thought were 'soft sleepers'. These have 4 beds in a compartment that has a door: two lower bunks at seat level, and two bunk beds over the seats. However, when we got on board, we found we had been given a 'hard sleeper' with 6 beds to each compartment, and no door to the corridor. Luckily we had a lower and a middle berth, so did not have to clamber up a ladder to squeeze into a top bed. It seems that all the soft sleepers had been sold.

The train left promptly on time at 4:48pm and would arrive at 6:24am the next morning.

We shared our section with three men who worked for a steel factory. The boss would write down full English sentences of questions, but refused to speak in English. We suspected that he was not confident of his accent, and did not want to loose face in front of his staff. A lady joined us at a later station, and went straight to her top bunk, and we never noticed her again.

We made hot coffee with the hot water provided on board, and I had a couple of beers from the food sellers who are always going up and down the train.

We slept fitfully, as it was quite hot. Much of the track is single track, so we often had to stop at a siding to let a train pass by in the other direction. A quarter of an hour before arrival, we were shaken by the staff and told to get ready as we were arriving at Emei, which is the nearest station for Emei Shan. So our worries about getting off at the right stop were unfounded.

Emei Shan.

Emei Shan is the most holy of the mountains in China. (Pronounced as 'Ermay' and Shan means mountain).

At the station we took a small van to the Teddy Bear Hotel. Luckily they had a nice room available even so early in the morning. They even have a very large stuffed Teddy Bear left in each room. This small hotel is run by Andy Foo and his wife Shirley, and specialises in foreign guests. We found the staff friendly, helpful, and always cheerful.

Spent the day strolling around to see the 'Crouching Tiger Monastery', the 'Fu Hu Monastery', and the other sights at the base of the mountain. Our path rose from 1,800ft (540m) up to 2,200ft (675m), but it was quite hot even walking in the shade of the trees and bamboo.

Later we sorted out our bags to carry the minimum on the mountain, leaving the balance at the hotel. Our plan to spend two nights away dovetailed well, as the Teddy Bear was full for the next two nights.

Liedongping

So we took the early small bus up the mountain for the 30-mile (50km), two-hour journey to Liedongping, which is at 7,760ft (2,365m). Stopped a couple of times, and once to fill up with water for the brake system. We arrived to see clear blue sky.

The journey up was very scenic: thick forest at the base, which gradually became sparser, and then pines and rhododendrons. Half way up was the park entrance and here we had to pay our entrance fees; 120 Yuan (US$16) for Lian, and 60 Yuan for me, as an old man, They take your photo, and a black & white picture is stuck onto your entrance ticket

Liedongping has a rather ugly concrete car park bounded on one side by crumby hotels and restaurants.

The recommended hotel was not acceptable, and we checked into the Min Shan Hotel. They were listed as 450 Yuan a night, but accepted 100 Yuan after some bargaining.

We walked up to Jinding and took a cable car up to the Golden Summit. They have two cable cars, but the small four-seater bubble one is broken down, so we had to take the big standing-up-only one. Quite fast.

From the cable car one walks up to what was still a construction site. A gold anodised Chinese temple, and a silver anodised one were nearing completion, whilst a huge golden 10-faced Buddha seemed complete.

Unfortunately the heavy haze spoilt the incredible views. Or is this pollution even at 9,900ft (3,010m)?

We had decided to walk down, and some of the steps were very steep. Our new trekking walking sticks came in very handy. Mind you, we were overtaken by a number of elderly ladies who were practically running down. Made me feel a bit ancient, as by the time we reached the bottom, my knees felt decidedly wobbly even after a great cold beer and some noodle soup.

In the early evening we had a walk down the entrance road, and also visited an old monastery opposite our hotel. It was here that we saw our first of the 'naughty monkeys'.

They will waylay travellers and expect to be given some food. It would be a brave man who would walk along with a plastic bag in one hand. The monkeys are quite large and heavy, and have quite long hair to protect them from the cold winter.

Hot water only came on at 8pm, not quite hot enough but still very acceptable. Lian even turned on her electric blanket.

We were woken by a 4am telephone call, and asked if we wanted to see the sunrise. Luckily enough we declined, and we were told later that the cloud cover meant that they saw only what we saw when we got up two and half hours later.

Walked down the road and found the ski resort. They had cleared pine trees for a length of only about 350 yards (300m), but it did have a small ski lift. We wondered how many clients they got there in the winter.

Noticed that all the crash barriers on the way up are decorated with a pine bark design rather than having the standard galvanised finish. This is a nice idea.

At just after 9am we checked out and took a bus half way down the mountain to the Wannian Car Park (2,800ft-860m)

Tried a couple of hotels before checking into the Tian Ran Ju Hotel. I will remember this hotel, as the pull-down blind had an amazing picture of a waterfall and herons fishing. It also had a WC pan sitting in the middle of the bathroom floor. One could practically walk right around it, and the shower of course sprayed right over the WC.

Took a bubble cable car up to the Wannian Temple and had views of the forest and cleared areas where they had tea plantations.

Started walking down through the dark pine forest. Six monkeys got a bit close, but we got through safely. Waved our sticks at them, and they waved their teeth back at us.

Passed the Bailong Si Temple, and continued down to the Qingyin Pavilion. Very picturesque with the Chinese pavilions and crystal clear rushing water and scenic bridges. A lot more people here and a good place to sit quietly and do some advanced people watching. Many were on a tour and had come in from the Winxian-gong car park.

When we reached the car park ourselves, we wanted to take a bus back to Wannian, but the car park was completely chock-a-block, and all the car and buses were blasting their horns. We decided to walk back, but had little idea of the distance involved. Luckily a local bus stopped when we waved it down, and this saved us about 3 miles (5km) of uphill walking.

We were quite tired when we reached the hotel, and had a rest before walking to the bus station to find out times of the buses for the following morning. We sat in the bus station admiring the views of a vertical cliff on the other side of the river. An enterprising man came over and had little trouble in selling me a big bottle of cold beer.

All day had been overcast, and it started to drizzle over dinner and then rained heavily all night.

In the morning we thought we would start walking up towards Wannian. Our entrance passes were still valid. But there were many busloads of tourists already arriving, and the path up was really crowded. So we took the first path off to the right and started walking through the tea plantations. Mules with empty woven panniers were being led down. Then mules passed us going up with their panniers loaded with bricks. These mules really had to work hard to get up the slippery concrete steps. We took off on another branch through some terraced agriculture and met a lady with her grandson, and later an old man and his grandson. No, they were not relatives.

As we returned to the mule train area, we could see below us that one of the mules had fallen awkwardly, and was lying on its side with it's legs facing uphill. One pannier was empty and it could not get up. The man then started to flog the mule with a thick rope about the neck and head. The mule struggled but could still not get up. The man then started to pick up bricks and hurl them at point blank range at the neck and head of the animal. What unnecessary cruelty. Other mules and men had been standing around watching and they helped yank the mule back onto its feet. No, I took no videos.

Checked out of the hotel, and caught the bus back for the forty five minute journey down to the bus station and the Teddy Bear, where we had our old room reserved for a further two nights.

Just in time for their full breakfast; two large hamburger rolls filled with fried eggs, bacon, tomato and mushrooms. Doesn't the sound of that get the old digestive juices flowing?

It was Sunday afternoon, and we wandered through the University grounds and the park at the base of Emei Shan, and had a chance to watch and meet the locals as well as the tourists relaxing.

Leshan.

We wanted to go to Leshan to see the 71m high sitting Buddha, carved into the cliff. (At 220ft tall, it is as high as a 20-storey building) This is the world's tallest now that the Taliban have destroyed the ones in Bamian, Afghanistan. We had to decide whether to move our base there, or to do it as a day trip. The day trip alternative won. Maybe it was because of the thought of an additional big breakfast.

The bus station was just round the corner from the hotel, and we took a bus for the one-hour trip to Leshan. We were pleasantly surprised to find that the bus stopped right outside the entrance, as we had expected to be dropped in town and to have to take a ferry across the river to the site.

The Dafo, or Great Buddha, was started by a monk in 713AD to protect people sailing past, and took over ninety years to complete. Two rivers joined here and the water could be very rough. Whirlpools can still be seen.

After paying ones entrance fee, one climbs a series of steps and slopes, and suddenly one is at the level of the Dafo's head. Only then does one realize the sheer scale of this carving into the red sandstone cliff. It sits with great serenity, overlooking the river and the multi storey buildings of the main town in the distance. We took lots of photos and videos of course, and then took a very narrow zigzag set of steps down the sheer side of the cliff to the foot of the statue. Lots more photo opportunities here.

Many visitors simply take tour boats from the town and try to take their photos from the deck as the boat tries to hold station in the fast current. These boats do not land.

We then set off around the hillside to visit various temples and other places of interest. Met a crowd of students from Inner Mongolia. One wanted a photograph of himself standing by me acting as his best buddy. And then they all wanted a similar photo. I really should start charging people. Then Lian turned the table on them by insisting on a group photo. They had been quite excited when they heard that we had visited Inner Mongolia, or 'Mongol' as they called it.

When we got back to the Buddha head level again, we were amazed to find that huge hordes of tourists had arrived. Fighting to have their photos taken with them pretending to touch the Buddha's head, and then pushing and shoving trying to get onto the steps down to the foot level. It was all a bit dangerous, especially for children and the aged.

China has such a huge domestic tourist trade that they certainly do not have to have rely on foreign tourists at all. And the Chinese tourists spend money.

It was certainly time to find the exit and a restaurant for a beer and a spot of lunch.

We had the bus to ourselves on the ride back to Emei Shan.

Next morning we took the first bus out to Chengdu, the capital of the province of Sichuan. We were just leaving the main terminal at Emei town itself, after picking up a number of passengers, when a police Jeep suddenly blocked our path, and the police started to check the bus driver's papers. Two male passengers got off and disappeared into the crowd. Then another police car arrived and the police jumped out and came and boarded the bus for a visual inspection. They did not find whatever they were looking for, and the bus was allowed to continue. Surprise, surprise when we stopped a few hundred yards ahead, and the same two men stepped from behind some bushes and got back on board.

China drive on the right, but on the dual or triple carriageways, all the buses and lorries want to use the 'fast lane', so most overtaking has to be done on the inside or 'slow lane' and this is accompanied by long blasts on their very loud air-horns.

Still not to many cars around, and about 80% of these are black in colour.

Chengdu.

Chengdu is a typical large Chinese city. I think Lian is right. What I had been assuming was haze, is in fact simply pollution. At only 1,700ft (525m) it was a little warmer than Kunming)

We dumped our luggage in the left luggage office, and went off to find some accommodation.

Jumped on a town bus to try to find the Dragon Inn which features in the guidebooks. Took a long time to find, down a lane where all the houses were being demolished, and all the rubbish and old bricks were piled in the road. Not only was the place a mess, but also it was an expensive mess. Our second choice was not much better, so we decided to try the recommendation of the South African we had met. "Don't know the name, but it's pink and next to the Sofitel Hotel".

The Bin Jiang Hotel turned out to be very acceptable for price, and in a good central location and not too far from the bus terminal.

It was mid-afternoon by then and we were both tired, so really enjoyed a hot shower and change of clothes.

Popped into the Bank of China and changed some US dollars with no hassle, as we were running low on the Yuan we had brought with us.

Had a walk round town towards the Washou Temple area. This has been rebuilt in the old style as a tourist area and was quite well done. Lian tried to find somewhere that showed the 'face changing' routine from the Chinese Opera, but we were not successful. So we had a snack of deep fried baby crabs.

Crossing a road is a dangerous problem in China, as even when one uses a Zebra Crossing the vehicles do not give you the right of way. This is compounded by having to remember to look 'left then right' rather than the 'right then left' that we are used to. Even the crossings which have traffic lights and 'walk' signs can be a problem, as traffic taking a right filter does not stop, even though you think you have the green 'walk' sign on your side. The many bicycles also do not bother to stop. There are now a number of electric scooters about, and they are so quiet that they also become a danger as they come up silently behind you also on the pavement areas.

Our original plan was to try to visit the Giant Panda sanctuary at Wolong, but we heard that it was closed to visitors in the spring in case the visitors disturb the Panda's mating. Anyway, the Pandas are also very difficult to find, and one can spend weeks there and still not see one in the wild.

We stopped at some tourist offices to look at the alternatives. We had time for a three day tour, but not a four day tour as we would have an overnight train journey back to Kunming to take our flight back, and we wanted to allow a spare day in case things went wrong. One agent suggested we fly from Chengdu to Kunming as they could give us a good discount. The price turned out to be similar to the overnight 'soft sleeper' train price, but we would have an extra nights hotel bill when we reached Kunming.

The four days, three-nights tour would take us to Jiuzhai Gou (pronounced 'Jew Hi Go') and to Huang Long, both famed scenic areas. We accepted this package for two days ahead, and arranged that we would have front seats in the bus.

This was a great decision, and the trip turned out to be probably the greatest scenic journey we have made.

There was light rain, so we did not want to stray far from the hotel for our dinner. Finished up in a small place that did a really excellent pizza.

My wrist alarm clock did not waken us at 6am, and it was nearly 7:30am before my eyes opened. Yes, when travelling we may go to sleep very early, but we like to get up and start doing things early in the morning. Had the hotel Chinese buffet breakfast: porridge (boiled rice in water), pau (steamed buns), salted vegetables, peanuts, and hard-boiled eggs and salted eggs. They also fried eggs.

Walked along to the bird and flower market, but this comprises mostly aquarium gold fish, and a lot of puppies, even including Huskies.

From there we went to the Wenshu Monastery to try the vegetarian restaurant. The signature dish we tried was the 'deep fried fish in sweet and sour sauce'. It was served on a long dish and one could not tell this whole fish from a real one. The head and the tail looked so lifelike as the soya bean skin looked just like crispy fried fish. No bones—and filled with mashed potato—and quite delicious. Walked round the temple grounds that had quite a few birds around.

Time to go back to the travel agents and pick up our airline tickets, and then to go downtown to the shops selling camping gear etc. But all was relatively expensive compared with our purchases in Lijiang, and as nothing struck our fancy, we did not buy anything.

Popped into the Sofitel, the hotel next door, to see how the rich live. Noticed that their charge out to the airport cost a lot more than we were paying for our accommodation.

Jiuzhai Gou & Huang Long.

The little van that was sent to pick us up was late arriving, and then we had to pick up another couple. The driver's phone was ringing every five minutes and when we finally reached the bus, he got a good bollocking for keeping everyone waiting for about three quarters of an hour. The twenty-eight seater bus was full up and a bit ancient. By a miracle Lian managed to get us into the front seats.

We left at 8:30am and it took us an hour to get out of town.

We saw rice and other grains were being laid out to dry on giant woven mats placed on the inner lane of the roadway

By 10am we were on an Expressway.

We have a real Chinaman driver: black leather jacket on the back of his seat, white cotton gloves, dark shades, and a cigarette behind his ear.

There is one other white-man on the trip. He turns out to be an American from New Jersey. He was with a Chinese woman who spoke no English at all, and he speaks no Mandarin. Their exact relationship was obviously a matter of speculation by all the other passengers.

The bus leaves the agricultural flat plain and starts to climb. We pass a lake with a dam. This is 'panda' country, with very steep conical hills and valleys with sides covered with trees and bamboos. No wonder it would be difficult to find a panda in the wild.

Regular stops needed to fill up with water for cooling the brakes.

We climb alongside a very fast river, and see that a number of small hydroelectric schemes have either been completed or are under construction. A new road system is being built and the main bridge columns have been completed. I can imagine the foundation problems encountered in the raging waters. This is like Tiger Leaping Gorge, but bigger and much longer.

The pretty young guide had been trying a hard sell for a special cultural show one evening. It was a silly price, and she and the driver were a bit upset when about a dozen of us refused to play ball.

Six of us, including the American and friend, had opted for the 'three star' hotels, instead of the '2 star'. So at 1:45pm we were dropped at one restaurant for lunch, whilst the bus took the others off for their meal. Only half an hour and we were off again, climbing from 5,200ft to 7,900ft (1575m to 2,400m) through a series of hairpin bends. The mountains still loomed above us.

The police then stopped us for speeding, and we wasted a half hour whilst this was sorted out. From then on the driver was playing catch-up.

By mid afternoon we reached a lake, and here the bus was hosed down and one had the chance of having a photo taken with a number of snow-white yaks. We resisted this opportunity. So far we enjoyed really outstanding scenery.

The lakeside road gives way to a gorge, and continues climbing. The two storey houses are made of pine poles with mud brick or stonewall infill. The roofs are a mixture of Chinese half round tiles, clay roof tiles, or giant slabs of slate.

We were now on a plateau that rose to 11,400ft (3,465m) by late afternoon, before dropping into a 'Forest Terrace' lined with large firs. The road continued to drop through a bare gorge and it was early evening before we reached our destination of Jiuzhai Gou, where we booked into the Jiulong Hotel that would be our base for two nights. A fast stream ran past the hotel entrance.

Had our dinner straight away with the other four. It was cold and uninteresting and we sent it back to be heated up. The room may have had TV, electric blankets and a heater, but it was certainly not clean. The bedroom carpet was filthy and there was a triangle of old food and grease behind the bathroom door. Obviously, the bathroom had been continually cleaned by the maid, swirling around her mop whilst she stood in the hallway. Thus this little triangle was not only continually missed, but any gunge in the bathroom would be swept into this corner, and was gradually growing taller. One could only spot it when sitting on the toilet with the bathroom door closed. Then it became painfully obvious. The next morning I led someone along to see it, and when we returned later the room had been cleaned a little better.

Breakfast was easily forgettable with porridge and cold pau, and no tea or drinks.

We were then collected and taken over to our bus where we were each given a plastic bag with our packed lunch. No, we were not going in on our bus, and joined a long line of people walking down the hill where we finished up at the park Head Quarters. Our guide handed out our entrance tickets and we walked up to form a huge queue for the park buses. The entrance fee to the park is marked at 220Yuan(US$60) with a further 90Yuan (US$12) for the internal transport. Seems that all internal transport is by shuttle bus.

The first leg of the road is about 3 miles (5km) long, where it splits into the two arms of a 'Y'. Each is about 9 miles (15km) long. The bus stops at each of the scenic spots on the way, so one had the day to come and go as one pleased. One could also walk between the locations on their constructed boardwalks and pathways.

But trying to get onto the first bus was no easy matter, with people trying to cut the queue, and there was lots of pushing and shoving. It kept the forest guards very busy trying to keep order. But after that, when people realized that the transport was in fact plentiful, matters improved.

That was the bad news. The good news was that the scenery was mind-blowing. The usual superlatives do not do it justice. If they called this Shangri La, then they might be right.

The Tibetans settled the valleys of Jiuhai Gou many years ago and their fenced villages are still there. The translation for the place is 'Nine Stockades' Gulley'. It is now a UNESCO World Heritage site. Officially no visitors can stay overnight within the park area.

The streams flowing through are crystal clear, and where they run over white sand, they turn a wonderful turquoise blue. The effect is breath-taking against the greens of the pine forest and the snow-capped mountains surrounding the area. Pines and alders and maple are just having their new leaves open, and the look especially bright and clean. A series of blue lakes cascade over falls into rivers and streams, that then feed into yet another lake.

There are vertical cliffs 1,600ft (500m) high, with pine forests on the 70degree steep slopes, and wonderful waterfalls. I have seen nothing like it before.

We made sure we visited the 'Primeval Forest' at one end of the 'Y', as well as Long Lake and Five-coloured Lake at the end of the other branch. The ends of the trails were about 9,800ft (3,000m) compared with the 6,500ft (1,965m) at the park Head Quarters.

We were very lucky with the weather, as we were able to enjoy the colours on the water, as these may not have been so startling had the weather been overcast. It had been hot, and my three layers of clothing were soon reduced to a long sleeved tee-shirt.

When we reached the park Head Quarters we watched a cultural show of singing and dancing that was being put on for the visitors. The local Tibetans are a good-looking race, with very pretty girls. They certainly contrast with the hardy Tibetans one sees in Lhasa and central Tibet.

We had walked a lot this day, and the long energy-sapping hike up the slope to our hotel did make it seem to be a long way.

Today we met a retired Pakistani colonel and his wife. We had sat behind them on one of our bus rides. Later we saw them and introduced ourselves. He was surprised when I said, "I assume you are a military man", but with a haircut like that he could not have been anything else. They were about to visit

Malaysia as their son was working in Kuala Lumpur. Naturally we offered to meet them when they came to Kuala Lumpur.

Later in the evening we met a couple from California, and he had been in the Peace Corp and had spent some time teaching English in a very small town in Malaysia. He still remembered his Bahasa Malayasia language after thirty years, and had forgotten more of it than I ever knew.

It all proves what a small place the world is these days.

Next morning we were woken at 5:45am for a 6:30am breakfast. Today we would be visiting another World Heritage Park at Huang Long.

There was a touch of mutiny as some of the people on the tour were trying to get the guide to take us somewhere else, as they said there was "No water in Huang Long", and they also mentioned altitude sickness. I could not understand why, and amused them by miming swimming strokes, then washing my face, followed by a few sniffs under my armpit. Still no explanation.

The driver was obviously fed up and started to increase the 'G force' he was applying at each bend.

We then got a bit fed up as the bus then spent the next few hours on a shopping spree, driving from shop car park to shop car park each selling crystals or jewellery or items made from yak horn.

The only interesting shops were the one selling about twenty different types of dried yak meat, and another where they were cutting up old radiator hosepipes and making them into vulcanised combs.

At every shop I stop for a pee, as you never know when one would get a further opportunity. It's not like a dog trying mark it's territory.

By mid-day we had had lunch and were told that we would now be on our way. But within five minutes, the mutineers declared they would go no further. It was agreed that all twelve would be put down and would walk back to town. The bus would pick them up again on its way back at 6pm.

The bus then started an amazing climb up to the snow line at 12,700ft (3,880m) to bare rocky mountainsides, with panoramic views down into the valleys below. The driver seemed to have the 'wind up his tail', as he kept the vehicle clinging to the sides of the precipices, and had no hesitation in overtaking on blind corners in spite of the cries from us passengers. The road then plunged back down on the other side of the pass.

At a stop to top up the brake spray water, we found bright yellow wild tulips at this high elevation. I had seen multi-coloured wild tulips (called 'guli lala') in Afghanistan, but those were quite small, whereas these ones were normal size.

Our bus parked at a crowded bus park and our guide went to buy our entrance tickets. (220 Yuan—US$33 per person)

NO CURE FOR THE TRAVEL BUG

It was 1:30pm when we entered the park and we would have a 2.3/4 mile (4.1/2 km) walk to reach the top most lake.

Huang Long is famed for a series of cascading circular ponds with the raised edges built up from calcified deposits. (They have similar calcified ponds in Turkey) The water in the shallow ponds was a light turquoise blue even in the overcast conditions. Certainly some of the lower pools had no water, as it seems they are only full in September and October. Now we knew what the mutineers had complained about. But what they did not know was that many of the pools were full, and one could certainly enjoy them.

One gradually climbed on their wooden boardwalk from 10,000ft (3,075m) at the entrance to 11,250ft (3,440m) at the lakes behind the temple. The air was very thin, and one needed to take it easy and take deep breathes. All along the trail they had wooden huts labelled as 'oxygen stations', where those who needed it could have free oxygen. One could also buy aerosol cans containing oxygen. Now we knew where the mutineers had got the idea of altitude sickness.

The walk down was much easier and we arrived in time for our 5pm departure.

Then it was a case of returning over the mountain pass to pick up our mutineers and start our journey south back along the road we had come on.

Darkness fell and we had a bit of a nightmare drive around the mountain passes. Our driver spent too long on his phone, and was swinging round the curves with only one hand on the wheel. Why am I sitting up the front?

We would come up behind convoys of buses all doing a reasonable speed, but our driver insisted on overtaking everything in his path.

It was nearly 9:30pm when we reached the West Hotel—Huanyingguan at Mao Xian. No time to wash up before going straight in for dinner. We were both physically and mentally tired, as it had been a long day.

Slept well, but we were woken at 4am when the TV came on at high volume. When we told the story next morning at breakfast, the others laughed, as the same thing had also happened to them.

We had a 7am checkout, and were once again subjected to a number of those cursed shopping stops until 10am.

By mid-day the visibility was dropping rapidly and we were back into the polluted air again. By 3pm the bus started dropping off the people in Chengdu, and we reached our destination by 3:35pm.

The whole group had been very good to us, and we had had plenty of laughs with them. Language is only a problem if you let it be. Yes, I realize that's a stupid and trite statement to make when you don't understand a word apart from 'hello' and 'thank you' in Mandarin; but sign language and a smile can go a long way.

Caught an airport shuttle bus to the airport and had a very easy check-in for the hour flight to Kunming. This was much better than the fourteen-hour train journey.

Kunming to Kuala Lumpur.

The same room was waiting for us at the Camellia Hotel. It had rained all night and continued to drizzle all day. Had a bus trip round town, then found a sports shop near the hotel. My Lowe Alpine bum bag was disintegrating, so I finished up with a local replacement, and Lian also bought one. A 'dry-bag' for storing cameras etc from the rain went into the basket, as well as a body-warmer and a rain-jacket for Lian. The Mastercard came to our rescue here. Generally had a lazy day and a half winding down and actually looking forward to our return.

The flight back to Kuala Lumpur via Bangkok went well. We had arranged for legroom in an emergency row, and had just settled down when the chief steward asked us to move up the plane. I tried to explain that I did not want to move, as I needed the legroom. "I assure you that you will be comfortable sir", and we followed him for a free upgrade to the business class.

This was a fitting end for a wonderful and memorable trip.

CHAPTER 7

East Malaysia: Sabah—An expedition to the Imbak Canyon

River crossing—Imbak Canyon.

When the Malaysian Nature Society (MNS) announced they were making an 8-day photographic expedition to the Imbak Canyon in Sabah, on the northeast corner of the island of Borneo, we leapt at the chance to join it. The trip was limited to about a dozen participants.

In central Sabah they have two conservation areas; Dunum Valley, and the Maliau Basin.

At present the Imbak Canyon is still designated as a potential logging area, and they were in the process of changing this into another conservation area.

The previous year, Raleigh International sent twelve volunteers for a 3-month initial exploration of the area, and described it as one of the most pristine rainforests in the world. The 74,000-acre (30,000-hectare) 'canyon' is about 6 miles (10km) long and 2 miles (3 km) wide, with a flattish bottom at about 500ft (150m) above sea level, and steep sandstone sides with a rim at over 5,000ft (1,500m).

Knowing there would be a good deal of forest trekking, Lian and I trained quite hard on our return from our trip to England, as we did not want any lack of fitness to spoil the trip. So nearly every morning we went walking around Bukit Gasing, a wooded hill area just south of Kuala Lumpur. This had plenty of very steep slopes to clamber up and down, and within a week we were able to do the 1.1/4 hour walk without pain.

So early on a Saturday morning in mid November, the group of thirteen MNS members met for the 2.3/4 hours Air Asia flight to Sandakan in Sabah.

Jimmy, our team leader for the expedition, met us with four 4WD vehicles. Firstly we drove off to a market to buy provisions and bottled water, and then on to a local open restaurant area for a fried rice lunch before starting the main journey.

Or route took us out of Sandakan to the police checkpoint, where the road either goes west towards Kota Kinabalu, or eastwards to Lahad Datu and Tawau. We turned westwards and after about 63 miles (100 km) on tarred roads, we turned south onto a laterite road through the palm oil estates, and later through logging concessions.

We were within 12 miles (20km) of our destination of the Imbak Base Camp, when we were told that the Imbak River crossing was impassable due to three days of rain further up stream. There was no telling how long it would take for the river to go down, so we had little alternative but to take the long route via Tawau.

However, as there was insufficient time that day, we returned to Sandakan. We were accommodated overnight at the Yayasan Sabah headquarters. Yayasan Sabah is a government organisation that administers the logging in the huge area surrounding the three conservation areas.

Lian and I had a room with a single bed and they brought us an extra mattress to put on the floor. The room even had an air conditioner, so no complaints. Shared toilet facilities were available.

Before daybreak the next morning, the convoy set out for Tawau. Once again the weather was very overcast, and threatening with rain.

We had an hours breakfast stop at Lahad Datu, before reaching Tawau at 10:45am. Spent an hour buying extra snacks etc., and waiting for the drivers to pick up fuel vouchers from their local office. Then at the petrol station, one of the drivers started filling his diesel powered Toyota with petrol! We then had to wait half an hour while the tank was drained off and diesel refilled. Needless to say, the driver was very embarrassed.

Although we were on a tarred road passing through palm oil estate roads, somehow the convoy got split up. We stopped at a small shop / restaurant next to a mosque, but did not fancy the food there, as there were so many flies. I walked down the road to what I assumed was a garage only to find it was a Chinese coffee shop /restaurant. Much cleaner and I enjoyed a good chicken noodle soup.

At 2pm the convoy got together, and soon turned off onto laterite surfaced estate roads.

Half an hour later we left the palm oil estates for the tracks in the forest logging concessions.

We came upon a huge logging truck and trailer full of logs, which had skidded off the road and blocked all access. This truck was just being pulled out, and we had 20 minutes to wait before it got going again and we passed by. There were perhaps as many as a hundred logging trucks in a jam behind it, and we were able to get a feel of how much log volume is being taken daily out of the concessions in the area.

We passed the entrance road signposted for the Maliau Basin, and followed the main logging road. This was not that easy, as there are many junctions, and those using them do not bother to put up any signposts.

Took one smaller track alongside what we found was the Imbak River. A couple of 4WD's were at the side of the track, and a few people were sitting by the river. We stopped and got out. Leading this group was Dr Waidi, who manages the conservation areas of Danum, Maliau, and now Imbak. They had made a small fire, and were roasting some sweet corn cobs they had brought. After a chat, we left for the Base Camp and they would join us later.

It was nearly dusk when we came across a huge branch that had split off a giant tree and completely blocked the track.

We were told it was only a couple of miles (2 or 3 km) from the camp, so one driver set off to get help and a chainsaw.

Dusk falls swiftly in the tropics. The sky was turning orange as we watched many huge flying-foxes flapping overhead on their way to their feeding grounds. As it got darker we saw fireflies, and some were so bright that we kept thinking our rescuers were returning, as we thought we could see torches shining through the forest. But was 7pm and very dark when seven

Forest Rangers returned with a chainsaw, and within minutes we were ready to roll again.

But the track on the last mile or so to the camp was very bad, and we were soon slipping and sliding through deep mud before reaching the base camp half an hour later. It was real 'Camel Trophy' conditions, and this was all in the dark. How the driver and the Rangers made the trip on foot I do not know.

Could not see too much there, but passed a big bonfire of log stumps as the area for the camp continues being cleared.

Three main timber building have been completed with an elevated timber boardwalk interconnecting them. The main building houses the Forest Rangers. The kitchen and canteen block has open sides, apart from around the kitchen area. The third building is the visitor's bedroom block, which also has open sides. The beds are canvas stretcher beds, lashed between bush pole supports. Although the beds were quite adequate and comfortable, they proved much too short for someone with my frame. Cooking water is rainwater, collected by gutters to a storage tank.

Washing is done in the river, and some wooden steps assist one getting down. The WC's are pit latrines, situated quite a long walk from the bedroom block.

Plans are in hand for collecting running water from a small stream for the camp, and this was one of the reasons for Dr Waidi's visit.

Lighting is by a generator, which operated on restricted hours, but would be adequate for charging our camera batteries.

So we chose our camp beds and put up new mosquito nets provided for us.

Then it was time to start cooking dinner. What—no cooking oil—who made out the provisions list? Luckily the Rangers lent us some. Then we found we were cooking not only for the Rangers, but also for Dr Waidi's group. That makes twenty-seven people. More food rations would be needed, or we would not have enough food to last us.

As we had lost a day in additional travelling, it was time to discuss the revised itinerary, and also our routing for the next day's two-day camping trek up to the ridge. As each person would need about six or seven pints (3 litres) of drinking water a day, water would be the main consideration on this trek, as no water would be available on the ridge.

Three of the group from Kuala Lumpur were not confident of making the top of the ridge, and elected to stay around the Base Camp.

It was nearly 10am the next morning when the group and the Rangers left camp. Only a few hundred yards and it was time to cross the river. Not an easy crossing, as the riverbed is full of boulders and the current quite strong. The Rangers took the baggage and photo equipment over first, and we were all glad that everything was wrapped in plastic bags, as several times one could see the bottom of the bags dip in the water. Then they helped us to cross. The water was certainly waist deep for me, and chest deep for many. Those who took their trousers off first were glad they had done so. I did not bother, as I had chopped down some old Rohan trousers to become shorts, and they dry very fast.

Then it was time to start a slow climb up a fairly steep ridge. Not much in the way of undergrowth, as there is insufficient sunlight for the groundcover to grow. This is one of the advantages of travelling in pristine forest.

We were only an hour away from our overnight 'half-way camp', when I stumbled or tripped and I felt a sharp pain run up my leg, and I fell over. After a quick yell or two or three, I sat mumble swearing to myself. I had certainly sprained my ankle and would not be able to go on. Luckily we had an elasticised sleeve with us and I slipped this on my ankle and foot to give additional support.

It was agreed that Lian and I would return to base camp with a Forest Ranger as guide. We had already agreed we would pay him extra to carry more of our equipment, as we did not want to have to struggle.

The Ranger cut a staff for me, and we slowly retraced our steps down the hill, sometimes walking, and sometimes shuffling down on my bum. He even offered to carry me, but as he was slightly built and pretty short, I said I was scared, and we had a good laugh. At the river crossing I suggested I lay on my back and he tow me across, and this worked well, even if it was cold getting right into the water.

Once across, he left us and went for some help at the camp, and I was able to keep the ankle in the cool water, and I think this kept the swelling down. The Ranger returned with Ismail, a senior Ranger, and I slowly hobbled back to the camp, where I had a wash from a bucket, changed my clothes and had a rest and a kip.

Went to the canteen block for some rice and vegetables for dinner. Lian and another girl went off for a pee, and told me to stay where I was until they came back.

If only I had done as I was told—but you know how it is.

After waiting for some time, I thought I would start along the boardwalk with my long staff to assist me. This went well until I reached some steps. I'm not sure why, but I lost my balance and started to slowly topple off the side—so I put the staff down sideways onto the ground to support myself, but managed to fall towards it. I saw the end of the pole coming towards my left eye, and I seemed to do a pole-vault with the staff in my eye socket. As I sat on the ground nursing my eye, I really thought I had done it! Had my glasses broken? What about my eye? Thank goodness I could still see, but it hurt and felt very bruised. Then Lian arrived and found me. She was also worried as there was some blood by the side of the eye. The girls searched around and found my glasses, quite unbroken.

I now fully appreciate the phrase 'better than being poked in the eye with a blunt stick'.

Ismail was going to Sandakan or Tawau early next morning to buy the additional foodstuff, and we said we would come with him to go to a hospital. It was however obvious that a return to Kuala Lumpur was required, as we were worried about any damage to the eye. Time for bed.

Lian was up at 4am and had to pack up all our gear by candlelight.

At first light we set out. Luckily the river level was down enough, and we were able to cross the river by 4WD and so take the shorter northern route back to Sandakan.

Whilst going through the palm oil estates we passed a lot—over 500 I would guess—of soldiers doing a full pack route march. They were strung along the road and having to walk in the full tropical sun and humidity. Even saw a few women soldiers with full packs. The funny thing was that most were wearing assorted sports shoes rather than army boots. Would have made some good photos, but that could have been very unwise!

On the way into Sandakan, we stopped at the airport and Lian managed to get us on the 5:10pm flight back to Kuala Lumpur.

Ismail took us into town and we booked into the Sandakan Hotel. Had a warm shower, took some eye drops that Lian bought, and slept.

Took a taxi to the airport, and had a wheelchair to the plane and also had one at KLIA as it would have been a long walk at that end.

Next morning we left early to get in the queue at the Tun Hussein Eye Hospital. Luckily we did not have to wait too long to see our doctor. She examined my eye for some time and said that "The plastic lense in the glasses had certainly saved you, and the abrasions on the cornea would heal in a few days."

Then on to the hospital to sort out the ankle, which obviously was not the priority. The X-ray showed a fracture of the fibula. "Yes, it's a spiral fracture, but you are lucky, as the ankle joint seems O.K. It was a good job that you were wearing high-sided trekking boots. I will put on a cast and you will have to keep this on for about six weeks. Pick up some crutches at the physio' department."

Thus ended our visit to the Imbak Canyon.

CHAPTER 8

Northern India: Rajasthan

A 'Haveli' in Mandawa.

When the Indian Government issued us a visa last September to visit Himachal Pradesh, it allowed a second entry within the year as long as there was a two-month gap between visits.

We were last in Rajasthan in May 1988, and it was so unpleasantly hot. We visited Bharukpur and Jaipur before succumbing to the heat, and fled to Kashmir to enjoy its wonderful ambience.

So winter would be a good time to enjoy the state of Rajasthan. We intended to visit the majority of the tourist areas, but this would not be a 'Palace on Wheels' trip, as not only is the price beyond our budget, but such trips do not allow one to experience India, but rather give a Disney Land / Kodak view, where the dirt and rubbish tends to disappear from view. There were of course several times on the trip when the idea of the 'Palace on Wheels' became a lot more favourable.

Delhi

We arrived in Delhi on a pleasant Air Asia flight to a cool 10deg C (50 F) and our hotel taxi was waiting for us. Lian had made an Internet booking for the 6am train the next morning from Delhi to Jaipur, but we had been on the waiting list for several days. So we were relieved when the night manager at the Hotel Ajunta phoned the railway station to find that our seats were confirmed. The manager then wanted us to move to a more crumby place behind the Hotel Adjunta, as he said his hotel were working 24 hours-a-day on renovations, and it would be just too noisy. We refused, and slept well with no noise in our room.

Our alarm was set for 4:30am and it only took five minutes on the little 3-wheeled 'tut-tut' to reach the station.

Then the problem started. We scrambled around the hundreds of bodies sleeping on the station floor to the platform gate, where we were told that our computer printout was not a ticket, and that there had been a lot of double ticketing by unscrupulous agents. We were taken upstairs to see one man, who then accompanied us out of the station and directed us to a travel agent along the road. He also said our seats were not confirmed, but there was a special allocation for tourists which we could purchase. Other foreigners were also being brought into the shop.

Smelling a rat, we went back to the station and ignored the man at the gate. When the train arrived we saw that our names were on the passenger list, so found our allocated seats on the Shababi Express. One wonders how long this scam has been going on with the railways staff.

Jaipur.

We had booked 1st class seats, and found that this included a 5-course Indian breakfast, drinks and newspapers. All quite civilised, although our carriage was quite old, and the 5-hour journey went fast, arriving in Jaipur in the late morning.

The temperature when we left Delhi was 4deg C, (40 F) and it was quite misty.

We took a 'tuk-tuk' to the Arya Niwas Hotel, but they had no available rooms. They suggested their sister hotel, the Jai Niwas, and we took their advise.

We walked all along the bazaar area. Teeming with people and vehicles and cows and slippery cowpats. We walked through the New Gate to the Albert Hall. Saw lots of rats living in shrubbery and quite without fear of people passing by.

Lian used a public toilet and was shocked for several days whenever she recalled seeing a naked young woman crouched on the floor. Her imagination ran wild as to the relationship between the woman, and the man collecting money at the toilet entrance. Unfortunately, her worst fears were probably correct.

Turning north we walked along the main city road, admiring the wonderful architecture of the three and four-storey buildings with their balconies and carved honeycomb stone windows. We then saw the famed Hawa Mahal or 'Wind Palace', an extraordinary five-storey building of pink stone that is one of the main tourist destinations in the city. It is basically an ornamental façade built over 200 years ago for the ladies of the court to view across the city. Many of the stone latticework windows are glazed with multi coloured glass. It reminds me of an old-fashioned jelly mould.

Camel carts abounded: with the imperious looking single humped camel pulling a 6 foot (2 metre) square wooden platform mounted over an old lorry axle and wheels. The white turbaned driver lolled off the edge of the platform.

We decided not to stay another night in Jaipur, but proceed to explore the Shekhawati area. This is a little off the normal tourist route, but is famous for the 'havelis'; merchants mansions that are decorated internally and externally with paintings, making them a living fresco art gallery.

Luckily, some have now been converted to hotels and guesthouses, and we wanted to enjoy what remains before the real 'havelis' turn to dust.

The next morning we checked out of our hotel, and took a 'tuk tuk' to the local Jaipur bus station and set off for the town of Mandawa. The local bus was not going there, but could drop us off Mukundgarh. We put our two bags in the compartment at the back of the bus.

We managed to get seats next to the door, but there was little legroom, so one of my feet had to be in the corridor. At 9:20am the bus engine rattled into life, and off we set. The bus soon became very crowded, and I became subjected to a continual barrage of elbows and swinging bags onto my head as the bus discharged its passengers and a new rent-a-mob scrambled on. If six got off, it always seemed as if a dozen got back on.

To say it was a pretty uncomfortable journey was an understatement. Pulling out our luggage from the bus brought with it a cyclone of dust. The bottom of the compartment looked like the Sahara desert.

Mukundgarh is a one street village. We were surrounded by 'tut tut' drivers, but they lost interest when we said we wanted to go the 9-miles (15km) to Mandawa. So we crossed the road to the only petrol station, and borrowed the toilet key. Things seemed much clearer once we had relieved ourselves.

Lian soon haggled with a driver, and we set off down the road to Mandawa. The air was crisp, and at last I could see the countryside. Sandy desert, with sparse grasses and shrubs, and with those most unusual Khejeri trees. They had been pruned such that the branches ended in big fists, with long thin shoots growing in all directions from this knotted fist. A species of acacia tree? Some trees had all the shoots cut off, and others were full of greenery. In the fields we saw what appeared to be hayricks, so assume these were built up from the tree's shoots and used for feed for the camels. I later found that this is the State Tree of Rajasthan, and not only is it used as animal feed, but the pods are used in cooking, the wood as firewood, and it even has medicinal properties.

Mandawa.

Reaching the town, we were held up for some time by a local bus that was discharging its passengers at a small roundabout. Women in their scarlet and red saris were clambering over each other trying to get on, whilst one young man managed to get in via an open window. Perhaps a forecast of things to come?

The 'tut tut' dropped us off at the Mandawa Haveli, waiting to see that we could get a room there, before accelerating away.

Wow, what an amazing place it was. Rooms on three levels all around a courtyard that has an open fireplace in the middle.

We were shown several rooms, every one is different in size and facilities, but all have every square inch of walls and ceilings covered with paintings. Even the floors are covered with painted stripes.

The walls are amazingly smooth, as they add a fine powder of marble to the plaster, so it looks and feels more like marble.

We chose a room on the first floor, and climbed the steep stairs. A narrow balcony runs all around the inner courtyard. The balcony wall is very low, and I remind myself not to trip as I step over the high threshold, or to step backwards when locking our door with the heavy padlock, or one could very easily plunge to the courtyard below.

We do have our en-suite bathroom and hot water is promised, as well as an electric heater for the room and a hot water bottle.

On our floor is a library, with a wide window seat overlooking the outer courtyard.

We climb the stairs and admire the view of the town around us. We look down into other 'havelis', which are dark with mould, as well as others with their painting still in good condition.

At one time Shekhawati was on the extension of the Silk Route branches that crossed the Himalayas and wend their way down to the Indian Ocean. The Maharaja of the area agreed to give protection to the various merchants and traders, but one condition was that they did not build any forts. Trade flourished under this system to everyone's benefit, and the merchants started building large mansions with outer and inner courtyards. They painted the external and internal walls, ceilings and often the floors, with paintings depicting religious and other pictures. They also often included such pictures as trains and planes. I suppose that each wanted to outdo the other, so these walls became living art galleries, tracing history and progress as it occurred. Then as other routes and railways opened, this area was bypassed and the merchants moved to the big trading cities, leaving their mansions or 'havelis' to slowly decay, with only watchmen or squatters to care for them.

Time to explore the town. Our 'haveli' is just outside the main gate, a medieval looking structure adorned with paintings. We were continually astounded by 'haveli' after 'haveli'. Our cameras were clicking and whirring, as each building seemed to outdo the next.

Saw several that had accommodation, so this was a good excuse to have a good look around.

Saw a man who was crushing rapeseed using a blindfolded bullock who was walking in circles around a giant mortar. The pestle comprised of a large tree trunk standing on end, and being dragged around by the animal. The man was scooping up quite large quantities of oil using this basic contraption. We remember having seen several yellow fields of rape flowers on our way there.

In the evening the 'haveli' guests can sit around the wood fire in the courtyard. A male dancer in a long red brocade coat swirls around, accompanied by a drummer and a man playing a stringed instrument.

We ate at the 'haveli's' restaurant. Whilst on this trip we had agreed to go vegetarian, as it is so much safer for health.

We ordered and enjoyed a potato curry, a vegetable curry and rice and chapattis.

Although Ragasthan is a dry state, they do have some 'beer shops', and most of the tourist places will serve alcohol, even though they may describe it quite differently on ones bill. So I also enjoyed the large Kingfisher beer.

The room is quite cold despite the heater and we pile on a couple of additional blankets.

Next morning saw us exploring the town. Kids can be a nuisance following us and demanding 'bon bons', and 'pen'. The answer to both was "No", and so they soon loose interest. Watch boys playing cricket as camel carts, donkey carts, motorbikes and decrepit buses trundle by. People of all ages are flying small kites.

There will be a festival in a few days and kite fights are a big attraction. Resin on the string will cut another kites string. They practice, and little boys fight for the loosing kites as they flutter to the ground. No wonder all the kites are small and cheap, as no-one would want to loose a big or expensive kite.

Lots of cows about, so one has to watch where one puts ones feet. But more attention to the cows would be prudent. As I wandered past one cow, with my hands clasped behind my back, I was suddenly hit with a horn that the animal rammed into the quick of my thumb. What a surprise. Was it because I was wearing a rusty red fleece?

The next morning we were setting off for Bikaner, so after sitting on the rooftop to watch the sunrise, we went down to the main circle to buy tickets for the local bus. The ticket seller was very helpful, and when the crowded bus arrived at 9am, he did a lot of shouting and we managed to clamber through a glazed door and get a bench facing the side of the driver. Here at least I had some knee room even though there were ten of us in this screened off area. All were ladies apart from the driver and myself.

One woman was trying to sell bracelets to the other women, who turned out to be teachers returning after a few days leave. So we had a lot of laughs with them and the conductor.

Bikaner.

It was 12:15pm when the bus pulled into its terminal, which was still 2 miles (3km) outside of town. A 'tut tut' took us to the Bhairon Vilas, where we took a 'heritage' room.

A huge room, two storeys high internally, with a bathroom, satellite TV (which only played a few local channels), and a full-length veranda complete with a swing couch.

We had decided that where possible we would take trains rather than a bus, so later in the afternoon we went to the station to book a night train to Jaisalmer for the next evening.

For our visit around the Junagarth Fort we hired the audio self-guide. Glad we did this, as one can proceed at one's own pace, and simply step back and wait if a crowd come through. The audio was very well done, using an Indian commentator with a very expensive English accent.

At the fort entrance were a number of handprints on the wall. These represented the wives and concubines who had committed 'suttee' by jumping onto the funeral pyre of a deceased Maharaja.

The fort is unusual in that it is not built on the top of a hill, but on level ground.

Pigeons are everywhere; it is more crowded with them than in Trafalgar Square. Buses, cars and motorbikes rarely have their hand off their horns. It's a good job the camel carts are without horns as they race along the roadway at the side of the fort. Roundabouts have a stand for policeman in the middle, but few drivers use them as intended, but may simply take any shortcut across as being the most direct way. As foreign pedestrians, it is all very confusing and unsafe.

Slept well as it was not as cold as previous nights. After breakfast we took a 'tuk tuk' through the old town to the all white Bhanaindasar Jain temple. The Jains prescribe a path of non-violence towards all living beings.

From the upper levels we had good views over the old town with its many powder blue painted Jain house. We then attempted, with some success, to retrace our 'tut tut's route all the way back. Passing through narrow lanes, and sometimes having to hide in doorways to make way for the camel carts and many 'tut tuts'. On the way we stopped off to look around the Bhanwar Niwas, an expensive heritage hotel, that was full of antiques. A beautiful hotel, but really surrounded by the squalor of the surrounding area. I admired the old white 1927 Buick at the entrance.

Enjoyed a long lunch, followed by reading in the garden until it was time to go to the station. We had only managed to buy 2nd class sleepers, with a lower bunk each. The train pulled in at 23:10hrs so we had plenty of time to find our bunks. The train for Jaisalmer departed on time at 23:35hrs but as it turned out, the whole carriage was fairly empty and we had no others sharing our compartment, which had 6 bunks.

We soon settled in to sleep, which was disturbed initially by two in the next compartment who talked loudly, and later snored even louder. But it was the cold that really got to us; it was like trying to sleep on a cold plastic park bench. Thank goodness I had my woolly hat pulled well down over my ears. The train had two speeds: very fast or stopped. This is the main problem with single-track railways.

Jaisalmer.

At 5:30 am we pulled into Jaisalmer station, and we were immediately surrounded by taxi drivers in the carriage. "Hello Sir, I have already been waiting for you for an hour". All bluffing, as they started guessing the names of various hotels and guesthouses. But Lian had made a booking on the Internet the previous day for a hotel right inside the old fort itself, and they said they would send transport. Looking around, we spotted a man quietly standing hold a sheet of paper with our name spelt correctly. So we climbed into his 'tut tut' and shivered all the way as the cold air made our eyes run. We rushed through the streets deserted apart from a few dogs, then through a number of gates and arches as he careered upwards into the bowels of the fort. We stopped in a small square and he indicated that we should follow him as he bolted off like the rabbit in Alice and Wonderland. We followed as fast as we could, pulling our luggage behind us. By now completely lost and disorientated.

Then, lo and behold, we had reached the 500-year-old Suraj Haveli. Shown three rooms, Lian disapproved of all, but offered 50% of the asking price for the best of the three. To my surprise, this was accepted.

It was a huge room, with painted walls. The big bed was in the middle of the room, and there were two tree-trunk sized props holding up the wood panelled ceiling just behind the head of our bed. The word termites came into the conversation.

We had a cup of coffee and by 6:45am were asleep until we were woken at 9am by a cacophony of noise coming from outside.

Went over to open the big timber doors to the balcony and looked down into the alley below. A group of American tourists were just leaving the Jain house beside us, and all looked up as their guide carried on with his chat about our 'haveli'.

We wandered around the fort, taking in the sights and sounds and managed to avoid the motorbikes that roared along the alleyways. The main Jain temple is just opposite, and was crowded with visitors. The place looks quite different during the daytime, with souvenir shops over spilling into the alleys. Found the main square, and walked down through the various gates to the main bazaar, where we had some lunch.

A cow tried to butt Lian, who managed to spring out the way, so it was my turn to have a giggle.

We bought bus tickets for the next morning to Jodhpur from an interesting old man.

As the sunset we sat up on our 'haveli's' roof, where we had good views into the Jain temple, as well as the outer walls of the fort. Watched a cat trying to catch one of the many pigeons, but he only managed a few feathers. What did he expect when he was a gleaming black and everything else is sandy coloured?

After a good night's sleep, we were up early, after having paid our bill the previous evening. The alleyways were still deserted, but we managed to find a 'tut tut' to take us to the local bus station. Had a wait for the bus to arrive, which then made a number of stops around town to pick up customers. But at least with this bus we had numbered tickets. Not much headroom though, as there was a platform above us where other passengers could buy tickets and so either lay and sleep, or sit cross legged. One advantage of this system is that the standing passengers lean against the platform rather than your seatback.

A couple of hours later, the driver stopped for a short rest, so we had the chance for a quick pee. We had limited our morning tea to strictly one cup each.

Jodhpur.

Just under six hours from starting, the bus pulled into a petrol station about six kilometres from Jodhpur town centre, and we all had to get off. We squeezed onto a 'tut tut' which took us to the Shahi Haveli, in the maze of the bazaar area. The 'tut tut' driver got lost a couple of times in the narrow lanes.

The house is said to be 350 years old, and was once part of the 'Janana Dodi', or women's quarters.

We took a bedroom with a magnificent view of the fort that clings to a hilltop right in front of us. The dining room is on the rooftop together with a viewing platform. Many of the houses are painted with hues of powder blue, denoting them to be Jain.

The air is crisp and again the sky is a powder blue, and we snacked on a plate of chips and deep fried potato 'pakoda'.

Time to wander around the bazaar area, trying to remember how to get back again. Around the old clock tower were many fruit stalls, and thence onto the expensive 'Pal Haveli', to see where the rich and famous stay.

That night we dined on our rooftop under the stars, with the floodlight fort as the backdrop. We shared a rice 'thali' (steamed rice with dal and other curried vegetables) and a vegetable pizza. Both delicious and warming, as the evening got colder. The large bottle of Kingfisher beer seemed to go well with both.

In the morning we could see sets of steps going up the hill towards the fort, so decided to use these to get to the fort. Found that they only went as far a Jain temple, but found a dirt footpath going around the hillside, and twenty minutes later this led us to the entrance to Mehrangarh Fort.

Took the audio self-tour, which again was done very well.

From the battlements we spotted where we were staying.

A new tarmac road brings the tour buses and taxis to the fort entrance. But leaving the fort we opted to walk down the steep old road, which had been the original access way to the fort from the bazaar.

Here we booked seats for our bus to Udaipur, and Lian again used the Internet to arrange our accommodation there.

Back on our rooftop, we watched a troop of long tailed langur monkeys making their ways across the rooftops and onto a wooded section of the hillside below the fort.

Early the next morning, we left our room and took a 'tuk tuk' to a bus pick up point as dawn broke. There we were told a long story about a bus breakdown and we would be put onto another bus, but our seats would be the same. This was of course not true, and although we got seats, they were not what we had booked. We and the some other tourists had the same problem, so refused to move when others boarded later.

This again was the low double-decker, with people sleeping above us. Not a pleasant 7.3/4-hour journey. Had a 15-minute break for a pee at a road T-junction. No toilet facilities, so the women had to find a friendly bush. I luckily managed to snatch another pee when the bus had to stop at a level crossing for a train to go past.

The first half of the journey was across scrubby desert, although it was difficult to get a good view, as the outside our window was smeared with old sick from an upper passenger. Then the landscape became more hill and rocky, and later there was some agriculture. The road is narrow, and passing vehicles have to put a couple of wheels onto the hard standing. Even the tarmac is full of potholes and very bumpy.

I noticed that the bus had several different air-horn notes / tunes. Cows got a different hoot to other buses or lorries.

Some tourists had been talking to an Indian woman, when there was a commotion and they started to jump up as the woman just managed to scramble over them and get her head out of the window in time before she threw up. The tourists were screaming. Then about an hour later, the same thing was repeated, but through a window on the other side of the bus.

Udaipur.

So at 3:15pm everyone was pleased to reach the outskirts of Udaipur. We pulled out our dusty luggage, and a 'tut tut' took us to the Mewar Haveli, where we took the last available room.

We had just about to unpack when we had a call from reception to say that they had just had a cancellation and we could change room if we wished. Although the room was smaller, it had windows on three sides and a long padded couch seat under the windows, giving a wonderful view over the lake.

In the middle of the lake is the old Lake Palace Hotel made famous in the James Bond film, 'Octopussy', starring Roger Moore.

We sat on the roof terrace with a Kingfisher as we watched the sun set over the hills in the background.

Next morning we were up at daybreak to experience the dawn and the changing light over the lake.

After breakfast we walked along to the City Palace Museum that was close by. Again we made use of the audio guide, and found it an ideal way of enjoying the building and the exhibits about the Mewar royal family history.

One memorable story concerned a Maharaja who had a very beautiful daughter. She was offered to the prince of another state, who immediately accepted. The problem was that two such invitations had mistakenly been sent out to different princes, and both had accepted. If either invitation had been retracted, then this would have led to war. Being pragmatic, the Maharaja decided that the only way was to have his daughter die, so neither prince would loose face. So the 16-year old Princess Krishna Kumari was given poison several times, but the Gods protected her and the poisons did not work until at last she took a poison herself. The father felt pretty guilty and decorated one area in her name, with mirrors and beautiful peacocks. Of course they say her ghost still roams the palace.

We were running out of time, and had to choose between visiting Bundi or Ranthambore. The latter won with its National Park, so Lian made booking by train for the rest of our journey, and a hotel in Ranthambore. We had now agreed to use trains wherever possible rather than travel by bus.

In the afternoon we walked over a footbridge to get views of our 'haveli' and the Palace from the other side of the lake. The footbridge was nearly closed as three cows had taken it over and we gingerly sidled past them and their sloppy dropping. One had fearsome horns painted red.

Women were doing their washing on the lakeside, beating the wet clothes with thick sticks.

We were unable to visit the Lake Palace Hotel, as they allow no visitors even to take a meal. Without bookings for accommodation, the small ferryboats refuse to take you to the island. So we had our lunch on the lawns of the Ambrai Hotel, the closest one across the lake.

We found that generally speaking, Udaipur was the cleanest place we had been in Rajasthan.

At 5pm a 'tut tut' took us to the railway station for the Udaipur to Sasai Madhopur Express. The train pulled in at 5:40pm. We found our 2nd class sleeper cabin, but the numbers showed we had a middle and upper bunk instead of the two lower bunks that Lian had requested.

At first we had the compartment to ourselves, then three others boarded to we were forced to use our allocated bunks. I clambered to the top one. There were six swivelling fans on the ceiling, but there was no need to use them, as it was still cool.

Children and babies were whining and sibbing, people talked and laughed, and Hindi music was washing over us. But this is still much more comfortable than a bus.

But we managed to sleep despite the snoring and farting that slowly took over from the talking.

Ranthambore.

We had set our alarm for 1:00am as the train would only be at our station for two minutes. At 1:20am the train pulled in and we hopped off.

A 'tut tut' took us to the Tiger Safari Resort, and we managed to wake up a night watchman who appeared wrapped up in a blanket. Shown a couple of rooms, and took one on the 1st floor of a so-called cottage. By 2am we were in bed, but I did suffer from icy cold feet.

Having had no dinner the previous evening, I splashed out on a boiled egg, curried baked beans and chips for breakfast. Lian had French toast and honey. The sun is hot on our backs as we sit in the garden and catch up on news with a Times of India.

Went for a walk in the direction of the National Park entrance, and did some bird-watching.

Went into the Oberoi Hotel to have a look. The interior design of public areas and restaurants were delightfully. They said they would show us the 'tents' and we should follow the reception lady. But these 'tents' are extremely luxurious and huge. At a price of US$975 per night (excluding breakfast) they certainly should be. A plaque on the wall states that the hotel had been awarded the Best Hotel in the World in 2010, and the Best Resort Hotel in Asia in 2009, 2010. No comment.

We visit the tourist office and find that we can book our safari for the next morning by being there at 5am and making a booking at half the price of booking through a hotel.

So at 4:40am our alarm went off, and wrapped in blankets and with our hot drinks in hand we were the first people in the queue for the 6-seater 'gypny' seats. It was 5:45am before the kiosk opened, but we got our seats and walked down to our Resort.

An hour later, the 'gypnys' started to arrive and pick up their customers from the numerous hotels along the road. We then found that we had a double booking, as our Resort had also made a booking for us, despite our saying we would book our own.

Anyway, we got on the one we had booked, wrapping a blanket around our knees and pulling down a knitted hat. Funnily enough we pulled into the Oberoi to pick up an English couple. They were passed blankets, hot water bottles, and a hamper with snacks and drinks. This was their 3rd safari here, and they had yet to see a tiger.

At the park entrance, I paid extra for my video licence. The 'gypnys' were each day allocated an area to visit so there would not be too many vehicles in one place. We had been allocated Section 4, which our guide said was the most scenic.

At 10am we watched a government vehicle go off the track and drive towards a clump of trees. Our guide suggested we take a few photos of this as it was obvious that there was a tiger there as the men and women were clambering onto the roof of their jeep.

They must have been feeling guilty, and as they left, they gave permission for us to go in. We could see a tiger lying in the long grass, but it was difficult to tell head from tail. Seems that this female is the biggest tiger in the park.

Later a government vehicle came up to ask if we had taken any photos of the government vehicle and we solemnly said we hadn't.

In the afternoon we walked into town and checked the railway station and platform numbers. The place is dusty and dirty. Without tourists and the national Park, one fears that the place would soon become a ghost time. Arranged for a 'tut tut' to pick us up at 6am the next morning.

The train for the 217mile (350km), and 2.1/4 hour journey to Delhi arrived late at 7:25am. We had allocated seats, but the train was quite full. Only 2nd class was available, so no water or breakfast supplied. Just enough legroom, and with non-reclining seat backs. However there was a continual stream of people selling various foods and tea, so there was no need to starve.

Delhi.

We had eight hours to kill before our return Air Asia flight to Kuala Lumpur, so we took a taxi from the station to the Radisson Hotel, located quite close to the airport.

Here we splurged on a buffet lunch and attempted to catch up on the meat and fish we had forgone over the last two weeks. Then enjoyed the lounge facilities and newspapers until it was time to leave.

CHAPTER 9

Northern Thailand and Laos

The slow boat to Luang Prabang.

Lian and I set off for a bird-watching trip to northern Thailand, from the Kuala Lumpur International Airport, with six Malaysian friends.

The trip had been arranged and was led by Lim Aun Tiah. His wife, Siew Pang, accompanied him. The two other men joining the party were Neo, and 'Uncle' Foo. Neo brought along his CDD digital video camera and telescope and was expected to take some impressive bird photos.

Yoke Lin and Wai Lee made up our group. Yoke Lin is a teacher, and she has the gift of incredibly sharp eyesight, being able to spot birds that elude us lesser mortals. Wai Lee is a shy pharmacist, with long and very thick hair,

The 2hr 40min flight to Chiang Mai was pleasant enough, and we were met at the airport by our minibus and driver, and they would be at our beck and call for the next week.

Thailand: Bird watching around Doi Chiang Dao and Doi Inthanon.

We booked into the Lai-Thai Guest House, which was quite adequate. Lian and the others went out to do some shopping, but I stayed behind for a kip, as I had a bit of a fever and was suffering from a bad cold.

The next morning we headed north to Chiang Dao about 56 miles (90km) north of Chiang Mai and stayed at the Malee Chalet. This is a very friendly little place run by a woman called Malee. At that time Jurgen, a Belgian bird-watcher, was assisting her. The food was good.

The next morning Siew Ping, Yoke Lin and Wai Lee took the minibus for a shopping trip, and the rest of us followed Jurgen for a walk in the surrounding valley. After 1.1/2 miles (2-½ km) on the flat, passing through several habitats and cultivated areas, we reached a protected forest area and the trail climbed steeply. It was too much for 'Uncle' Foo, who slowly returned at his own pace. I was soon panting as the uneven track became steeper. Jurgen and I were ahead of the others, and I was pleased when a 4WD drew up and offered us a lift. The others had stopped it, and had climbed up onto the sacks of pig's feed that was being carried together with several other hill tribesmen, women and children. There wasn't much room left, and Jurgen and I had to hang on the back, which felt very precarious going fast up steep muddy slopes. Once we came to some level ground we stopped the vehicle and all of us clambered off.

The birding was quite interesting, and Neo was kept busy with his video.

By the time we had returned to Malees we were all tired and hungry.

Next morning we were up at 5am for a 4WD trip up to Doi Chiang Dao. Two vehicles awaited us, both pick-up trucks. They had open backs and no form of seating. It took a very uncomfortable hour to reach the top of Doi Chiang Dao. (Doi means mountain in Thai) The specialty here is the Giant Nuthatch, that lives in the tall pine forest. The others saw some in the mist, but Lian and I couldn't be sure, so cannot add it to our bird list. Plenty of things to see otherwise. By the time we reached Malee's we had plenty of bruised buttocks and sides, as one could not avoid sliding around and being slammed into the shallow sides of the pick-ups.

Our minibus then felt most comfortable in comparison as we returned to the 'Lai-Thai Guest House' in Chiang Mai. Actually the mini-bus was quite good. Due to his age, 'Uncle' Foo claimed the seat next to the driver, although he didn't need the legroom. Lian and I took the next row with Aun Tiah. The other four occupied the next two rows. It would have been too cramped if we had more than eight in our party, as we all had our daypacks with us inside the bus. The main luggage went on the roof.

Lian and I were taken for dinner on the banks of the Mae Ping River in Chiang Mai, by a distant relative of hers.

His is quite an interesting story, as he had disappeared some years ago and the family did not know whether he was alive or dead.

However, it seems he is a bit of a rogue. The story was that he had problems in Singapore over some gambling debts and had to run away. He settled near Chiang Mai and now says he has a local fruit plantation, growing longan, lichee and mango. He is also in the travel business, and claims to have started tours for people to see the long necked hill tribes near the Burma (now Myanmar) border. Whist there he had been caught by the Burmese and spent some time in prison for being involved with the Karan tribesmen. Now he goes to Singapore quite often, accompanying Buddhist monks and holy-men who give 'fung shui' advice to businessmen on the layout of their houses and offices, and to say prayers at the launching of ships.

On one such Singapore visit, he was asked by a business associate to look after and entertain a visitor from Kuala Lumpur, as the associate had a previous engagement. He immediately recognized the visitor as being one of Lian's brothers, and jumped across the table to greet his long lost nephew. So now he was introduced back to the family.

We then left for Doi Inthanon, which was to be the highlight of our birding trip. It is the highest mountain in Thailand at 8,500 ft (2,590m). We had heard that the National Park might be closed as the Queen of Thailand was visiting the area, and that no accommodation would be available in the park.

Luckily the park was still open to visitors, and we booked into four rooms at the Littlehome Guest House, close to the park entrance gates.

The summit is 29 miles (47 km) from the gate and passes through a number of different zones/ habitats, each being home to various bird species. (The bird list here is said to total 382, of which 104 are winter visitors)

We had done some homework on what we were likely to see in the various areas, as I had sorted out some trip lists from various British birders, which I had obtained some years earlier.

Lian was sick our first day here, and stayed at the hotel to rest. I reached the summit before finding that I had left my binoculars in the room. What an idiot! There was no option but to return to our little hotel and pick them up. I think the driver enjoyed it, as he an excuse to drive like the wind.

By 8:30am I was back at the summit, to find that some of the group were sitting shivering, and had left the sphagum moss bog area to sit in the sun and attempt to warm up.

As I rushed down the path to the boggy area, I could actually feel the drop in temperature. 'Uncle Foo' was all dressed up and looked like a little green goblin with his green hood and long walking stick. There was even a ground frost on the boardwalk and the long grass area.

I returned to the mini-bus to put on some more warm clothes, and returned. The binoculars felt very cold, so I used a spare pair of socks as mittens, and this actually worked very well.

We saw the Gould's Sunbird, and also the Greentail Sunbird, both of which are only found on this particular mountaintop. Then we had great views of a Eurasian Woodcock sitting, preening and the feeding. All magic stuff and I was so sad that Lian wasn't there to enjoy it.

The mountaintop had been so productive that the group agreed to return the next day. Luckily Lian was feeling much better and could come with us. Then amazingly we found the

Woodcock feeding again and we had plenty of great views of the Sunbirds.

On the first day here Aun Tiah had left his sun hat at the car-park of the Vachtathrn Nam Tok Falls, and luckily when we went back later in the day he got it back from an ice cream seller who had picked it up.

Then, two days later on our way down, we drove past an ice-cream man on his motorcycle, when Neo called for our mini-bus to stop. He jumped out and flagged down the ice-cream man. We watched as the man took off his jacket and passed it to Neo. It seems that Neo had lost his jacket at the same time as Aun Tiah had left his hat, but hadn't said anything. We all teased Neo about it as we drove back to Chiang Mai.

After a week in Thailand, the others were going to fly back to Malaysia from Chiang Mai, and Lian and I intended to go north and try to cross over into Laos.

Lian and I had seen about a hundred bird species, of which about 34 were 'lifers' (Ones we had not seen anywhere before.)

The 'Golden Triangle'.

Lian's relative arranged for us to join a day tour the next morning, going up to the Golden Triangle and then be dropped off at Chiang Rai.

We were picked up at our hotel by a mini-bus that proceeded to pick up seven others from different hotels. There were four Japanese, an American, and a Norwegian and his German wife.

Stopped at hot spring at Mae Khajan on the way to Chiang Rai, and watched people buying eggs and then cooking them in the hot spring water.

Then on to Chiang Saen and Sop Ruak, to see the 'Golden Triangle', where Thailand, Laos and Burma (now Myanmar) join.

It was here that we saw quite large cargo boats on the Mekong, and were told that they had come down from China. It was obvious therefore that the upper Mekong was much more navigable than much of it's lower reaches. Our curiosity had been stirred, and this became subject to a later trip.

After a lunch we went to Mai Sai, the border town going into Burma. Watched the people walking across the border bridge. There the German lady noticed a small boy's hand rummaging inside her handbag, but managed to stop him taking anything. Hand and owner ran away across the bridge to safety, and we all learned a lesson.

Then visits to two hill-tribe villages (Akha and then Yao). These were a little disappointing, as we had seen more authentic villages earlier on our travels.

We said goodbye to the others, and were dropped off in Chiang Rai, whilst the group returned to Chiang Mai.

We had arranged a booking at the Wiang Inn Hotel. Every now and again it is good to have a night in a comfortable bed with crisp white sheets, in a hotel with a few 'stars' to its credit. The night market was interesting and fascinating. The Thais certainly know what tourists want to see, and so have plenty of facilities.

Lao: Down the Mekong River to Luang Prabang.

After breakfast the next morning we took the local bus from the bus station for a 3-hour ride to the border town of Cheang Kong. The last couple of miles to the immigration point has to be taken using the little 3-wheeled motorized 'sanlow'. Then we crossed the Mekong by ferry, to the little Laotian town of Huay Xai. No problem with immigration, as we had obtained visas whilst we were in Kuala Lumpur.

Checked into the nearest hotel, which had a double bed, hot water and a fan for 20,000 kips/night (about US$5).

Walked around town, and enquired as to the best way to travel the 168 miles (270km) down the Mekong River to the old city of Luang Prabang.

Seems that one has two alternatives: the slow boat for two days, or the fast boat for six hours. The fast boats are expensive unless there are six passengers, and you wear a life vest and helmet—and even then you are deaf for days as the engines have no silencer and the propeller is driven direct from the engine. Alternatively the slow boats each takes thirty passengers and you have a night's stopover. We chose the latter.

We took a small tut-tut to the 'slow' jetty the next morning at 8am in order to book our passage. The fare was approximately US$ 11 each.

Lian's Thai language had been coming back to her over the last week, and she was now finding that this made our journey much simpler, as the Lao language is very similar to Thai.

The two boats were not going to leave before 10:30am, and we settled down to watch and chat with some of our fellow passengers, many of whom we had seen walking around town or drinking the previous evening.

Just about anyone who can read was carrying a copy of the Lonely Planet guide to Laos. Lonely Planet guides are like bibles for any traveler in this part of the world, but in Laos it seemed even more prevalent. They are great guides because not only do they tell you about the history of the country, but have super maps of every god-forsaken hole you could ever expect to visit. The only problem comes when they have recommended a certain hostel or café, as then its standing room only. You have to accept that there are other places in town and many new restaurants and hotels may have been opened since the guidebook had been written.

The boat was long and narrow with a row of seating along each side. You sit on this 5" (12cm) wide plank with about 2ft (1/2m) between the your knees and that of the passenger on the other side. The captain sits in the bow (up front), then passengers, then baggage, then engine, and lastly the toilet. To reach the toilet you have to crawl over the piled luggage, and squeeze past the very hot, smelly, thundering diesel engine. Not something you wanted to do too often. Later found it simpler to climb up onto the wooden roof and walk along this to the stern. At least the men could stand up and have a pee, but the women needed to scramble into a hutch about 3-foot cube. Not easy.

At the first Lao immigration office one is given a card to keep until departure, and every time one crosses a county border or reaches a town, then another stamp is put on the card. The penalty for missing a stamp is to go back and get one. The authorities then have a fairly good idea of the location of all the visitors, and this could even be useful if one got lost or worse.

One example of this was an Englishman from Brighton who had to go back to the towns immigration department, as he had not even gone through immigration on arrival in Laos. He came back from town very thankful. He was a real Cockney 'barrow boy' type, and looked a real toughie, even though about sixty years old.

"I've always 'ad trouble with authority, and is inclined to get confused," he said, and "Me brain sometimes lets me down, as I'd taken too many 'ead punches whilst boxing". He is real salt of the earth type, who had made his money selling stuff on the pavement in London's Oxford Street.

At last we got chugging away, all a bit cramped and soon my bum was getting corns.

The passengers were a real international motley crew. If I hadn't got a beard, I would probably have had to walk the plank, as I had no Rasta hair, earrings, chin studs, and safety pin through my eyebrow (an Irishman). Also we had no tattoos (more Irish, Swedes etc), and no body odor to talk about.

The Swedes were into rolling twiglets of what looked and smelt like camel dung and discussing who made the best roll-your-own cigarette papers. Yes, I was lucky to be allowed to stay aboard.

Christofe, the German, works only two months a year as a cowherd in Switzerland. He takes the cattle up to the high summer pastures and works 20-hours a day milking cows and making vast quantities of Swiss cheese. Then he travels for the rest of the year.

Two Canadian girls were on their way to Australia as exchange students studying law. The more attractive one was half-Chinese.

Patrick, a Northern Irishman now working in the USA, was going on to meet his girlfriend in South Africa.

Andrew Sabitini, was a young longhaired Englishman was just 'travelling'. During the boat journey, he found out that the father of the man from Brighton had been a close friend of his grandfather. His grandfather was said to be a notorious Mafia man from the Midlands.

A young English girl from Southampton turned out to be a doctor, and was shortly going on to Belize in Central America to work in a hospital.

An American girl from Colorado was on holiday from teaching English in China.

The Mekong is dark chocolate brown, and was at low level; so skillful river knowledge is necessary to avoid the nasty rocks. Many protrude above the river surface, but some lay waiting below the surface, ready to rip away the wooden hull. The sandbanks are often cultivated with some green vegetables. Behind the sandbanks are hills covered with scrubby secondary forest. Any big trees that may have existed have been taken.

Our first immigration stop was very pleasant once we had climbed up the steep riverbank

At 5:30pm we arrived at a small village of Pakbeng, and we all rushed off to find some overnight accommodation.

After climbing the long steep concrete path we booked into the first hotel we found. At least we had our own squat toilet, but this bathroom was bigger than our bedroom. (US$17 per night)

Had a problem when I burnt out the small hot water coil that Lian always uses, which allows us to have a hot drink night or morning. I had the accident trying to heat up some water for a hot wash.

Enjoyed a dinner of fried rice at a small thatched restaurant, together with a big bottle of the very good and very cheap BeerLao. Slept well as I was quite exhausted.

After a bread and jam breakfast, we went to the morning market to buy some bananas and water. Then we had to get immigration stamps, before we set off at 9:30am.

A different boat this time, as yesterday's boat would now return to Huay Xai. Some were staying on at Pakbeng, but others took their seats. This time there were three boats travelling together, but one broke down several times, and by journey end we had taken on some of these passengers.

Once again we saw very few birds by the river, but did manage some River Lapwings and a couple of Chinese Pond Herons.

Luang Prabang.

We arrived at our destination of Luang Prabang just as the sun was setting. After two days on the Mekong we thought we should spoil ourselves again, and stayed at the Phousi Hotel in the middle of town. It felt so good to have a hot shower and a cold beer.

Next morning we were up early to explore the town and watch the monks going out to collect alms. A few years ago, Luang Prabang was made a World Heritage town in appreciation of its history and the importance of its buildings. So much in this part of the world had been destroyed by the Americans saturation bombing, but luckily irreplaceable Luang Prabang escaped. Lots of Wats abound, which are Buddhist temples that have monks living in them. Many of the young monks are studying English and spoke surprisingly well. Met many of the boat passengers, as everyone seemed to congregate at the stupa on the hill to watch the sunset. All dry and dusty, but we had had a great day.

The next day we hired a couple of bikes and were able to explore areas that would have been too far to walk. We were able to pedal through places that we had seen from the stupa the previous day, and see how the Laotians lived in the smaller villages. Very interesting.

Decided that a thirty-hour bus trip to Vientiane would be a bit much, and we were not too sure of the security situation, so decided to fly down to the capital. The forty-minute flight was in a Russian plane similar in size to the Fokker Friendship.

Vientiane.

Booked into the Day-Inn Hotel, which was quite adequate and centrally located and stayed three nights there.

As a capital city it is very small and very dusty. Very little maintenance has been done to the old French colonial houses since the French left. They are carrying out some road works, and so perhaps some of the dust will clear. There were however some impressive temples.

Lian still had her bad cough, and I managed to get a bad stomach after a visit to the Scandinavian Bakery.

We enjoyed beautiful red sunsets as we sat at the little open-air restaurants on the Mekong's bund.

Once again we hired bikes, but this time with rather uncomfortable saddles.

It was time to leave Laos, and we took the half hour taxi trip to the Friendship Bridge. After going through Laos's immigration, one goes by shuttle bus across the bridge to the Thai side. Took a 'tut-tut' to the station and left our luggage before going into town of Nong Khai. Wandered along a great riverside market. Sitting in a restaurant, we spotted eight Spot-billed Ducks on a sandbar in the middle of the Mekong. These are pretty rare this far south.

Thailand: Night train to Bangkok.

At 6:30pm we took the night train for the twelve-hour trip to Bangkok. Had second-class sleepers, both bottom bunks and luckily we had no one above us. Drinks and food were delivered to our tables before they made up the beds. I was disappointed that the train wheels didn't made the traditional night train noises, but instead it was a real 'rock and roll' job with the rhythm changing every few yards, which I found stressful rather than being soporific.

It was raining as we arrived and Bangkok seemed really miserable. So we went along to the Royal Bangkok Club, which has affiliation rights with the Royal Lake Club we belong to in Kuala Lumpur. Had a breakfast and a shower, and used the reading room until it was time to take a taxi to the airport for the two and a half hour flight back to Kuala Lumpur airport.

CHAPTER 10

Taiwan

Taipei street scene.

We bought a six day / five night tour to Taiwan at the MATA Travel Fair in Malaysia. Neither of us had been there before. Taiwan is generally known as an expensive place to visit, with not much to see. But the tour price, including all meals, seemed to be quite reasonable value, and it was a good opportunity to visit the country.

As a Malaysian citizen Lian had to purchase a visa, but my UK passport did not need one. When visiting many of the local countries, the visa requirements are usually visa-versa.

We were about to take off from Kuala Lumpur when a storm arrived, so we had to taxi back to the terminal, and sit on the tarmac for nearly an hour before it passed. The four-hour 2,000 miles (3,200km) flight on Eva Air was pleasantly uneventful once we did take off.

We had been told that the Taiwanese tour guide would be speaking Mandarin, so we bought the Lonely Planet guide to Taiwan so at least we would have an idea about what we would be looking at. In fact the guide spoke only in Cantonese, and his English was zero. We also had a Malaysian tour assistant, and so she could confirm times for returning to the bus, wake up time, breakfast time and departure times, etc. This was very important, as we stayed in a different hotel each night.

The tour guide was a bit of a character, and would chatter on sometimes for an hour at a time. He was obviously a bit of a stand-up comedian, as he often had the thirty or so other passengers on the bus in stitches. Lian understood most of what the tour guide was saying.

The bus was quite comfortable with passengers up stairs and the luggage in a room below. No on-board toilet, so we had a pee-stop every two hours, which gave me the opportunity to unwind my legs for a while, as the legroom for me was only just O.K. They showed some video movies on the bus TV, all in

English with Chinese subtitles. Most of the films seemed to be adventure films, and with a sprinkling of soft porn.

Taipei is a big bustling city, with not too many signs in English. However, every other shop all over the country seemed to be a '7-Eleven'. Traffic not as bad as I had expected. Lots of overhead roadways, many of which are constructed using structural steelwork rather than the more normal reinforced concrete structures. We saw very few real motorbikes, but lots and lots of motor scooters. Rather like an updated and streamlined smart Italian Vespa—most seem to be Japanese Yamahas. Each scooter has a large silencer, so they are very quiet, and not at all like the noisy motorbikes in Kuala Lumpur.

The first morning we were woken at 6am, and after breakfast set out at 8:00am sharp, on a city tour. After a visit to the Chiang Kai-Shek Memorial Hall, we watched the changing of the guard at the Martyrs Shrine. This was very impressive, and quite a show of American style rifle drill. Lots of twirling and tossing which is obviously dangerous when you have a shiny fixed bayonet. I would be inclined to bet on them in a competition against the Americans. They also had a very unusual method of slow marching, which was worth studying.

The National Palace Museum is a treasure trove of Chinese artifacts, which were taken out of China and saved from the communists. They say that they have more antiquities now than in the whole of China. We could have easily spent more time here.

The things that annoyed many of us were the hour-long stops at speciality shops that cater for the tour groups, and who obviously pay top commissions to the tour guides. There are usually two similar showrooms side by side, and the customers are supposed to keep to their own showroom, and only meet at the shared toilet facilities. The visit usually starts with a sales pitch, followed by a video, more 'hard sell' and then listening to the cash registers ring. The Malaysians are great shoppers. Obviously I could not understand any of the sales patter, so I would mooch around the exhibits, and perhaps wander into the opposing showroom and cause as much consternation as possible without causing offence.

The main showrooms we stopped at were:—

Pearl showroom. As well as buying the normal pearl jewellery you could buy so many grams of pearls, which they would grind down to a fine powder. You then eat a small portion each day, and this is said to give you a beautiful complexion.

Mushroom showroom. This specialized in *'Granodesma Lucidam'* mushrooms, which are said to be much better than ginseng, and would cure anything that ails you. They also sold powdered stag horn, dried stag penis, and dried deer foetus. (The latter cost about US$740 each, and were said to be able to cure some cancers)

Marble showroom. Taiwan is a big exporter of marble and granite, and I was the only person who found the cutting of the large slabs to be of any interest. Then we went into the showroom to see the carved figures.

Fung shui showroom. Here we were greeted outside by the manager, who had everyone rubbing their hands three times clockwise round the head of a stone lion and then continue to stroke it right along the back and haunches. You then had to plunge your hands into your pockets. This was said to bring you luck. He then ushered everyone inside the showroom for the usual stories about his very expensive small stone and jade figures in an attempt to also bring him a lot of luck.

The tour went right around the island in a clockwise direction, starting at Taipei in the north. The east coast is relatively undeveloped, and has some very impressive scenery. Much of the time the coastal road hugs the sides of steep mountains, every now and then disappearing into one of the numerous tunnels built through the rock.

The Toroko Gorge was especially spectacular, and is probably the one and only real international tourist attraction in the country. Deep ravines, with towering marble cliffs, and clear water rapids.

Just north of Kaosiung we visited some interesting lakeside temples by Cheng Lake, and an especially beautiful Chunchui Confucian temple.

The west side of the island is flatter, and has a mix of agricultural land and light industrial. They mix together in an unusual manner, as you normally expect them to be in separate areas. But in Taiwan many of the rice fields seem to be in a checkerboard pattern with 3 or 4 storey buildings and factories between them.

The temples at the Light of Buddha Mountain at Fokuangshan are well known as a centre for Buddhist learning, and we saw many of the students there. It was set up by the Venerable Master Hsing Yun to realize his vision of Humanistic Buddhism. I'm not at all sure what that means! A huge golden coloured Buddha stands on the hilltop, and there are literally hundreds of life sized white figures lining all the pathways.

The weather was very kind to us, although it was drizzling when we visited the mountainside ex gold mining town of Chuifen. Here they had a winding covered shopping arcade selling some quite interesting handicrafts.

The food was plentiful and fairly good Chinese food. Breakfast was usually Chinese rice porridge with lots of vegetables, pickles, meat and fish to add to it. Lunch and dinner were normally seven or eight course Chinese meals. A couple of times we had barbeques, where we could pick up whatever we wanted buffet style, and then either cook it on a hotplate or steamboat style. We certainly had no complaints about the food.

In the evenings we either visited the local night market areas, or one evening we visited an Ani Cultural Village show. The Ani is a hill-tribe group, and put on a show of their dancing. Unfortunately it is all too similar to the dance shows you see from any tribal group: harvesting dance, fishing dance, wedding dance etc. etc.

The various night markets we visited (Lui-Ho in Kaoshiug, Chung Hwa in Taichung, and Shihlin in Taipei) were interesting, but things were more expensive than in Malaysia. Surprising however was how many young people go there to eat every evening, with thousands of scooters parked neatly side-by-side down the roadside.

Taiwan is very much an earthquake area. South of Taipei, near Taichung, we visited a school that had been destroyed in an earthquake in 1999. The reinforced concrete frame of the school was twisted and smashed, and a portion of the school running track dropped about 6 feet (2m).

On our last evening in Taipei, we went to the Yang Min Shan hot spring spa. Lian and I shared a hot tub, which we filled with a mixture of the natural hot spring water and cold water (about 50:50). Not too strong a smell of sulphur, but a definite mineral smell. A half hour was sufficient, and we put on sweaters after we dressed and came out, as the outside temperature had dropped to about 15deg C (60F).

I was the only Caucasian we met on any of the tour groups visits, and in fact we saw only about a dozen on the whole trip. Lian and I did however meet one young teacher from the English Midlands, who told us that there were quite a few British teachers in the country and they earn quite good money. They are supposed to speak no Chinese to their pupils. This chap teaches English to youngsters, and keeps discipline by the award or taking away of coloured stickers. He said that taking a sticker away, or awarding a frowning face sticker rather than a smiley face sticker, would make a student cry.

On any future visit, we would like to visit the national parks in the central mountain area.

CHAPTER 11

Indonesia: A journey to northern Sulawesi and the Spice Islands of northern Maluku

Ternate—Alfred Russell Wallace must have lived in a similar house.

So within six weeks from returning from our trip to the islands east of Bali, we set off on another trip, loosely following in Alfred Russell Wallace's footsteps, this time visiting northern Sulawesi and the spice islands of northern Maluku (previously known as the Moluccas) and Halmahera.

We consider Wallace's book, 'The Malay Archipelago', to be one of the best travel and adventure books that one can read. We took with us extracts from his book, as we hoped to visit some of the places he so vividly describes in his book.

Northern Sulawesi: Manado

At the end of March we flew by Air Asia from Kuala Lumpur to Manado on the western coast of the northern end of Sulawesi. We could see that the hilly areas were forested, and all the flat areas covered with coconut trees.

As we would be returning from Manado, we had decided it would be safest if we travel to our farthest destination, and then work our way back to northern Sulawesi.

So on arrival at the Manado airport, Lian started investigating and booking flights.

As we had mentioned previously, booking Indonesian local flights when out of the country is very difficult, as the airlines are not very Internet friendly. And we were now to find that some of the airlines mentioned in the guidebooks had already closed down.

We had planned to visit Ambon in the southern Maluku during the trip, but found that flights from the northern Maluku were very infrequent and expensive. Ambon would have to wait for another trip, where flights could be easily taken from Jakarta.

So we booked an early flight the next morning for the volcanic island of Ternate in northern Maluku, before checking into a small hotel near the airport. The airline did not accept credit cards, so cash had to be paid.

After a rest, we had a trip into town using the local form of transport the 'angot', a small blue Suzuki bus, that can cram in about eight or nine passengers.

The first thing a driver does when he buys the little bus is to throw away the steering wheel and fit a tiny 'racing style' wheel. Then he will fit a hi-fi with a set of 12" (300mm) diameter speakers that are always played at high volume. A number of 3" (75mm) diameter convex mirrors would be stuck around the inside of the windscreen, so the driver can admire himself at all times. One bus actually had fifteen of these mirrors. But of course room must be left for a lot of dangling items to be hung from the rear view mirror. The ashtray is used to store the fares, as the driver can use the road as his personal ashtray.

We had to change buses on the way, and got off by a three-storey departmental store.

Asked a man for directions to the museum, and he insisted on dropping us off there in his car. However, the place was a complete disappointment. It seemed deserted, with no lights, and what we could see was covered with dust.

From here we took an 'angot' to the nineteenth century Kienteng Ban Hian Kiong temple, the oldest Buddhist temple in eastern

Indonesia. It then took three 'angots' before at last we found our way back to the hotel.

Here the cold shower was very welcome, even though we had no other choice.

Woken in the night by a brilliant white light, and the noise and smell of the hotel's generator. We were having a power cut. There was no switch I could find to turn off this light, so took the pragmatic approach of standing on a chair and unscrewing the bulb.

Set our alarm for 5am, and went out to try the breakfast which comprised cups of very bitter coffee and a toasted chocolate sandwich. We were to find that this is a pretty standard breakfast dish. Two slices of bread are buttered, and a filling of chocolate chips is heaped in. The sandwich is then put into an electric 'Brevette' type waffle toaster. It's not as bad as it sounds. Strawberry jam is sometimes an alternative filling.

The hotel has a shuttle bus up to the beautifully named 'Sitou Timou Tumou Tou International Airport'. Doesn't the name just want to roll off your lips?

The 'Wings' flight from Manado to Ternate is on a Dash 8-300 aircraft and takes only forty five minutes.

However we then saw something we have never encountered before in our travels. The seat pocket contains an 'Invocation Card' containing a set of prayers for each of the various religions in Bahasa Indonesia (Malay): for 'Islam', 'Buddha', 'Protestan' and 'Katolik'. So if the flight gets too rough, you can invoke the help of your own God to sort things out and land the plane safely.

The Northern Malaku: Ternate

The island of Ternate, is approximately 6 mile by 8 mile (10km by 12 km), and comprises a 5,645ft (1,721m) high conical volcano, with a narrow coastal strip of fertile land.

It took a lot of bargaining with the taxi drivers to get a reasonable cost for the ride into town.

We checked into the Losmen Kita Hotel, but had to wait until noon until a room became available.

So sat in their restaurant to drink endless cups of the excellent local coffee and play with the two tame Cockatoos they had in the restaurant.

One was a Moluccan White Cockatoo with a huge and powerful beak, and the other a Sulphur-crested Cockatoo with a much smaller and more delicate beak. Both were extremely tame and loved to be scratched and petted. The larger one loved drinking water from a glass, or sipping one's coffee.

Went for a walk to explore the town. A man in uniform on a motorbike soon stopped me. He wanted to practice his

English, so we had a chat for a while. I had to politely decline however when he wanted to come to our room to continue the conversation.

Walked down to the waterfront and the main jetty. Above us, Lian spotted five Frigate birds soaring in the sky. Looking back behind the town, the volcano is shrouded in cloud.

Four girls, who want to practice their English, stop me. In fact I soon got used to this, as it happened daily, and we always tried to oblige, even though most of the students were very shy. Surprisingly, Malays in the small towns in Malaysia never stop me, as even though English (American) has now become the international business language of the world, the Malays there still seem to consider it a colonial language.

We took a walk along to the Benteng Oranye, a fort built by the Dutch in 1607. The battlements still exist to three sides of the fort, and one can walk along them. The buildings inside are quite run down apart from the military hospital. The police and army families of those serving on other islands now live there.

Everyone is very friendly, and we are invited into one of the biggest buildings. Plywood partitions have been used to divide the inside into separate rooms. These have no ceilings, but look up into the darkness of the blackened wooden roof structure. A woman takes a precious framed photograph off the wall to show us. "That's my husband". A few soldiers are posing with some people from the highlands of Papua. The older women are bare-breasted, whilst the young Amazons sport black bras and hold spears. The naked Papuan men hold bows and arrows.

From the battlements we could clearly see the volcano on the adjoining island of Tidore, with its tip covered with a turban of cloud.

Continuing our walk, Lian spotted a road name, 'Jalan Alfred Russell Wallace'. ('Jalan' translates as 'Road' in Bahasa Indonesia.) This Jalan will need further investigation.

Our bathroom is very small and very economical. The basin outlet is not connected and the water flows across the tiled floor. There is no water supply to the WC; so flushing comprises collecting water from the shower outlet into a small plastic pail, and pouring it down the toilet. We do however have hot water to the shower, which sprays out into the middle of the floor and wets the toilet seat. A string of ants march across the ceiling, and I have to remember to duck when using the 5'9" (1.75m) high door.

The room is OK, and we found HBO on the TV. We ask for a top white sheet to go with the white bottom on. We could hear the rain during the night on the tin roof. The power went off as couple of times in the night, so we had to get up and restart the air-conditioner.

But this 'par for the course', and we are quite comfortable.

Breakfast comprised the famous toasted sandwiches and coffee. The people at the next table were talking in the Ternate dialect, and the timing and rhythm of it sounded just like a cheap 'spagetti western', when the Mexicans are talking in the 'cantina'.

Tidore.

Today we visit the sister Island of Tidore.

We took a couple of 'ojeks', motorbike taxis, down to the port. There was no ferry running, so we took a twelve-passenger speedboat with two 40HP outboard motors. We managed to sit at the back, and enjoyed the fifteen-minute trip. Once landed at the northwest corner of the island, we had a great view back to Ternate.

Leaving the jetty, we crossed the road to the little blue bus terminus, and took a bus on an anti-clockwise trip around to the east coast town of Soasio. I enjoyed a seat next to the driver for the fifty-minute ride.

The island has only a narrow strip of land around the coast, and pretty little single-storey houses line both sides of the winding road. The houses and fences are painted, with yellow and sky blue being the favorite colours. The elections are coming up and the multi coloured flags of the political parties fly everywhere.

Had a walk around Soasio market. Quite large, and dealing mainly in vegetables, eggs, spices etc. The main walkways are covered by orange or blue tarpaulins, and are much too low for someone like me, so I have to half crawl. There was lots of laughter when I manage to stand up straight at a gap between the coverings.

Not much left by the time we arrive at the fish market, although the giant kippers look quite interesting. It is hot and humid.

The bus back took forty-five minutes, and the speedboat only ten minutes back to Ternate jetty.

Ternate.

Later in the afternoon we took two 'ojeks' to the Sultan of Ternate's palace. But it was closed, and we find that the Sultan receives guests only between 8-11am. But I am not sure what we have to say!

Took a walk down to the seafront. We see many kids playing in the dirty seawater by the long wooden jetty. We move along onto the new bund. This bund has cut off a lot of wooden houses on stilts above the water, and the water around the water village is filthy with pollution and rubbish.

Had a long power cut early in the evening, and when it came back on we had no air-conditioning. An electrician was called and I helped him sort around to find the fuse-board in another building in the hotel grounds.

On the Friday after breakfast, I put on some more respectable clothes, and we set off on the back of two motorbikes for the Sultans Palace.

The retainers were sitting around at the entrance gate and were not sure what to do when we asked if we could have a look around. An elderly woman was on the verandah of an out-building, and Lian spoke to her. It turned out she was the Sultan's sister, and she got an old retainer to show us into the palace, a wood framed building with painted wood paneling. We were informed that the Sultan was still dressing, so the old man would be showing us around.

There were a number of old photos on the wall and a list of past sultans and the years of their reign. The furniture was relatively sparse, but there were some interesting crystal and Dutch candelabra. An elegant woman wrapped in a gown comes out of a side door and passes through an adjoining door. Could this be the Sultan's wife going to the bathroom? The answer is probably yes.

We went onto the wide verandah overlooking the grounds and looking towards the sea. A wonderful location, but unfortunately we were not allowed to take photos.

Walked along to the 'little blue bus' terminal, and from here we had a 35-minute trip along the coast to find the lake of Danau Laguna, at the base of the volcano.

Even thought the villages may not be as pretty as those in Tidore, they are still very picturesque.

The water in the lake is rather greenish, and the sides are vertical and forested. We sat on the rim and did a spot of bird-watching, before exploring the path alongside the edge. It was hot and humid.

When we flew out of Ternate, the aircraft flew over this lake and we had a good alternative view.

Walking back to the main road, we were able to flag down a blue bus for our return trip. I sat in the front with Farid the driver. He said he was seventeen, but looked a bit younger. Passing through one village, he had no chance to miss a cat, which must have run across right in front of us. I did not even see it coming, but only felt the double thump as our little wheels went over it.

I looked back to see the cat jumping high into the air, twitching with an arched back before collapsing dead on the verge.

Farid jumped out of his cab, and ran back to the cat. Seeing it was dead, he took off his T-shirt, and opening it, he gently lowered the cat into it, and carefully wrapped it up, before putting it into the back of the bus beneath Lian's feet.

He said he would have to take it home and bury it. This would appease the cat's spirit and ensure that Farid himself would not be run down, and would also remind him to go to the mosque to pray.

That afternoon, after a power cut, we were having some lunch when some really loud music started up in the street. A giant set of speakers had been set up just opposite the hotel entrance. Then a huge procession of people passed by motorbikes, trucks and cars. All the people were in the yellow T-shirts denoting their political party, and they trailed huge yellow flags with the party emblem. They were off to the main stadium for a rally.

We went in to try to rest, but the floor was throbbing. So we decided to go for a walk and try to find Alfred Russell Wallace' house. The yellow shirts were still passing by, and as we passed the speakers, one could feel one's diaphragm vibrating. Not a pleasant feeling. The police had a heavy presence at all the corners. The people all waved at us, and the sound of "Hello Mister" was pretty well continuous as the people drove pass. If I waved back, then they would let out a huge roar. So friendly, but one always felt a little apprehensive, and the hairs on the back of my neck did tingle a few times.

Found the road, and checked Wallace's description of the house:

> "There is of course only one floor. The walls are
> of stone up to three feet high: on this are strong

squared posts supporting the roof, everywhere except in the verandah filled in with the leaf-stems of the sago-palm, fitted neatly into wooden framing. The floor is of stucco, and the ceiling is like the walls. The house is forty feet square, consists of four rooms, hall, and two verandahs, and is surrounded by a wilderness of fruit trees. A deep well supplied me with pure cold water, a great luxury in this climate. Five minutes walk down the road brought me to the market and the beach, while in the opposite direction there were no more European houses between me and the mountain."

So we had all the clues we needed. The main one was that it was 'five minutes from the beach'. But the road named after him only starts about five minutes from the beach, so it could not be too far up. Saw two houses that still fitted the description, but the owners pointed us in the direction of a modern single storey modern bungalow with a mini-general store attached. What a disappointment.

We knocked at the door and the owners' son greeted us. Yes—this was the house where Wallace had a base for five years. When they bought the house in 1974 and rebuilt it, they were not aware of its history. They already had other tourists from Japan and Holland visit the house.

He told us that the road had only recently been re-named as Ternate realized too late the tourist potential of their famous historical resident. He took us round the back and showed us where his family had concreted over the top of the well to stop everyone around coming in to take water.

We then took some photos of one of a neighbouring old houses, complete with an elderly man on the verandah with his wispy white beard. This did seem more like the real McCoy.

People here are very inquisitive about us, and where we come from. They say "Blunder?" to me.

"No I am not Blunder (Dutch), but English."

"English?"

"Yes, from England: David Beckham, Manchester United, Liverpool"

Then their faces light up. "Yes—England, Michael Owen—yes"

Some will then name the whole line-up of their favorite team. It's bewildering how popular British soccer has become.

When the Dutch controlled the 'Spice Islands', the cloves and nutmeg etc were collected from a number of islands where they were growing wild. The local pickers made very little even though at one time the spices were literally worth their weight in gold once they reached Europe.

The Dutch then started plantations on only Tenate, Tidore and Ambon. They then paid the people on the other spice islands to cut down their own spice trees. Wallace describes this happening, but was of the opinion that in fact the 'ex-spice' islanders came out financially better with this arrangement.

The Island of Halmahera

At the end of March, it is time to move on to the main island of Halmahera in Maluku. This is the shape of an 'E' written by someone with a bad nervous twitch. It's about 220 miles (350km) from north to south, and 95 miles (150km) from east to west.

Found the jetty and boarded a fast boat to Sofifi on Halmahera. We had to wait until the boat was full, and it was 9am before the four Yamaha 40HP outboards were pulled into action. Thirty-five minutes later and we stepped onto the jetty and were surrounded by a number of taxi drivers offering to take us to Tobelo on the northeast coast.

By 10am we were crammed into a Toyota Avanza with five other passengers. At least I was in the front with the driver, so had some legroom. Our two bags were tied on the top with raffia string and I was more than a little worried that we may be arriving without our toothpaste.

The main road northwards was very narrow, passing through secondary forest (already logged of the big trees), and villages. Plenty of clove trees, like a tall bush with small leaves.

Also saw the larger nutmeg trees, and everywhere coconuts cover any land not forested. Much of the route was beside the sea.

Many of the villages had wooden crosses set into the grass verges every 50 yards (50m) or so through the spread out village. The crosses were between 3ft to 5ft tall (1m to1.1/2 m). Some villages had them painted white, and others black or a natural colour. Some had purple ribbons draped loosely around the intersection. These are Christian villages and the crosses are in preparation of the forthcoming Easter celebrations.

At 11:30am our taxi stopped for half an hour at a small restaurant for lunch. Lian bought some bananas and we had those.

It was early afternoon before we arrived at our destination. We had to take a diversion going into the town as the Golkar political party was having a procession with its usual car, lorries and motorbikes. Not as big a meeting as Ternate, but still impressive for a pretty quiet place.

Arrived at the Elizabeth Inn, a new hotel, and after inspecting the room, we checked in. It was clean with a tiled floor and walls up to the dado line, a TV, air-conditioning and hot water in the bathroom.

Told by the ethnic Chinese owner that we have to register with the police and make a payment if we were staying more than twenty-four hours. However, later his wife said not to worry, and she would make any payments on our behalf.

Went for a walk down into the town with its wide street. It was obvious from the shops that this is not a very affluent town. Walked into the port area without being stopped by the authorities, and took a few video.

I have just bought a new video camera, a High Definition Panasonic TM300 with a solid-state storage system. And the learning curve is fairly steep.

Whilst in town, Lian topped up her Indonesian phone-card, arranged transport for the next day, and booked a 4am taxi for our return to Sofifi in two days time. As you can see, I have a very good travel agent.

Found a supermarket and bought a couple of large cold Bintang beers which we wrapped in newspaper to keep cool. As Ternate was 'dry', we really enjoyed sipping them whilst sitting on the hotel balcony overlooking the mangrove lined sea view.

We had arranged to eat in the hotel, as the owner said she would only charge us the material cost. Had a great grilled fish, green vegetable and steamed rice.

The next morning, after a fried rice breakfast, we were all ready to leave. But our booked driver did not turn up at 8am as promised, so we had to walk into town and find alternative transport.

So it was nearly 9am, before we set off northwards for Galela, which is famed for a black sand beach used by a bird called a Maleo locally, or a Moloccan Scrub-fowl. This bird is a megapod, and comes down to the beach at night and lays an egg every eight days at the bottom of a hole it digs in the black sand. After covering it, the bird returns to the forest, leaving the heat of the sun on the black sand to incubate the egg forty days later.

But the eggs are said to have a large yolk and to be very tasty, so once again man becomes the major predator.

Forty minutes later we passed the village of Galela, and fifteen minutes after picking up a very short man in a camouflage combat jacket who was to be the guide, we turned off the road into a coconut plantation and drove as far as we could in the Isuzu. From there on it was strictly 'shanks pony'. Our guide and driver set off at fast pace, and slowed only when we have to traverse a muddy area or knee-deep small stream. I found it easier to walk barefooted.

Passed a number of platforms where workers were breaking open the coconuts and cutting out the 'white meat' to make copra. The white meat is laid out on the raised platform and a smoky fire of coconut husks as lighted beneath the platform.

It was three quarters of hour before at last we reached the beach.

The sand is so hot that I could feel it burning through the sole of my Croc plastic slippers. We could see the Maleo tracks in the hard sand, and the areas where they had laid their eggs. A couple of 'collectors' were sitting in the shade of a leafy bush.

Lian flushed out a Nightjar that had been crouching quietly on the sand. It flew into the coconut trees, leaving behind a single egg on the sand.

As we walked back along the beach we came across the prints of a python that must have passed behind us, as the track had certainly not been there earlier.

The guide got us back to the car, and one could not help but realize how vulnerable we were if anyone wanted to take advantage of us. Lian had earlier said how the guide looked like one of the Philippino insurgents one sees in newspaper photographs.

At the Galela village we stopped by a house advertising the Maleo eggs for sale, and Lian finished up buying one. I wanted to make an omelet of it, but Lian insisted she keep it and maybe we could have our own little Maleo chick running around our condominium. Sad to say that the egg was damaged on arrival in KL, and we now have an empty shell, with a large hole in its side.

That evening we had another large and excellent grilled fish, but this time a different species.

The Island of Morotai

The next morning we left the major part of our luggage at the hotel, and set out with small bag for a trip to the island of Morotai, off the northern tip of Halmahera.

It had just passed 8am when we took a motorized tricycle, with it's two seats at the front, down to the docks.

But we were told that the 'Rizky Wildan' would only be leaving at 10am. The passengers all crowded below the eaves of a go-down (warehouse), trying to catch what shade they could. Even so early it was so hot and the humidity high. The men all smoke like chimneys.

In fact we left twenty minutes early as all the passengers were there. The sea was calm and oily. A child throws up on the deck next to us. Her elder sister takes off her jacket and tries to soak it up. It was a long two hours before we arrived.

As we pull into the Daruba jetty, the island looks long and low with hills in the distance.

It's even hotter now, and we walk down the jetty and along the main street. It's like when Clint Eastward arrives in an old cowboy town and walks down the high street. No one on the street, but you can feel the eyes watching you. Many of the single storey shops have shutters up. Some look burnt and derelict and threatening, and it's blazingly hot.

Lian wonders if there is a boat going back this afternoon.

We come across the Tongah guesthouse. We took the best room with an air-conditioner and a fan. It was very basic. Our attached bathroom has a squat toilet and a 'mandi'. This is a tiled water tank with a plastic dipper. One stands on the floor and pours the cold water over oneself. The cold water is luke-warm but still cooling. The dark blue painted walls have a big cut out Minnie Mouse stuck on with Sello-tape, so is relatively well decorated.

We were informed that power is cut off daily from 1pm to 6pm. So no chance for a cool rest in the heat of the afternoon.

Moratai was famous in WWII for a number of battles between the Americans and the Japanese. Reminders of the war are everywhere. Most fences, and some house wall are made from the rusty perforated metal planks used as driveways for lorries across soft sand.

In 1976 it made the world headlines when one Japanese soldier came out of the jungle here not knowing that the war had ended.

Lian negotiated for two 'ojeks' to take us for a few hours sightseeing up the only coastal road. So at 2pm we set off, both without any helmets to wear.

Leaving town we passed a large burnt out church, and several gutted shops. We had been warned to refrain from taking photos of such sensitive scenes.

Our first stop was to see the airport. This had been built by the American during WWII, and was said to comprise seven parallel runways. At least one is still operational as they have weekly flights taking the locals off the island in their Military aircraft.

A guard stopped us, and Lian said she was my guide, and could we see the old runways. He went off to telephone for permission. He said he would show us, and we walked through the gardens to the runway boundary fence, where he then said that this was as far as we could go. I was not allowed to take a photo of the airfield name. He told us one of the runways was 1,300yd (1.2km) long, and Lian asked him some further questions. I suddenly realized that some people might think we were spying so I signaled to Lian not to ask any further questions. The guard had already asked if we had a police /military pass.

When we got back to Kuala Lumpur I had a look at Google Earth, and one can clearly see the runways, and one looks recently surfaced. The length is 2,500yd (2.3km), so I guess this could be used by the USA for strategic purposes as it could now take their very large military aircraft.

Our next stop was to a natural hot water spring in a cave like hole in the ground. A couple of women were washing their clothes in the pond at the bottom. Unfortunately it all looked very cloudy with soap.

The road is very bad, but no problem for the motorbikes. We pass coconut plantations, some grass lands and plenty of big mango trees. Bullock carts are the main form of local transportation.

A small political procession passes in the other direction. Waving flags and horns blaring.

The 'ojek' drivers know we are interested in birds. "Do you want to see a Cassowary? We know a man who has one in one of the villages"

We stop in a village and are invited to follow the owner through the mud-floored house into the back garden. There, in a fenced area was a juvenile Cassowary with a twisted and malformed beak. It did not look too well. By this time half the village were surging around us. They were a happy laughing crowd who all wanted to touch and hold me. Played back some video I took of them, and they were in hysterics. We were definitely the best show that had come to town in a very long time.

It was time to meander back to town, and just before we arrived we took a detour around the back and into a coconut plantation. The drivers had to do a bit of searching, but in the end we arrived at the site of a rusting hulk hidden in amongst some undergrowth. The ground was soft and muddy, but by keeping close to the bushes I managed to only get one trouser leg and shoe wet and muddy. It turned out to be a quite small landing craft.

Someone had surrounded it with wooden posts and barbed wire: probably to protect it from being sold as scrap. 'I love you' was daubed in blue paint along the side.

My driver stopped in the plantation to pick some fresh guava fruit, and when we reached the guesthouse the others were nowhere to be seen. My driver immediately turned around and we set off back to find them. We had reached the market when we saw them coming. They had got a bit lost finding their way out of the plantation.

The drivers had also had a good time, and they insisted on saying they would give us a free ride to the ferry the next morning.

By the time we had taken a super 'mandi' shower it was dark. We put on a 'Vap-mat' as there were quite a few mosquitoes flying around. There was a large spider in the bedroom, and a giant cockroach ran behind the big water tub in the bathroom before I could whack it with a slipper.

No streetlights, so we set off towards town using our torch to guide us. We could see fires burning in some of the abandoned houses. A young off duty soldier suggested a shop where we could get dinner and was kind enough to escort us.

It was a very basic place, and looked as if someone had taken over a gutted house and put up a few half partitions with horizontal planks. We ordered fried rice. The husband and wife were from Surabaya in Java, and were part of the transmigration plan where peoples from crowded Java were sent to the more remote areas and given inducements to farm or start a business. This had caused resentment between them and the local inhabitants.

At half past midnight the cockroach met it's maker with the assistance of a descending high velocity plastic dipper. Minnie Mouse on the wall was the sole witness.

We slept inside our own traveling sheets, and I had a surprisingly good nights' sleep despite the creaks anytime either us moved even a fraction.

For breakfast we were given red bean buns and coffee.

At 8am we checked out, and needless to say the motorbike taxis were nowhere to be seen. We strolled through town to the jetty, and were told the boat would only be leaving at 9am.

The speedboat was much smaller than the one we had arrived on yesterday.

Once we left the protection of the island, for about half an hour the boat started to roll quite a bit and some of the women started crying. The man next to me, who had also arrived yesterday, proceeded to open a big plastic bag and put on a bright orange inflatable life jacket that he brought with him. At the sight of this the wailing got even louder. A couple of children had been stuffing their faces with peanuts ever since they boarded, but surprisingly neither was seasick.

The man with life jacket showed me some photos he had taken at a logging camp on the island, with shots of the log loaders, lots of logs, and a whole lot of the various pretty young girls living at the camp. As everything between us was done by sign language, I could only assume he was a log buyer.

Return to Halmahera.

We reached Tobelo within two hours and took a 'benti', the three-wheeled motorised tricycle, to the Elizabeth Inn. This time they were full, with only their VIP room available. Luckily we had it at the previous rate, as surprisingly this room had no hot water.

Time to shower, do some washing and lay in the cool of the air-conditioning. After tea and cakes we set off to try to find an Internet café. This was not easy, and despite asking shopkeepers in town, we finished up an hour and a half later in a residential area. No important messages.

That evening, after another delicious grilled fish, we had a call from our friendly taxi driver. He was still at Sofifi, but had arranged for a friend to pick us up at 4am the next morning.

At 3:15am we woke and had the hardboiled eggs, bread and Milo that had been provided for us. But no taxi arrived. So the manager phoned around and got a replacement to come. Then of course, at 4:30am both pulled up together. We took the one arranged by the manager, so it was 4:45am before we left. Once again our bags were tied on the roof with raffia string, and we had a breakfast break at the same restaurant we stopped at on our way to Tobelo.

By 8:30am we were on a speedboat, and forty minutes later were back at Ternate jetty.

Ternate.

Somehow we managed to squeeze onto two 'ojeks' with our luggage, and we went straight to a travel agent to arrange our flight back to Manado in Sulawesi. Arranged to get a booking for the next morning, and this agent actually accepted credit cards, but with a three percent addition. Left our luggage at the agents and set off to find a night's accommodation. The Losmen Kita greeted us like long lost brother and sisters, and sent off a driver to pick up our bags.

Woke early, and after breakfast, hired a whole little blue bus to take us to the airport for the 9am flight from Ternate to Manado. Although they had X-ray machines at the airport, they were unmanned. At the airport, saw the first Caucasian faces for eight days.

I must remember to put the clock back an hour during the flight, as I forgot on the way there.

Northern Sulawesi: Manado

In the taxi going into town, the driver suggested the Wisata Hotel as being well located, and he was right.

Had a relaxing day and used an Internet café before enjoying a spectacular sunset.

Decided to go north and spent a couple of nights in a national park. So did some repacking so we could leave the main bags at the hotel.

Had the usual toasted sandwiches for breakfast.

A typical Indonesian businessman sat at the next table. Heavily built, and with a paunch. On the table before him were lined up his hand phone, a packet of cigarettes, and a lighter. A chunky ring on the little finger and a flashy imitation gold watch hung from his wrist. I assume that if the watch were gold, he would have being staying in a rather better hotel.

Took a little blue bus to the bus terminal, and we were climbing aboard a rickety old bus, when Lian saw a woman alighting after she realized that the bus would not be departing for a further hour. As this woman had a ferry to catch for a four-day trip, she was trying to get a taxi to take her, as she was running late. So we shared the taxi with her. An hour later, we were dropped off at the pretty village of Giran.

From here we had a delightful ride on two 'ojeks' along the 11mile (17km) dipping, diving and twisting lane to the small village of Batu Puteh. It was very pretty as we passed through the forested and coconut plantation areas.

Tangkoko-Batuangas Dua Sudara National Park.

There are a number of home-stay places adjacent to the track going into the Tangkoko-Batuangas Dua Sudara Reserve and National Park.

We checked into Tarsius Homestay. They had no other guests, and we chose what we thought was the best room. This had sparse furnishings, a big bed with a mosquito net, a fan, and a small bed for us to put our bag on. The bathroom had a WC and a cold shower only.

Coffee was brought and Lian got down to negotiating a best price for the room and three meals a day, and a guide who knew the local birds.

After checking out the restaurant, which was on the other side of the road, we walked down to the beach.

The translation of 'Batu Puteh' means white rock or stone. But there was no sign of any rock, and the sand is all black.

There were many outrigger canoes owned by the fishermen, and pulled up the beach. A woman was carving up a smallish shark and selling some nice looking steaks. The balance was piled in a big bucket. The shark's teeth were quite small, but the mouth was still about 6" wide (150mm).

A man is building a huge floating platform called a 'bagang' from rough sawn branches on floats. A timber deck has a small hut on it and there is a hand turned windlass. A huge net is suspended below the floating platform and the net lowered. A number of bright lights are placed on the platform and this attracts many small fish. The net is slowly raised using the windlass, and the fish caught.

Just behind the beach is a small graveyard. The graves are tiled with Christian motifs and pictures of Christ, and there is normally a concrete flat roof on piers shading the grave. All in all, probably better than the house the people used to live in.

Back for a lunch of omelet, rice, and noodles.

We were then introduced to Fun, our guide. We then pulled some chairs out into the garden and we did some birding with Fun. A huge mango tree seemed to be a magnet for birds, and we even saw some endemic birds. i.e. birds found nowhere else in the world.

Once it cooled down we walked along the main village street that runs parallel with beach for about a kilometer. Nice little houses with bamboo slat fences. As usual I am a Pied Piper with a "Hello Mister" coming every 30 seconds or so.

The most obvious thing is the number of churches of different denominations, which seemed to be spaced out every 100 yards (100m) or so. Some big, some small, but most with building work going on. We were told there was a mosque, but did not see it.

A girl explains to Lian that the village was "100% Christian and 30% Muslim".

At the end of the village was a boatyard, and the herringbone strutting of quite a large wooden boat had been set out. We stood on the jetty and admired the scenery as we watched some boys doing some fishing.

Can you guess what was for dinner? Chunks of salted and deep-fried shark meat, with deep fried grated vegetables, and rice. And yes, it was the shark meat we had seen on the beach. As we were eating we could hear some hymns being sung beautifully. Later on Fan explained that there was a sick person staying in his house, and people had come from his church to sing and pray for the this person.

Then Fan arrived to take us to find the endemic Sulawesi Scops Owl. It did not take too long down a track before we came across a pair of these tiny owls. We had good views in the torchlight, but I could not get an acceptable video of them.

So back for a celebratory coffee.

It was hot and sweaty under the mosquito net. A giant wolf-spider skulks in the bathroom, and I cause it to come to a sticky end.

Woke at 5am and had delicious banana pancakes and chocolate sauce for breakfast. Just as we set off an hour later with Fan, heavy rain started, so we returned to the restaurant for more coffee. We consoled ourselves by saying that although the rain will keep the birds sitting still, when it stops they will be very hungry and we can expect a flurry of movement as they will be feeding madly.

Forty five minutes later we set off, bird-watching along the access lane to the park. The morning was very successful and we saw a number of endemics including some forest kingfishers, a hornbill, and a large woodpecker.

Stopping at a very large ficus tree, we looked up into a crack and saw two tiny Tarsiers looking down at us with their huge eyes, The bodies are about 6" long (150mm), with tails twice this length. Fun said they can move very fast and can leap over 10 feet (3m).

We were also lucky enough o see a large fawn 'cuscus' with its prehensile tail, high in a tree. This is the Eastern Opossum and is the furthest westward extension of the marsupial range.

Later we came across a troupe of seventeen of the six families of Black Macaques living in the park. Wallace describes them as being baboon like:

> "These creatures are about the size of a spaniel, of a jet black colour, and have the projecting dog-like muzzle and overhanging brows of the baboon. They have large red callosities and a short tail, scarcely an inch long, and hardly visible. They go in large bands, living chiefly in the trees, often descending on the ground and robbing gardens and orchards."

In the park these Macaques are being studied and are followed all day by some foreign volunteers with notebooks, stopwatches and hand-held GPS devices. Their French leader pointed out that there was a reticulated python hidden in some undergrowth. It was certainly well hidden and it was difficult to see where the head was. Fun said it was probably 10ft (3m) or so long. The Macaques knew it was there, but would not go too close. One would creep forward for a look, and would pull at a dead branch in the hope of getting a reaction from the python. Then another would step forward and pull another branch or a vine. He then sprang back and the whole troupe let out a screech and jumped back. This was repeated several times, and was very amusing to watch. The python never moved.

Whilst this was going on, one of the large Macaques came up behind Lian and pulled at her trousers. This was a bit frightening, so we left them.

We returned to the Home Stay for some lunch, as mid-day is a very quiet time for birds, as they usually rest until later in the afternoon. We had time for a shower, and to go through the list of birds seen, and to check out the scientific names.

The afternoon walk was quieter than the morning, but still productive, especially when Fun whistled out a Blue-breasted Pitta.

We enjoyed a diner of small barbequed fish, vegetables and rice. Fan came over for a chat and to collect his money. He is certainly a man with very keen eyes.

At about midnight the power went off and Lian accused me of not closing the mosquito net as she was well bitten. This was surprising, as I am usually the one to get all the mosquito bites, and I had none.

But in the morning I counted over six hundred and fifty bites from her waist down. And they were itching her to distraction. Lian has always reacted strongly to bites, especially sand-flies, but this was considerably worse.

I later counted over a hundred on each of my ankles, but the reaction was not nearly as bad.

When shown the bites, the locals laughed and said we had been bitten by 'gonone'. They would itch for some weeks. But no one could tell us what it was, and whether it had laid eggs under our skin. Later we spent some time on Google, and ascertained that the gonone is part of the life cycle of a type of mite or tick. Only at this stage does it bite and inject a substance that liquidizes the animal cells, and it then feeds on the liquid. Although my bites have disappeared, Lians' are still too obvious even three weeks later.

After breakfast, where I sat watching the women out sweeping the large leaves from the road and taking them away in a wheelbarrow, poor Lian was trying to stop scratching.

We took a couple of 'ojeks' back to the bus terminal at the first town, stopping to look at the view and some birds on the way.

The bus was about to leave for Manado, and I managed to sit in front with the driver after he turfed out the woman already sitting there.

We passed pretty villages. It was Sunday morning, and the churchgoers were streaming towards the churches, prayer books in hand. One could not help notice that 80-90% of them were women and children. Very few men were walking along.

From the large bus we had to transfer to a little blue bus. The first one wanted to charge me double for sitting beside him, so we got out and into another bus. This driver had witnessed the incident and asked for the same before bursting into laughter. He dropped us outside the Wisata Hotel, and we could not wait to check in, pick up our bags, and have a decent shower.

It started raining, and as soon as it stopped we were off to a pharmacy to get what we could to ease the itching and to check the Internet for information on the 'gonone'.

We had had a busy trip, our toothpaste was running low, and it was not easy to concentrate on things when one itched like hell. So we decided to return to Malaysia a few days earlier, but found the next available flight would be 3 days time.

The Minahasa Highlands.

We also arranged to hire a car and guide the next day for a days drive around the Minahasa highlands.

The Minahasa people live in the northeastern tip of Sulawesi. They are a pale-skinned and handsome people. According to Wallace, before the Dutch brought them Christianity, they were fierce headhunters, and clothed in bark. He said they had since become quiet and gentle and submissive to authority.

At 7am the next morning, Alex our guide / driver picked us up in a beat up old van, and we drove out of town and climbed eastwards for the 15 mile (25km) to the town of Tomohon.

We passed many vegetable gardens, and clove trees grew at the roadside.

At 2,500 feet above sea level (760m), Tomohon was pleasantly cool. Our first stop was to the market, which is well known for selling unusual animals.

But it was certainly a culture shock for us. We had seen dogs for sale in China and other parts of Indonesia, but certainly not on this scale.

A man on a motorbike had half a dozen blackened dog carcasses on his motorbike and was delivering them to the market stalls. There were several stalls with rows of dead dogs laid out on them. After killing the dogs, the hair was all burnt off, and the dog becomes unrecognizable. I watched as a butcher sliced open a belly to degut the dog.

Other stalls were selling rats. These had a bamboo stick pushed up their bottoms, so they looked like giant lollypops. Although they also had the fur burnt off, the long tails were a giveaway.

Bats were also a very popular item. These large fruit bats had their wings cut off, and were lying in blackened rows, and with their sharp little teeth protruding. The wings were being chopped up and sold separately. Lian asked a woman who was buying bat wings how she prepared them. "Deep fried with a chili sauce".

Three or four miserable looking dogs were lying in a cage awaiting their fate.

Alex said that this market was extremely busy at Christmas time.

"How about some crispy bat wing as a starter Sir? Would you prefer roast turkey or dog as the main course? And I would recommend a couple of stuffed rats on the side. As the visitor, we would invite you to say grace."

We had a cup of coffee in one of the small shops. Now I am feeling brave, I know I should have at least tried a few mouthfuls of each of the specialties.

Close to the town is the dormant volcano of Gunung Mahawo, and we drove up as far as we could before climbing a path for ten minutes or so to the summit. We walked part of the way around the rim and looked down. A small pond occupied part of the bottom. One could see how at some time the mud had bubbled and boiled, and it had now dried and hardened.

Driving on we visited a small pottery selling fairly plain wares, but surprisingly painting most of the items either black or yellow. We thought the plain earthenware colour was much better. But as they said they only make items to order, then they must know what they are doing. The pots are not fired in a kiln, but stacked on a platform of branches, and firewood and dry coconut fronds put on top. They are then fired for only an hour. We watched as they prepared and light the fire and went on our way.

We passed what we assumed to be a geothermal power station. Lots of large insulated pipes and plenty of escaping steam. One factory processing palm sugar was using geothermal energy.

We stopped at an embankment where steam was escaping from the ground. It was too slippery to get anywhere close.

Close by was Danau Linow, a sulphur lake. One could smell the sulphur and see air bubbles escaping from the sandy bottom. I wondered whether the water was a weak sulphuric acid.

Our last stop before returning to Manado, was to a village with the main street lined with one and two storey wooden houses under construction. These houses were of different sizes and layouts and were all for sale. We were told that many even are sold to Europe. Once a house is purchased, it is taken apart and packed for shipment. On arrival it is then re-erected at an all-inclusive price that however excludes foundations, plumbing and electrics. The hardwood timber quality certainly looked OK.

Manado.

Manado has an old Dutch church with a big memorial outside to commemorate those who died during WW1 and WWII. At first they did not allow us to go into the church, but then they unlocked it for us. This was because a long table had been set out down the whole length of the aisle. The table was covered with white tablecloths and a number of candlesticks. This for use in the Easter celebrations, when the members of the congregation would be called to take turns in partaking of bread and grapes at the table. This was a representation of 'the last supper'.

From there we walked down to the port, which turned out to be a fascinating place. Whilst many of the ferry and cargo boats were steel, there were still quite a few wooden boats. Wandered along the waterfront to the market, passing many chandlers and shops selling all manner of things. If Robinson Crusoe could have had an hour here to pick up things for his island, he could have lived in comfort for years.

Later in the afternoon we went to one of the largest Internet cafes I have ever seen. The main room was full of young men playing computer games. The manager said they have a hundred and eighty computers, and they all have to be fast to play the advanced games being played. It was very noisy, with some crowds standing around some of the better players. The manager's desk was crowded with tall trophies won by the café's teenage players.

The smaller room for Internet use still must have held about forty computers. This time nearly all the users were girls, and most of them seemed to be happily staring at their own photograph on Facebook.

Our last full day in Manado was very quiet and we took it easy. A public holiday had been declared for the national and local elections. We passed a number of polling stations, and were amazed how quiet everything was after considering how incredibly noisy the political processions had been. Once the people had voted, they had indelible ink put on their little finger. So many were showing the finger and laughing.

We celebrated our last night in Manado watching an incredible sunset from a waterfront bar and with a few beers and plates of French fries before us.

CHAPTER 12

Taiwan and the islands of Kinmen and Liehyu

Liehyu - The Ang Clan House elders with Lian.

To our surprise, our Air AsiaX flight turned out to be their inaugural flight to Taipei, the capital of Taiwan. On the way the airline gave away a few vouchers as prizes for a quiz, and Lian was lucky enough to win a voucher to go towards a future flight.

The main purpose of this July trip was to try to find from where Lian's grandfather Ang originally came. She knew very little apart from the name of a small island near the Chinese mainland that her father had told her about when she was a child.

Some years ago we had been on a trip to China to find the seat of the Ong family, which was on her mother's side. This had been a very successful visit, and whilst there, we had taken a boat trip to see the Ang family's island, but were unable to land, as the island is owned by Taiwan. Instead, the guides used a few high-powered loudspeakers to scream and shout to the islanders that the island should be returned to China.

It is only recently that the islands have been open for visits from Xiamen in China.

On landing, we took a shuttle bus from Taoyuan International Airport on the western side of Taipei into town, near the old airport of Songshang. We were unable to fly to the island of Kinmen, as all flights that afternoon were fully booked with all the three airlines flying there. It seems that not only was it the first day of the school holidays, but people are using this as a route into China. They fly to the island of Kinmen, where they then take a ferry over to Xiamen on the Chinese mainland. So we booked a flight for the next morning, and found a hotel in Taipei for the night fairly near the domestic airport.

Lian's father had an interesting background. He was born in Kelantan, Malaya, (pre independence) but at the age of one, was taken back to China by his mother. Unfortunately, his mother died when he was about three, and his father came over to take him back to Malaya.

At that time education in Chinese was hard to come by in Kelantan, and it was common for well-to-do Chinese families to send their children back to China for their education. Many of these schools were built from money sent back by the overseas Chinese who had left their country to seek their fortunes in far-away countries.

So at the age of eight, Lian's father was sent off to mainland China for his further education.

Later, when the school was closed due to the civil war, her father managed to find his way back to the island of Liehyu, from where the family had originated. But once there his uncle kidnapped him, and as a ransom demanded that the family house and farmland be all signed over to him. Lian's grandfather went over, and after signing the appropriate documents, Lian's father returned to Malaya, but refused to visit Liehyu again, even though Lian had offered many times to take him. It was only when she pressed him that the skeleton at last slipped out of the closet.

So we had very little information to go by apart from: an island's name, a photo of the grandfather, some of her father's wedding photos, and a photo of the Chinese inscriptions on her grandfather's gravestone.

Kinmen.

The Mandarin Airlines flight to Kinmen takes forty-five minutes. The island is dumbbell shaped: about 16 miles (26 km) long and 11 miles (18km) at the widest, but only 3 miles (5km) across at the central neck. Then to the west is the other smaller island of Liehyu which is about 3 miles by 2 miles (5km x 3km) at the widest.

Lian had planned to stay at a 'home stay' in an old house in the south-west corner of Kinmen, as this was quite close to the jetty for Liehyu. But despite sending emails to make a booking, she received no reply.

At the airport we tried to book some accommodation, but were told this was difficult due to the start of the school holidays, and most of the better choices were fully booked.

The lady behind the counter said a 'home stay' was available in the area where we wanted to stay, and someone would come and pick us up.

When Joey introduced herself, and mentioned her husband Roland, Lian realized this was the lady she had sent the emails to. So we jumped into her old Renault and set off. The airport is in the middle of the dumbbell, and I was puzzled, as we seemed to be travelling to the northeast. We drove into an old town and were taken to the home stay. It was then that we realized that this was the wrong village. Then Joey said that six months previously she used to help her mother, but now she and her husband were running their own home stay in another village.

The single storey building was new but built to the old plan and in the old style. It was a pleasant place, but not where we wanted to be. We had booked for two days, and would at least give it one night when Joey said she would take us across the island to the ferry the following morning. In the meantime she took us for a walk around the cultural village next door, which dated from 1770.

As there were no restaurants nearby, we joined Joey, Roland and their two children as they were driving to a nearby town for dinner in a local restaurant. Both children were good fun to play with, and earlier we had played with a couple of footballs in the house yard area. The four year-old girl had shown off her skill with the 'English' alphabet, even though she only spoke Mandarin.

Following the much-improved relationship with China, Taiwan had been greatly reducing their armed forces. A year previously, Roland had been retired on a very generous pension from the Taiwan air force where he was a radar engineer.

The next morning, over a breakfast of 'mee sua' noodle soup with squid and fresh winkles, we said that we would only stay one night, as we wanted to be in town where it would be easy to get food.

Joey continued to be extremely helpful, and was aware of our reason for visiting Liehyu, so made some calls to a journalist with a surname of Ang that she knew there. He would meet us when we get off the ferry. Then, when we were in the main town of Kincheng, she helped us find accommodation that turned out to be recently renovated and excellent. Although the Haifu Hotel was full, they let us keep our bags there, and said they would do what they could for us.

Liehyu.

The ferry to Liehyu was full of local tourists and soldiers, but only took about fifteen minutes. We were met by a man, who asked Lian if her family name was 'Ang'. The man had been told that Lian was with a European, and as I was the only one on board, he was right first time.

We were then taken by car to the village of Chee Gia, and stopped by a temple surrounded by a large paved area. This temple was the Ang Clan House and temple. As we alighted, a long string of firecrackers cracked and exploded and filled the air with smoke and flying red paper. A half-dozen elderly men came forward and greeted us and took us around to the temples main entrance.

Lian was asked to pray to her ancestors—perhaps they thought that because I would be a Christian, then that Lian would have been converted. She was then passed joss sticks and started to follow the ritual taught by her grandmother. The elders stood around her watching every movement, which ended with some full 'kow tows' on her knees.

Passing this test, she was taken over to a large book showing the genealogy of the Ang clan, and she showed them photos of grandfather's grave and the photos we had brought. One man claimed to have known Lian's grandfather, his wife, and also her father when he was at Amoy middle school on the mainland. One man confirmed that his father was the cousin of Lian's grandfather. They were all getting quite excited, and some records were written in the big book. All this was taking place in the Hokkien dialect, so I took the opportunity of videoing some of the proceedings and the temple. Lian was then presented with a copy of the Ang Clan genealogy Book that added 4lb (1.75kg) to my backpack.

"Would we like lunch?" This was good idea, and a chance for us to return their hospitality.

But first we walked through the village to see the site of great grandfather's house. This has been demolished and the site is now partly grassed and partly a basketball court. The granduncle has a huge three story house adjacent, and we were taken in to meet his wife.

We were driven to a local restaurant where they had arranged a room upstairs. A large dish of braised pigs trotters was the first course dish served, and I must admit it is not one of my favourites. This was followed by a huge dish of noodles well laced with squid and oysters. I should explain that one of the local industries here and on the nearby China coast is the cultivation of oysters. This variety may only be thumb-nailed size, but they are sweet and succulent, and much preferred by the Chinese to the much larger oysters we are more familiar with. But more dishes kept arriving: fish ball soup, deep-fried spare-rib, prawns, fried grouper, and sliced liver and vegetables. All washed down with some local beer. Lian tried unsuccessfully to pay, but the owner insisted that it was already accounted for.

Two of the group said they would take us to the ferry after giving us a tour of the island, so we made our goodbyes to the rest. From the northeast corner, we could see across the straits to the tower blocks of Xiamen on the Chinese coast. It was a pity that the visibility on this day had not been better as a light drizzle commenced. From here we visited a new museum as well as a military museum.

Kinmen.

We did not have to wait long before the ferry set off back to Kinmen, and a taxi soon had us back at the Haifu Hotel where they had a good room waiting for us. How lucky can one get?

A little history concerning Taiwan / Formosa and China may make one realize the resilience of the Taiwanese.

During the Sino-Japanese War, the island was taken over and occupied by the Japanese for eight years until 1945.

NO CURE FOR THE TRAVEL BUG

The Chinese were fed up with the corruption of the Qing dynasty, and a civil war broke out between the communists under Moa Zedong, and the Nationalist army of Chiang Kai-shek and his Kuomintang party. Chiang Kai-shek was forced to retreat to Taiwan and to Kinmen. Then began a heavy artillery bombardment when over 450,000 shells were fired within forty-four days. Following this a partial truce was made, whereby each side would only fire on alternate days. This 'truce' continued for twenty years.

Every cloud has a silver lining, and there is now a famed industry in Kinmen where they make various kitchen knives and cleavers using the iron from the shells that landed. We bought one knife, and it really is dangerously sharp.

Kinmen is trying hard to use the history of their confrontation with China as a tourist attraction, and we think they have done this very successfully. Every morning and afternoon they have four separate bus tours of the island. If you buy a ticket, it lasts for 24 hours, so you can take an afternoon tour one day and a morning tour the next.

One such tour we took stood out as being very good value. As soon as we had paid and taken our seats on the bus, we had to dismount and go to a small theatre where they showed a video film about the bombing of the town by the Chinese and the building of tunnels linking all the main buildings in the city, and how they could be used as bomb shelters by the main population. We were then issued helmets and set out for a walk along over three quarters of a mile (1.2 km) of narrow damp tunnels. And that is a long way. I kept scraping my head on the low roof, and nearly wore the plastic through. Then at two points we 'came under fire' with the sounds of bomb blasts, heavy machine gun fire, and flickering lights.

Of course all the videos were in Mandarin Chinese, and as the tour guide spoke only in Mandarin, I must have missed quite bit. However all the exhibits we saw had many labels subtitled in English, so all was not lost.

Once in the bus we went to the Guningtoa Battle Museum to hear about the attack in October 1949 when the Chinese communists attacked with ten thousand troops, using two hundred fishing boats for the one and a quarter mile (2-kilometre) journey across the straits. Then a two-day battle, where the Nationalist troops from Kinmen managed to take the invaders prisoner. This was all explained using models, old films and paintings.

To cheer us all up, the bus took us to a nature reserve. Most of us were then lent rentable bicycles, and we wove our way through an old village and round lakes for about an hour. Some of us had not cycled for a while, and there were a few near misses either as we set off or stopped at the many places, where a female guide told stories about the old houses.

The last stop of the bus was to see one of the beaches where the main landings took place, with its rusty iron and concrete anti-landing craft defences. The latter items are now being removed as a sign of the improved relations that Taiwan is having with China.

Having found the tour so interesting we kept our tickets and presented them again for another tour the following morning. This one was not as adventurous, but was a chance to visit a number of the buildings and scenic spots that we would probably have missed.

One of the places we visited had an exhibition of the history of the Chinese emigration. This was of special interest to Lian.

My favourite was a 'U' shaped tunnel blasted into a granite hillside next to the sea. Small ships and naval vessels could float in for shelter and be quite safe from artillery or aircraft attack.

Then one evening we joined a walking tour of the old buildings. I understood zilch, as all was in Mandarin, but the next morning we retraced our steps and one could photograph the places and details of interest that the guide had pointed out.

The local food as very good, and the dish I am about to describe was delicious.

We saw a huge group surrounding a stall where three people where working like automatons. One woman was pouring a little batter onto a very large spoon. She then sprinkled on a thin layer of chopped up vegetables, followed by a sprinkling of small fresh oysters. She then shaped a heaped handful of the chopped vegetables on top, before covering all with a thin layer of batter. This was passed to the middle woman, who gently lowered the pancake-covered concoction, still sitting on its spoon, into deep boiling oil. Once the pancake mix was cooked long enough not to break open, the spoon was passed to a man who took the 4 inch (10cm) diameter pasty off the spoon and dropped it into more boiling oil until it was ready for draining, The spoon was passed back to start the process all over again. Of course, many spoons were in circulation.

We thought we would wait until the stall was less crowded and went off for some window-shopping in the old part of town. But when we returned the crowd seemed even bigger and many were sitting waiting on stools set up on the other side of the lane. We just had to wait our turn, but it was worth it.

The island is also famous for 'kaoliang', a strong liquor distilled from sorgum.

Taipei.

When we flew back to Taipei, we had a day for sight seeing. So of course we simply had to visit 'Taipei 101', as it is was still at that time the tallest completed building in the world.

The tower had the fastest lift in the world—travelling at 37.6 miles per hour (1,010m per minute). On the way up my testicles were left near my left knee—that would not be so bad if I hadn't been dressed on the right.

Joking of course, as it was so smooth one felt very little acceleration or braking, but the ears did pop. The viewing platforms are on the 88th to the 91st floors, and even with slightly reduced visibility it is very impressive.

Taiwan is simply full of motor scooters. Pavements may be wide, but they are covered by rows and rows of parked scooters, many of which are electric. Everyone seems to use them, and the drivers are of all ages and social standings. The surprising thing is that the owners can casually leave helmets and gloves on their vehicles without fear they may be missing on their return.

The people are industrious and seemed friendly to Caucasians, so is a place that is worth a visit.

A baby Pygmy Elephant.

We received an invitation to attend the 70th wedding anniversary of a friend's parent. As we had previously attended their 60th anniversary, we accepted Kenneth Tiong[1]s kind invitation.

The celebrations were being held in the seaside town of Sandakan in Sabah in August.

Sandakan.

Sabah is the northernmost of the two Malaysian states on the island of Borneo.

After an early start for the 3-hour direct flight to Sandakan, we booked into the Sandakan Hotel, and took the opportunity of having rest in the afternoon before meeting up some other guests for sundowners at the Yacht Club.

Then on to the celebratory dinner, being held at the new Imperial Bayview Restaurant. The restaurant is on the 1st floor of the new waterfront complex, and is above the fish market. From there are wonderful 180deg views of the bay. The Chinese dinner was surprisingly good when one considers that there were nearly four hundred guests. We had been put on one of the VIP tables; with the Minister of Infrastructure, the Mayor of Sandakan (called the President of the Town Council) and the past Mayor, all with their wives. Such a grouping could have been a little inhibiting, but we did manage a few laughs. And the Tiger beer sales girls always kept the glass full to the brim.

The next morning a big group of us were taken down the coast to a seafood Ba-ku-te restaurant. Normally 'Ba-ku-te' is made with pork cooked in a strong herbal tea, but this was a local version using seafood: fish, fish balls (a minced fish and tofu mixture), shellfish and large succulent prawns etc. It was all quite delicious.

The majority of the guests were returning to Kuala Lumpur or Hong Kong later that morning.

So in the afternoon Kenneth arranged a boat trip round the bay, and then on to see five of the local islands, finishing up at the Turtle Islands National Park. A nice trip and a fast boat with it's twin 85 HP outboard engines. A cruising speed of 30 mph (50kph) was reached with no problem.

By road to Kota Kinabalu.

The next morning five of us left Sandakan by road for the 205-mile (330km) journey to Kota Kinabalu: Kenneth, Steve Tennant (Kenneth[1]s old university friend who lives in Hong Kong), a Taiwanese, and the pair of us.

Kenneth has a big black Lexus LX470 V8 SUV for his use in Sabah. Very comfortable, with all the gadgets you can think of. For example, if anyone stands too close to the vehicle, a voice tells them to move away. The trouble is, the voice speaks in Japanese, so there is not much point in switching this gadget on.

Had lunch near the base of Mount Kinabalu, but as it was shrouded in cloud, we could not see the highest mountain in Southeast Asia.

Reached Kota Kinabalu without problems, and we dropped the others off at the Sutera Harbour Resort, while we found our own hotel.

Later we picked them up and had drinks on the terrace of the Yacht Club. (When I was working for Kenneth, his company financed and built the two hotels, the yacht club, and the golf clubhouse at Sutera Harbour)

Then on to the 'Cowboy', one of the many a pub / restaurant / karaoke joints in town.

Kenneth, Steve, and Mr. Taiwan, were having a couple of days in Kota Kinabalu (known locally as KK) and had other transport, so we had the Lexus for a few days to take back to Sandakan.

The road to Tawau.

So Lian and I left KK and took the road south to Papar, and thence inland and up and over the forested Crocker Range to the plateau round Keningau. The road is still under construction, but the steep sections have been surfaced, so no problems. In fact, the car drives extremely well. It had lots of grunt and power for quick and safe overtaking. Felt a bit big compared with our own Nissan X-Trail, but one soon got used to it.

We continued to drive south, down to Tenom, where we had a pretty miserable lunch before returning to Keningau. The first hotel we tried was full, but found the Juta Hotel and this was both comfortable and close to the market area and shops.

After an early breakfast, we proceeded southeast for our destination of Tawau. This would entail rough logging roads and un-surfaced laterite estate roads. We were told this would take about eight to ten hours if the weather held. By 9am we reached the end of the tarmac, and we would have over 93 miles (150km) of logging track before seeing tarmac again.

Actually, the road is under construction as a new highway, and in a couple of years time will be a super road through beautiful rainforest. But now it is a construction site for much of the way, with lots of heavy equipment using the track, and so making lots of clinging mud.

At one time we came across a full logging truck that had broken down and nearly blocked the road. We were told that the driver had run away. Had to get out and check it out, as there was a deep drop on the left. Got Lian to walk over and guide me, then retracted the side mirrors. It was time to inch pass the truck, keeping as close as I could to it. Lian told me afterwards that there was dirt tumbling down the slope as I drove over.

Came across another broken down logging truck, but this time it was dragged out of the way by a big tracked dozer, so no problems. We would have hated having to return to Sandakan via Keningau and KK.

It was a bit of a relief to meet a tarmac road again, and we had to pull into a car wash, where it took nearly an hour with a high-pressure hose to completely clean the underside and the wheel arches.

Drove into Tawau and checked into the Emas Hotel, a hotel we had used previously. Phoned some friends who live there, who were also at the anniversary party.

Sabah is famed for the fresh seafood, and Tawau is the tops. And the 'King Ling' serves the best. Started with lobster sushi, and it kept up this standard until we could hardly move. Wow!

Sukau and the pygmy elephants.

After an early breakfast we were on the road again heading east, then northwestwards past Lahad Datu. Crossed the Kinabatangan River bridge, and soon after turned right onto rough unpaved palm-oil estate roads for the 25 mile (40 km) trip to the little village of Sukau.

Saw a Changeable Hawk—Eagle on the ground, and then a rare Storm's Stork sitting on a dead tree stump.

By early afternoon we had found some accommodation in a chalet at Discovery Resort. Just in time for some lunch.

I then had a rest, whilst Lian checked out for a river trip.

Lian told a boatman. "I want to see elephants".

"You should have been here yesterday," he said "They were all over the bank on the other side of the river. Now they have gone upstream".

"How much to take us?"

"Can't do it, as I don't have enough petrol. The man with the key to the petrol-store has gone to Sandakan".

So we jumped in the car, and drove the 9 miles (14km) to the even smaller village of Bilit.

Within five minutes we were in a boat heading upstream. And fifteen minutes later we heard bellowing and then we saw our first elephant. Then we saw a couple, and then more and more. They were on both banks. Hard to count through the high grasses and trees, but we spotted about twenty five to thirty individuals.

It was only in 2003 that DNA tests confirmed the Sabahan Pygmy Elephant to be a new subspecies, and only found in Sabah. 'Elephas maximus borneenis' were isolated from the Indian elephants from Thailand and Peninsular Malaysia about 300,000 years ago. Where the Indian elephant grows to 8 to 10ft (2.5 to 3m) tall, the pygmy elephants are only 5.1/2 to 8.1/2ft (1.7 to 2.6m). But the ears and tail are proportionally longer, and the tusk straighter than the Indian elephant.

Then the elephants started to clamber and slide down the bank into the river where they frolicked for a while prior to starting to cross the 220 yard (200 meter) wide muddy river.

Then one elephant set off and the rest of that group followed, swimming low in the water, and raising their trunks to breathe, and blowing out under water. They swam surprisingly strongly, and it was a truly amazing sight. The video camera was working overtime.

Then another group lowered themselves down the bank, and waited their turn to cross.

All the time we could hear trumpeting from both banks as the animals kept in touch with each other.

We had seen one baby being shepherded around by the mother and two matrons. They then slid into the water and soon set off with the little one between them. But then a little trunk could be seen to return to the shore, leaving the three to continue. The baby started screaming extremely loudly, but to no avail.

A boatman went over to see if he could tow the youngster across, and our boatman went over to see if he could assist.

Apart from my getting some excellent video, the baby would not be helped.

And then as we suspected, the three females swam back to save their precious little one. They soon regrouped and disappeared into the trees. They would probably only try again the next morning, as it was about to get dark, and they were no doubt all tired and stressed.

For us it was all a magical encounter and really made our trip.

Next morning we did some break of dawn bird-watching before leaving for Sandakan.

We stopped off at the Sepilok Orang-utan sanctuary, but were too late for the feeding time.

Had to spend another hour at another carwash before reaching Sandakan in order to deliver back a clean and refueled vehicle.

Picked up a driver, who then took us to the airport for the direct afternoon flight back to Kuala Lumpur.

CHAPTER 14

China visit—The 'Water Towns' of Eastern China

A typical waterway in Tongli.

Two old Chinese proverbs translates as: 'Born in Suzhou, live in Hangzhou, eat in Guanzhou, die in Liuzhou', and 'Above is Heaven, below there is Suzhou and Hangzhou'.

This is an area also famed for silk and pretty girls, so we thought it would be worth a visit.

Hanzhou

It was a May morning when we took a pleasant five-hour flight to Hanzhou airport near the eastern coast of China.

We took the airport shuttle bus into town. The area is very flat, and much of this highway was elevated on columns.

As we got closer to Hanzhou the cultivated land slowly gave way to suburban areas, and there were many new multi storey houses. They were usually three or four storeys, and appeared to be in a neo-Gothic Walt Disney style of architecture, with spires and turrets. The external walls were decorated with fancy brickwork or tiles and many of the windows had triangular glazed upper sections. The effect was further enhanced by having the relatively dense rows of houses being located on opposite sides of narrow cultivated fields. This was more like a scene from an exotic part of central Europe rather than China.

Once we reached town we took a taxi along to Hostelling International, where we had a nights booking via the Internet.

The location was excellent and close to the famed West Lake. Our en-suite bedroom was very comfortable, and overlooked the Qianwangxi temple. The bathroom was modern and the wall mounted flat screen had 'on-demand' films, TV and TV series.

The only TV series in English was 'Everyone Likes Raymond', and one could choose from about 30 very old episodes.

Free Internet facilities were available in the foyer via three computers on a shelf. Long sessions were discouraged by there having no available seating. The only problem I had was that the lettering had long worn off the keyboards, and being a two-finger typist I could not always remember where the various letters were situated. It was time to book accommodation for a further night, as this hostel is deservedly popular.

Once settled in, we took a walk through the gardens bordering the lakeside. Many people were out for a late afternoon stroll as the sunset shimmered across the lake, and silhouetted the small boats as the boatmen stood at the stern and propelled the boats forward with the single oar. There were still a few boats ready for hire, and their boatman either slept or sat chatting.

Photographers had racks of clothing available for tourists to dress up in imperial Chinese dress and have their pictures taken by the lakeside or by the banks of yellow irises.

The next morning we had breakfast at a table in the hostel garden. This was buffet style with a mixture of Chinese and western cuisine. You are given a glass, a plate and a bowl as well as some cutlery, and after the meal one is expected to put everything into its allocated tray.

After breakfast we thought we would take an anti-clockwise walk alongside West Lake. The Lake is roughly circular and is about 2 miles (3 km) diameter and surrounded by low hills.

Stopped for a while to listen to a 'fiddler' and a singer who were using one of the many small pavilions along the lakeside.

Passed a group of women who were practising an umbrella dance with the music supplied from a cassette player. Their choreographer showed them the timing she wanted and kept adjusting the angle of the spinning umbrellas.

At the northern side we could see a musical fountain display going on, but this finished just about as we arrived.

Around the lake we saw rows of gleaming orange bicycles. The local government have set up a number of stations where one can hire a bike and have the opportunity of dropping it off at another location. Many tourists were taking advantage of this, at 1 Yuan an hour, although there is a deposit to be paid, in case a rider decides to simply keep on pedalling.

Alongside the western and southern parts of the lake, two causeways have been built. Access between the various sections of the Lake cut off from the main Lake, is by way of cute stone bridges.

It was getting quite hot, and we had been keeping to the shade beneath the trees were ever possible.

At the first causeway we came across the Zhejiang museum, which has artefacts covering the province's 7,000-year-old history. Time to take advantage of the air-conditioning, as well as partaking of a quick dose of culture. Zhejiang, meaning 'crooked river', is the province where Hangzhou is situated.

We stopped to watch a number of couples having their wedding photos taken by the lakeside or on a stone bridge parapet. The photographers were lying on their backs, or hanging from a tree branch in a desperate effort of trying to get a unique shot. The other happy couples were looking bored as they waited their turns for their photo-shoot to continue. We were amused to see that the brides seemed to have jeans and trainers on under their ivory white dresses.

By the time we had crossed the second and larger causeway, and walked back to the hostel, five and a half hours had passed, and we felt quite tired.

After a late lunch and short rest we went out to find where we needed to take the bus to the main bus station, as we intended to leave for Suzhou the next morning.

Found the street-market at the end of Hefang Street, which is in the Qing Dynasty style, and is an UNESCO Heritage Area. Crowded with Chinese tourists, and selling all types of souvenirs: jade and jewellery, carved wood, silk, and a man in a long blue coat sells tea. Artists sketch tourists, a grey cat sits on a high window cill watching everything, and a little boy is dressed in jungle fatigues. The temple on the hill behind magically appears with a string of lights outlining the sloping eaves and rooflines.

Suzhou.

The next morning we had a leisurely breakfast before we took a local bus for the half hour trip out to the eastern bus station. The earlier buses were full, and we had to wait until 11am before we could get a seat. But the bus was new and comfortable, and three hours later we pulled into the small bus station at Suzhou.

Had problems getting a taxi as soon as we said we wanted Hostelling International on the Ping Jiang Road. We found that this was because Ping Jiang Road was a pedestrian lane by the side of a waterway. But a helpful taxi driver dropped us off, and indicated that we should take the stone slab and cobble lane. It was only a couple of hundred yards (meters) before we found the hostel.

A quaint two storey place with one half of the hostel across the other side of an alleyway. We were given swipe cards to operate the pair of glass sliding doors on either side of the alley, and to enter our room. Charming and lacking the TV facilities of our previous hostel, but still more than adequate.

We are on the ground floor, and our window is quite high. Looking out I see a really exotic model with a gypsy style 'off the shoulder' deep red patterned long dress, leaning provocatively against an old knarled timber screen. She has a shock of black curly hair and long dangly earrings. What a girl. Then I see a photographer jumping forward to take an exposure reading close to her face, whilst a flunky angles a silver board to reflect more light onto her.

We later saw her sitting on stone steps going down to the canal. Before she adjusts the hem of her dress we see that she also wears jeans and sports shoes under the dress.

There were some Caucasian visitors in the hostel, probably Russian. The women were big, but still wore skimpy clothes. They had huge red bruises on their backs and arms, which looked really ugly. They had obviously been trying out the hot glass suction cups, which give bruises like giant leech bites, or the suckers of a huge octopus.

A couple of big dogs came over to wag their tails as we entered our corridor. Later Lian returned to our room to pick up a shawl, and when she came back she said one of the dogs had jumped up and started a tug-o-war, and had made a hole in the shawl. I went to see the dog. It was dark and I could not find the lights. Then the dog literally jumped at me and I hurt my knuckles trying to punch him in the head. The dogs were just being a little over friendly.

Went for an afternoon walk to get our bearings. It is such a pretty place, with canals, waterways, and quaint stone bridges. Small boats ferry visitors around or are used for clean-up operations. Found the central area with its noisy shops and a pedestrian area adjacent to a temple. The Xuan Miao Temple was built in 276AD. Outside, the street sellers have dancing mice toys, and a small toy helicopters zoom around the pedestrians. How long before someone looses an eye?

The houses are of stone or thin blue bricks, rendered with plaster. In many cases the plaster has fallen away, exposing the inner core of the wall.

A house is being restored and we walk in for a look around. Lots of nice architectural details on the timber screens, and also on the balcony seating that overlooks the canal.

We look into a building that is a musician's classroom. A man plays a small round pottery flute about the size of an orange. The haunting tune is so delicate and the musician so skilled. Later he moves over to play a stringed instrument shaped like a Hawaiian guitar.

Lots of electric powered motor scooters and bicycles. The problem is that they are so silent. Thank goodness for the rough stone pavements, as it is only the rattling of the scooter or bicycle that gives any indication of fast approaching danger. And they drive on the right hand side, and no one bothers about wearing a protective crash hat.

This hostel's room rate does not include breakfast, so the next morning we set off looking for 'yau tiau', that I usually call 'long johns', and comprise a long thin lightweight doughnut fried in boiling fat.

As we left the hostel it started to drizzle, so we stopped at a corner shop and I bought a small collapsible umbrella for less than a pound. Thank goodness, as the rain became quite heavy. We stopped at a shop that made 'long johns'. This was served and eaten with thin round 'nan' bread, coated with seeds and with pickled vegetables inside. They were a little salty, but very tasty. I also had a 'tea egg', a hard-boiled egg using tea rather than boiling water, and Lian has a glass of taufu milk. The shop owner took out a large square of old red carpet and laid it down in the street for the cars and motorbikes to run over. So much cheaper than sending it to the dry cleaner.

The famed Chinese architect I.M.Pei, who designed the glass pyramid at the Louvre in Paris, is said to have been born in Suzhou, and so when the town wanted a new museum, he considered it his duty to carry out the design.

It's worth visiting the new museum just for the architecture and the detailing. Basically grey and black stone and plasterwork, together with stainless steel and glass. But a couple of rooms are completely lined with a light wood wall panelling and sloped ceiling, giving a very calm yet cool feeling.

A complicated series of water channels cascaded along a vertical wall, and the grey stone became black wherever it was wet.

The use of natural light coming through northern lights is especially impressive, as are the stone staircases: which seem to float.

The only detailing that jarred with me, were the thin stone lintels that had central vertical joints above the doorways.

A great deal of thought had gone into the landscaping and gardens. The main garden area was mostly given over to ponds, but in a completely different way to the other gardens we were to see, that have a profusion of plants and trees. In this case the landscaping was stark and simple: rough cut triangular stone slabs against the boundary wall gives the appearance of mountains in the distance, and trees and shrubs are surrounded by pebbles and paving. Small courtyards containing a single stark tree and perhaps a few bamboos may be viewed through a circular window or full height plate glass. The general impression is more of a Japanese garden. Unfortunately it was still drizzling, and so perhaps our enjoyment of the gardens was somewhat curtailed

The exhibits were interesting, but one tends to remember the impression of the display cases as much as the artefacts themselves. The main memorable exhibit was a set of jade funeral coverings.

Stepping through an archway into the old part of the museum was like stepping back a thousand years. The exhibits were housed in a series of small single storey buildings. The rooms were dark and furnished in the traditional manner. The external walls were normally of timber panelling, with beautiful carved lattice screens on the windows.

We were surprised to find that one room had been made into a church.

We had been told by the hostel reception that there we could see Suzhou Chinese opera at nearby temple, and this would start at 1:30pm.

The place was already quite crowded, but we were shown to 'good seats' near the centre of the hall. People were sitting in pairs on chairs, with a long side table set longitudinal from the stage. On this table were set flasks of hot Chinese tea and saucers of wrapped sweets. The cups had no saucers, but a small cover to keep the tea warm and also to be held so that the large straggly green tea leaves stayed in the cup and were not strained into ones mouth. Lian was given a seat on one side of the table, and I on the other side. I wanted to stand or move to the next seat in order to take some videos, but a woman told me to sit down in my allocated seat.

The people were all elderly, and it seems that the opera is put on daily especially for the senior citizens.

Then the two performers appeared: a pretty woman in a white silk dress, and a man in a long red silk robe. The woman played a Chinese guitar, whilst he performed on a Chinese banjo. They both sang well, but her voice was especially powerful and sometimes screeching in a 'Chinese opera' style. The man spent quite a lot of the time recounting stories, which often had the audience smiling or in fits of laughter.

Of course I could understand nothing of what was said or sung, and I did not know the traditional folk stories then were being re-enacted.

Several times Lian whispered to ask whether I wanted to leave, but it was all quite fascinating. After an hour the performers had a break, and we took the opportunity to leave. I was a little surprised to hear that Lian also had no idea what was being said, as the performance was all in a local dialect and not in Mandarin or any dialect that Lian could follow.

The weather forecast was for further rain, so Lian made an Internet booking for the next night in Tongli, another 'water town'.

Tongli.

It took a while to get a taxi to the bus station, as it was the morning rush hour, where we bought our tickets and had only a half hour wait for the next bus. An hour later we reached Tongli. We walked into the old part of town, pulling our wheeled luggage over the rough paving stones. Passed over a couple of bridges before we reached a ticket office where we had to pay 80 Yuan each to get into the old town.

Spotted a tourist office and asked for directions to our hostel. The lady made a phone call and a couple of minutes later a man came to take us there.

We crossed the main square and passed an old man with a flowing white beard and a yellow silk robe, then over a stone bridge and into a very narrow alley. After 55 yards (50m) we reached the end and turned left, then a further 55 yards (50m) and a right turn. No obvious hostel, so where were we? Ahead were a couple of red lanterns, and a single door in a high windowless wall. The man opened the door and pointed up a steep winding rickety wooden staircase. At the top was our room. Not so bad as we had assumed it would be from the entrance. A big black carved wooden Chinese bed with a canopy over it, and a lot of heavy black furniture.

The bathroom was a bit crumby, but we did not have to share.

Went for a wander down one of the main tourist streets. These are Chinese tourists, and we saw very few foreign tourists until we later reached Shanghai.

We saw one small delightful hotel with its own courtyard, and made a booking for the next night.

The Tongli entrance tickets include the entrance fees for a number of the tourist attractions, and at the various entrances is a ticket collector who will punch a hole in the relevant place, so that a return visit is not allowed.

We visited the Tuisi and the Gufeng Gardens, and then enjoyed walking along the sides of the small canals and over quaint stone bridges. No cars, but quite a few electric scooters and bicycles. Reached a junction point of two canals, where there are three stone bridges. An old woman in a long black woollen dress and a brightly coloured ethnic head dress, has a small boat with seven cormorants perched on poles on each side of the boat. The birds are preening, or sitting with their wings out, like they are being put out to dry.

Then the woman started to feed the birds with fish. After feeding a bird with a fish, she grabs the bird by the neck and throws it overboard. It is back like lighting, and begging for more. This time she puts the cormorant on a stick and then moves it back to a pole over the side of the boat where she ties it to the pole. This is then deftly and quickly repeated with the other birds.

It is an ancient tradition that brides be carried in a sedan chair over all three bridges.

So an enterprising chap has a long hanger full of tradition clothes for the tourists to dress up in. They then make a couple of circuits, bouncing about in a sedan chair carried by two men, with a musician dancing and skipping at the front. The tourists seem to enjoy it, but I am sure they must feel a little sea sick by the time they get down.

Visited the Pearl Tower, a small model pagoda in a building set in a traditional Chinese garden, with a big pond full of golden carp.

It was near closing time by the time we visited a Dendrite Museum, and they could not wait to turn out all the lights. This museum comprises many rooms full of dendrites set into glazed picture frames. The dendrite pictures are made from split slate or layered stones, and look like fossils. But they are not, as the 'landscape like' pictures are formed by the different chemicals and salts that had permeated through the crevices in the rock.

A couple of schoolgirls offered to show us where there was an Internet café, and we had to walk out to near the main entrance road. We got the tourist office to scribble on our tickets so they would let us come in and out of the old village.

Early next morning we checked out of the hostel and checked into the Family House.

Spent most of the day covering the various tourist spots by walking around the canals and over all the little stone bridges: some arched, some flat. Also visited the Sex Museum which needed a separate entrance ticket. Not sure what we were expecting, but whatever it was, it as neither exotic nor erotic and so was a bit of a let down. There was a live white bunny rabbit in the gardens—but it was alone.

Following a couple of days of rain, everyone was hanging out their laundry to dry, and this made for some interesting observations. We saw some of the most horrendous bloomers out to dry. I am used to seeing such things hung on a clothes hanger or suspended from a clothesline, and as such they stay relatively flat. However, in this area, such items are suspended from crossed hangers, with a peg clipped to four corners, and so one sees them in glorious 3D. I admit it's a clever contraption, as it should certainly let more air circulate in and out of the leg and waist holes for extra fast drying.

This day must be an auspicious day in the Chinese calendar, and although not a weekend, there were a number of weddings being held in the town. Firecrackers were exploding behind high walls, and later we saw several wedding parties leaving restaurants and the brides being driven off in big black BMW's that were covered with pink bows and ribbons.

In the evening we went along to the Internet café, which turned out to be a very big place, packed out with young people playing on line games. From here Lian made a booking for a couple of nights in Shanghai.

The next morning we walked alongside a canal and passed a street market on the way for breakfast. Caught the reflections of rows of old houses in the canal. This is a delightful town.

Then bought our bus tickets for Shanghai, and sat in the Family House yard area enjoying the blue skies and ambience as we the sipped at our tea and read.

From the sign outside many tourists assumed that this was a museum of some kind, and some would wander in and inspect the lounges and bedrooms before someone would tell them that the rooms were for rent. Or they would peer round the circular entrance gate and snap a few pictures, or give a little wave as soon as one smiled at them.

Yes—even in China, most of the tourists were now using digital cameras.

We carried our luggage for as much as we could, as the rough stone pavings were very rough on the wheels.

Shanghai.

The mid-day bus took less than an hour and a half to reach Shanghai. The road went through numerable flat industrial estates before reaching suburbia. We met and chatted with a Chinese couple on the bus, and when we reached our destination it turned out to be a small bus station some way from the city centre.

A policeman came up to me and wanted to check my passport. Edward, our new friend, wanted him to show his card and his police badge before he said I should hand my passport over for inspection and allow him to write down the details. He was not interested to see Lian's passport. I suppose it was all due to the additional security prior to the Olympics.

Taxis refused to take the four of us into town for some reason or other, and so Edward and May guided us and walked along with us to find the main railway station where we could take the Shanghai underground.

The main bus station and train station are close together, and were teeming with people. We took the underground for five stations before changing onto another line for a further five stations. It was all clean and efficient, and the only problem is that there are only escalators going up, so trying to walk down the long staircases carrying luggage is not easy when there are large crowds. And the citizens want to get into the carriages before others have alighted.

The Mingtow Hiker Youth Hostel is situated in an old block in a road two blocks away from the famed Bund.

Our room was large, with a big settee and a TV, but was depressing with its black and gold wallpaper. But the bathroom was good, and the mattress was the only soft one we had experienced on the trip.

We went for a walk to find the Bund. It is a very impressive wide walkway alongside the river, crowded with tourists and people selling kites and other souvenirs.

Across the river is new business centre of Pudong. A radio tower and a number of outstanding skyscrapers are nearing completion. The weather is fine, and the cool breeze off the sea to the east meant visibility was excellent, and the buildings glow in the light of the setting sun.

Then, as it gets dark, the restaurant / cruise boats start passing up and down. Each boat is decorated with different coloured lights, and each company has tried to outdo its competitors. And then one sees the dark shape of a huge black barge passing, and these seem to be without any running lights.

The old buildings on the Bund side of the river had been magnificent in their day, and would not have been out of place in any European capital. These are best seen in the early morning, bathed in sunlight.

In the evening we walked along to the main pedestrian shopping street and People's Park. The neon signage certainly compares favourably with Piccadilly Circus in London.

The next morning we set out to have a closer look at them. We tried to get in to see the old Customs House, but the security guards were not happy about this, and would not let us take any photos internally. We went next door and took up an old lift, the level indicator being an arrow hand that swung across a dial—such a beautiful museum piece.

Then we entered the Shanghai Bank, complete with Trafalgar Square type bronze lions sitting either side of the entrance. And what a magnificent banking hall, with a glazed barrel vault roof, wonderful marble flooring, and even the original tellers booths.

The visibility had changed considerably now the breeze was coming from the west, and the buildings of Pudong looked decidedly misty.

Lian was keen to see the old French quarter. We did a lot of walking and some bus rides before we found it. The area was rather disappointing, and we took the underground back to our area.

Stopped to have a look at a 'Roewe' in a car showroom. A Chinese group had brought out the British Rover Car Company, and they are producing the Rover 75 under the name of Roewe. I guess the Chinese have problems pronouncing the 'v'.

Went to see the old Peace Hotel, but this was closed, perhaps for renovations. They still had a poster up advertising the famed jazz band. Lian asked around to try to see if the band was playing elsewhere, but the general reply was that probably most would have died of old age.

We had decided to go north and bought overnight sleeper train tickets to Qingdao for the next evening.

Standing at our hostel window, I could see a narrow lane. The building on the other side was undergoing repairs, and they had used traditional bamboo scaffolding.

There was a group of young school-kids playing the fool. One of them would grab hold of someone else's satchel, and hurl it as high up onto the scaffolding as they could. The kid had no option but to climb up and get it down. This was repeated several times with different satchels.

Later in the afternoon we decided to take the under-river tourist train to have a look around Pudong. The small carriages move on rails and for 50 Yuan each one can enjoy the underground sound and light show on the way. The commentary is partly in English, and amongst other things one passes an 'asteroid belt', the red glowing 'magna', other flashing 'things', and a lot of silly ghosts who get run down by the train.

Pudong was like a ghost town, but we sat on the embankment and watched the river and the passing boats, and the sun going down before returning to civilisation and walking the full length of the Bund.

It was mid June, the sun was out, and the cool breeze made it seem like a spring morning.

We heard that there had been a major earthquake in central Sichuan, but we had felt nothing in Shanghai.

We took the local bus to the huge railway station. Our train, number K294, was due to leave at 13:19hrs. Half an hour earlier we reached waiting room 5, which was full of people. Then the crowd started surging to the narrow exit gate like a tide. We both decided to use the toilets, and passed by the glazed 'smoking room'. Some people were leaving, but many there were taking the last long draughts of smoke into their lungs. A woman sweeper was literally filling buckets with the abandoned cigarette stubs.

It was time to join the crush at the barrier and so get onto the platform and find carriage No. 11.

Our cabin is comfortable with four 'soft' berths; we have one upper and one lower. A woman delivers us a thermos flask of boiling water and we enjoy a cup of our coffee.

A man joins us and places his things on the other top bunk.

Exactly on time the train gently pulls away from the station. It was eerily quiet and smooth. It is to be a 19-hour journey covering 870 miles (1,400 km).

We stop at Suzhou, and at Chang Zhou where our fourth berth mate joins us.

One would expect that the other two men would sit and share the lower berth until such time as it was time to turn in for the night.

Lets call the one who started at Shanghai Man A, and the man who joined the train later to be Man B.

Man B stretches out along the lower seat as soon as Man A leaves the carriage to visit the toilet. So Man A is forced to take his laptop computer and climb up to the upper bunk where he can only recline.

Every twenty minutes either Man A and /or Man B will receive a call on his mobile phone.

Man A is playing a Chinese movie on his laptop, and I wonder how long his battery will last.

Much of the track seems to be still single track, so we spend quite long periods waiting until a train passes in the other direction. Some seem to be bullet trains.

Both Man A and B have small thermoses with Chinese tea in, and they keep these topped up from the carriage's big thermos. When this is empty, one of us will refill it from the boiler situated outside the toilets.

We have a brief stop at Nanjing.

Man B is a salesman for a company who make hydraulic cylinders. He proudly shows us his products on his computer screen.

Man A is travelling up to Qingdao to see his fiancé.

It was past 9pm when we turn in. I found the volume switch for the piped in music and turned it right down.

Man A reads for a while using his reading light. I would have preferred that he should have done that all night, because soon after the light went out, his snoring began. His 'in-snore' was loud, but his 'out-snore' sounded like the release of airbrakes on a heavy tractor-trailer lorry. I feel sorry for the fiancé.

Man B simply has a quiet snore. Then the carriage door latch started rattling, but this was cured with a little rolled up toilet paper.

I woke early and stood in the corridor. The countryside was flat, and I could not tell whether the green fields were rice or wheat.

Half an hour later we stopped at Zibo, and quite a lot of passengers got off.

Lian made us a drink of packaged oats and we had an apple and some biscuits.

By now the fields were all covered with plastic sheeting as far as the eye could see.

Mr A left us at the stop at Weifang, and we wished him well.

I noticed that the stations this morning only had their names in Chinese characters, whereas yesterday evening I could follow our route with the anglicised English names.

Qingdao.

Then at 10am we reached a station outside of Qingdao, and the train went no further. We later realized that the main station was undergoing reconstruction in time for the Olympics. This station was really chaotic, but we piled into a minivan with some others on condition that we had a look at the hotel that the tout was trying to sell.

Surprisingly, it was not too bad. Before agreeing or making any payment, we got them to take us to the hostel where we had paid a 10% deposit. Their room was worse, and the staff confirmed we could cancel at no cost apart from loss of deposit.

So we returned to the Guxiangcun Hotel and checked in, as it was also in more convenient location.

Qingdao had been a German colony for 99 years. This was similar to the British having their colony in Hong Kong, and the Portuguese having Macau. It is also famous for its Tsingtoa beer.

It is much colder here, and we had to put on our fleece jackets in order to venture out.

Many of the buildings here have a German architectural flavour, which we wanted to see.

St Michael's church was nearby, but seems to be closed most of the time. Perhaps there are simply not enough Christians about?

Walked down to the seashore, and to the end of a long pier. The place is packed with local tourists despite the relative cold and overcast skies. Several people have large piles of seashells for sale.

The sandy beach is orange in colour. We set off to find the old railway station, but although we could see the original station building that had been recently repaired and repainted, it is now only a small section of quite a major development. This has however been carried out in quite an architecturally sympathetic way.

The Olympic yachting and boating section of the Games were held in Qingdao, so everything was being tarted up for this August event.

We went for a wander to find the old Observatory that is set on a hill in a small park. This is also used as a hostel, and the views from its terrace would have been good had the weather been better.

We tried to make a booking back south the next day using the Bullet Train, but there were no seats available until the following day.

Next morning we set off for the museum, but the place turned out to be the German Governors House set in some nice gardens and beautiful giant pine trees. It was an amazing cross between a Walt Disney Ginger Bread House and a gothic German castle. The inside was gloomy, but had some interesting design features, including a big selection of fireplace designs. At the ticket office the woman said the museum had moved out of town and gave us the bus numbers to catch.

It was an interesting trip eastwards along the coast, and we were surprised to find that a new and obviously affluent business district with some impressive multi storey offices buildings, hotels, and a Word Trade Centre.

When at last we reached the huge new museum we found that it was closed for pre-Olympic renovations. We went round the back and managed a quick look at one of the large stone

Buddhas they have. It seems that during the Sino-Japanese War the Japanese had cut off the heads off three of them and packed them off to Tokyo. Then recently they have been returned to China, and heads and bodies have now been re-united.

By now a toilet would be very welcome and so we popped into what we wrongly assumed was a hotel. It turned out to be a spa, and they directed Lian to the toilets. I sat for a moment or so and then decided I might as well relieve myself as well. I could see where Lian had had to take off her boots. I walked over to this sofa and was just kicking off my shoes when a woman came out, shouted at me and started laughing—this was the ladies massage area, and Lian later told me that both the masseuse and the customers were naked. Well that would have brightened up my day.

When the bus arrived to take us to town it was packed, and we had to really squeeze on. There were a few University students on board who were keen to practise their English on us. By this time we were very hungry, so jumped off at a shopping centre for a bite to eat. The next bus was pretty empty and luckily it was going to our part of town and dropped us off close to our hotel.

Next morning it was drizzling so took the opportunity to use an Internet café, and only then began to comprehend how big the quake had been in Sichuan.

Went for a walk eastwards along the beach path. Stopped at a Chinese temple. This one is unusual in that it dedicated to the

Goddess of the Sea normally worshiped in Fujian Province and the coastal South of China.

The television in on 24-hours a day, showing the rescue efforts being made in the aftermath of the earthquake. The Chinese Premier is everywhere, giving encouragement to the people. He is obviously very moved, and finds it hard to hold back his tears. We were later to be more impressed, as this was not simply a fly in, photo session, and fly out. He was there on the ground, directing operations; even if in hindsight he may have been more effective monitoring things from the capital. The Party Chairman, who was not to be left out of the hearts and minds operations, soon joined him.

This will certainly bring the Chinese closer together. The people are making big personal donations from towns and villages all over the vast country, and the Army have been fully mobilised

The major problem in the Sichuan area was the access to the towns and villages. We had visited this area two years previously. The roads run through mountainous areas, and hugs the steep hillsides by the rivers. I can just imagine the amount of work needed to clear an earth-slip. They can only be worked on one at a time. When we were there, there was a vast road rebuilding exercise being undertaken, whereby new roads were being built on elevated columns alongside the rivers and usually on the opposite side of the river to the existing road system. It's not difficult to envisage the effect that tremors and landslides could have on these.

The next morning we took a trolleybus to the stop closest to the railway station outside the town, and even this was actually quite a way from the little station. I even had to crouch down to get under a steel railway bridge on or way there. The waiting room was gloomy and the toilets old and unclean. One was expected to squat over a wide channel or stand astride it. Then every so often they could hose it through.

The gates opened fifteen minutes before departure. We soon found carriage No. 1. The seating arrangement was two seats on one side and three seats on the other, with a central isle. It was all very new and modern. The toilets were superb, with a separate urinal room for the men. And automatic glass sliding doors operated between the carriages. These Bullet Trains use French technology.

At 10:24am, the train left the station. Soon the sign (in Chinese and then in English) was announcing a speed in kilometres an hour of 170kph, and then up to 228kpm (140mph). And all the time it was very smooth.

We have our Bullet Train bookings only as far as Nanking, where we intend to overnight, and then find our way the next day by bus or slow train to Hangzhou. Lian is worried and manages to buy tickets on the train so we can continue from Nanking to Shanghai on this train. The only problem is that from there we will have to find ourselves empty seats, as we have no allocated seats.

Although we had to move a couple of times, this did not prove to be a problem. The train slid into Shanghai station at 8:40pm. The journey had taken an overall time of only 10.1/4 hours for the 870-mile (1,400km) trip.

At Shanghai railway station we bargained at the railway information desk for a hotel not too far from the bus station, and a mini-van took us there. The XinLi Cheng Hotel was cheap and not very cheerful, but the room was OK and the bathroom excellent. And it will probably be remembered best as the only place we stayed at on the trip that had a lift.

Hangzhou.

The next morning we checked out, and walked along to the bus station and booked seats for Hangzhou. But we would have a two-hour wait until 10:40am, as the earlier buses were already fully booked. No problem, and Lian unpacked a couple of mugs and we had coffees whilst we waited, using the boiling water dispenser always available at such places.

We had front seats, so had a good view. The bus soon entered an elevated highway, so we were not delayed by the heavy traffic.

On our previous trips we had noticed that the larger cars were invariably black in colour. This has now changed and a good number are in silver or white. I suppose the richer people in business are not so keen to be associated with the Party and government vehicles. The visibility was poor due to the general pollution, but we could see numerous high tension power line pylons disappearing into the gloom, and new ones under construction.

We reached Hangzhou two hours later, but found that the bottom of Lian's bag was soaking from water that had spilled from a container of live fish. Lian complained at the bus station, and surprisingly a man returned her full bus fare.

He even asked if my bag was also wet, so I suppose we could both have had a free trip.

We took a taxi along to hostel we had stayed at previously, and I checked the email whilst Lian did the checking in.

Took a walk along to the market, but it started to drizzle, so gave up trying to find a famous scissor shop we had heard about, and returned to the hostel.

The next morning, after the buffet breakfast, we found an information centre, and they were very helpful, giving us directions to the scissor shop and ideas about how best to see the Grand Canal. But the scissor shop turned out to be a bit of a disappointment.

Took a couple of buses northwards to find the waterbus station on the Grand Canal. The Canal is one of the marvels of China, after the Great Wall. The majority was built between 605 and 609AD, joining the Yellow River and the Yangzi Rivers. It forms a waterway meandering southwards from Beijing to

Shanghai and ends in Hangzhou 1,120 miles (1,800km) away. It was further developed in the 13th & 14th centuries, and about 685 miles (1,100 km) is now said to be navigable.

The first waterbus was full with a group, so we had an hour to kill before the next one came along.

We passed under a number of bridges of different designs, and disembarked at the famed Conghengtao stone bridge. This old stone pedestrian bridge forms a big triple arched access over the river. The central large arch is guarded on either side with a pair of carved stone dragons sitting atop columns set in the river to protect the stonework from damage by a passing barge.

The canal is still very busy, with barges full with aggregates, or coal, or construction materials.

We walk over the bridge that has steps up, and also a ramp to take wheelbarrows and motorbikes. There are a number of people selling jade and bracelets and other jewellery.

We were disappointed that the Grand Canal Museum was closed, so we could not have the chance to brush up on the history.

There is said to be a walkway alongside the entire canal, so I thought it would be a good idea to try this out, returning on the route we had taken with the waterbus.

The pedestrian way follows the riverbank, and there are also diversions through landscaped gardens. The walkways are usually well shaded with different species of trees, and there are many stretches with weeping willows. All in all a delightful walk which gave us time to admire the different types of design structure used for the many bridges spanning the canal.

Then, it was just before 2:30pm when we heard the crescendo of the wail of sirens, soon followed by continued hooting of car horns from stationary cars and busses. We could not think what it was, until we came up to a man who was standing with a bowed head and hands held with palms together. The noise stopped, and we asked another man what it was about, and he confirmed that it was about the earthquake.

It had been 2:28pm a week earlier that the quake had struck, and we later saw on TV that the whole country had come to a halt for five-minutes 'silence'. It was very moving, and then the government declared three days of mourning, and all public functions were cancelled. Only one TV programme continued showing the rescue efforts, while the rest showed flickering candles, even including the video-on-demand in our room.

We were nearly back to our destination, when the pathway gave out. We should have crossed the canal at the last bridge and walked along the other bank. But we were a little hot and weary, so made our way out to the traffic and boarded a bus. By good fortune the route stopped outside our hostel, so the cool beers went down very easily.

After a suitable rest we went along to the Lake and notice the West Lake Museum, a new structure, with a full height glass curtain wall on one length. It was near closing time, so we had to rush the visit a little.

We learned that the West Lake had been dredged from a depth of one and a half feet (half a meter) to an average of seven feet (2.1 m).

As we left the museum, a mother was carrying a little boy. He looked at me, and said "Hello granddad" in Chinese. This had everyone laughing.

Hangzhou is an affluent town with many upmarket restaurants. Opposite the hostel are a number of specialist car showrooms. The Ferrari Showroom had only one Ferrari and a new 4-door Maserati. The Porsche Showroom had six different models, and the no-name showroom next door had a Bentley 'Flying Spur' and an Aston Martin.

The next morning we returned to the West Lake Museum. As well as a natural history collection of stuffed birds, animals and reptiles, the history of the Lake and the adjacent areas, the museum has a superb collection of copies of old maps of the world, Asia, South-East Asia, and China, including one of each of the Provinces.

Crossed the road to see the Art Museum, but this was a little disappointing.

Time to check out of the hostel and leave our luggage in their storeroom.

Then caught a bus for a visit to the Silk Museum. This was very well done, and as well as the 'usual mulberry / silkworm / unravelling bit' one gets in other silk museums, they showed the history of silk and tried to explain how all the different types of weave could create so many different styles of material i.e. twill, damask, gauze, silk tabby, satin etc. Then they had a section showing dolls dressed in the typical clothing of a number of the dynasties.

Now time collect our luggage and take a shuttle bus to the airport for the evening flight back to Kuala Lumpur.

CHAPTER 15

East Malaysia—Sabah:
Mount Kinabalu Park

Porters carrying goods up Mount Kinabalu.

It was September, and we were off for another flight to Sabah, Malaysia's state on the northern tip of Borneo.

We arrived at Kota Kinabalu soon after mid-day, and were disappointed that the car we had hired was not at the airport waiting for us.

We phoned the owner, who we had been in email contact with for some time, and he announced that he had no car, as we had not confirmed it with him. Absolute nonsense of course, so we had little choice but to speak to the people at the car hire counters.

One company showed me an old Proton Saga, but when I checked the spare, I found that it had no jack or tools and one wheel was dented. This gave very little confidence. Another company offered a Perodua Viva, which is quite a new car on the market for the same price as the Proton. So we took this. Although it only had a small engine, it was reasonably nippy, and it climbed the hills without problems.

We drove into town to get some lunch and buy some wine prior to driving the 63 miles (100km) or so to the Mount Kinabalu Park.

As we left town it started to rain very heavily, and the roads became flooded in places. But we kept going, and we were thankful that the little car did not stall. The roads in Sabah have plenty of potholes and one can see why most cars there are 4WD vehicles. The small wheels of the Peradua needed care on the rough road surfaces, and one had to really slow down instead of simply accelerating and sailing over the top.

It was nearly 6pm when we reached the Park Headquarters (HQ). Lian had prepaid for our accommodation in the Park itself, and we were directed along to a chalet in Hill Lodge. This proved to be very comfortable.

Went for a walk, and remembered that by 6:30pm it would be dark, rather than at Kuala Lumpur's 7:30pm.

There are two restaurants in the park, the 'Balsam' by the HQ, and the 'Liwagu' near our chalet. So after a glass of wine on our balcony, we walked down to the Liwagu, and enjoyed a good curried chicken.

After dinner we drove up the road about 2.1/2 miles (4km) to the Power Station, where the main summit trail begins. Saw no birds, but only a Long-tailed Rat.

Next morning we woke early, and had a wonderful view of the Mountain. But by 6:30am the clouds came in and the mountain was shrouded.

The Park HQ is at over 5,100ft (1,550m) above sea level so it is much cooler than it is on the coast.

Walked to the HQ, and had some fried rice for breakfast at the Balsam Café. Tasted OK at the time, but had a bit of a runny tummy later, so decided not to eat there again. Took a 'short cut' back, passing the staff quarters for some bird watching.

Back at Hill Lodge, we changed rooms for one with a better balcony view, even though the room was not so good.

Went for a walk to see the Botanical Gardens. These were a little disappointing, as few orchids were flowering, and few plants were named. And some of the nametags are planted in the ground, and one cannot see which plant or tree they were referring to.

Had a call from the hire company, to say that a set of car keys for another vehicle had been left in the ashtray of our car. We were asked to leave them at reception and a driver would be coming to pick them up.

Took a drive down the other side of the hill, to the small town of Kundasan. Basically a street with vegetable and fruit stalls selling to passers by. Decided to have some lunch there. The café turned out to be full of flies, which are not something we normally see a lot of in Malaysia or Sabah.

Back to the Park, and a walk up the road towards the power station. On the way we came across a pair of beautiful Whitehead's Trogons sitting quietly in a dark wooded section. We saw the female first; all cinnamon brown, with a grey breast, black sides to the wings, and blue skin around the eye. She looked so delicate, and we had excellent front and back views. It was then that we saw the male. He was similar, but with a bright red head and belly. What a couple they made.

The trogons were named after a John Whitehead (1860-1899), a British explorer, writer and collector, who spent some time in Borneo, the Philippines and Hainan. As well as the trogon, Whitehead has a Spiderhunter and a Broadbill named after him in Sabah, but we have yet to see those.

Next morning we were out bird watching by 6am. Plenty of bird activity in an area adjacent to the botanical garden. Then at 7am to the Liwagu for breakfast. I tried their full western breakfast, and Lian had pancakes. The meal was spoilt by the very loud sound of a leaf blower that was being used in the Botanical Gardens. Apart from the noise pollution, I doubt if it was very successful in moving wet leaves.

Drove up to the power station to walk the Ular (snake) Trail. A very pleasant walk, even though we did not see a lot of bird activity.

Out birding again at 3pm, before driving out to the restaurant opposite the Park entrance for a snack and a Tiger beer.

Up again for clear early morning mountain views. This morning we did a couple of trails; the Silau trail by the side of a stream, and then the Kiau View Trail, coming out from the Pandan Trail. It seemed a long trek back to pick up the car, but Lian had a nice hot coffee waiting for me when I got back.

Lian had lost the cap on the end of her trekking pole, so we drove to Kundasan to try to find a rubber stopper such as one can put on the leg of a chair. No luck there, so we continued to the larger town of Ranau. Here we were lucky, so bought a couple of spares. Had some lunch in a coffee shop, before returning to the Park.

The next day we were due to go up the mountain. Lian booked a guide for us and negotiated with him to carry some of our things.

Normally, before such a trip, we would have done some training for the steep uphill and downhill walking that we were about to do. But his time we had stupidly done no training, so were physically unprepared for the exertion to come.

Did a repacking exercise to see exactly what we would take with us, and what we would leave locked up in the boot of the car.

Heavy rain in the afternoon, and it was 5:30pm before we could do any bird watching. Then went along to the Park HQ, where we could make use of a deposit box for passports, wallet and telescope.

The girls in the Park HQ and those looking after the chalets, were exceptionally good at their jobs. Whoever hired them seemed to use the same criteria to those hiring and training airline stewardesses. They were all smart, helpful and cheerful, as well as being pretty.

On our trip to Kundasan, we had spotted some of the Park staff in a small food shed (no name or sign up) about half a mile (1 km) from the Park, so thought we would check it out. It was hard to drive close, due to the big trailer lorries parked along the roadside. However the food was the best we had had on the trip; a big plate of fried 'keoy teow' (flat noodles), some barbeque pork, and fresh green vegetables stir-fried with lots of garlic. The only problem is that it closes at 7pm sharp.

As I had my shower, I found that I had collected a couple of leach bites on my ankle during our morning trail walks.

This was to be the day we started our climb up Mount Kinabalu. At 6:30am we had a breakfast outside the Park entrance. Back at the H.Q to find that our guide, Dimmy S, already had our tags and soon after 7am we drove up the road to the power station and parked the car. (6,200 ft-1,885m)

Seems we were the first away, and we kept up a good pace. After a drop down to a waterfall, the well-trodden path rose up before us. Some steps had been protected with wooden timbers, and others comprised tree roots or rocks. It was hard work, and the higher we got the more the lack of oxygen made breathing deep and difficult.

Our destination was the accommodation at Laban Rata, distance of just under 4 miles (6km). We were told that most people take five to six hours to get there, so our 4 hour 50 minutes did not seem too bad at the time. However, where the first half took 1.1/2 hours the second half took nearly twice as long.

Why oh why had we not trained for this!

But it was only the hotel staff or some porters that overtook us.

As we walked higher, the vegetation changed from montane forest to stunted cloud forest, and the rock types beneath our feet also changed. This mountain is not volcanic, but is formed from an ever-rising granite core.

One has to keep ones eyes down to see each step, so did not see much in the way of wildlife. At one of the small 'pondok' shelters, a small Brook's squirrel came over to take a piece of apple. He ran right up Lian's leg, and gently took it from her fingers. Then, at one of my frequent rests, I saw a Mountain Blackbird, black with a maroon belly. I only had to make a few sucking noises, and it came bounding over for a look and to see whether I had any crumbs for it.

At 12:30pm we reached Laban Rata at 10,750ft (3,273m). Here we had the chance of a rest in the canteen and to have some lunch of mushroom soup and a plate of chips. We were allocated a room for four, containing two bunk beds. We took the lower bunks and after a hot shower, lay down for a rest.

The last time Lian climbed the mountain, she went the further 1.1/2 miles (2km) up to the peak in the afternoon, and came back down to Laban Rata for the night. However, 95% of people leave the camp at about 2:30am, and climb up by torchlight in order to be at the peak for the dawn. They then walk all the way down that day. We had planned to go to the top that afternoon, and so could take our time on the way down. But I felt pretty knackered and drained. Even after the rest, I did not feel up to the walk up.

So we hung around the camp area. Most people seemed to arrive between 2:30 to 5pm. It was quite interesting to see the people coming in. Some parties had got split up during the climb and as a straggler stumbled in, they were mobbed and hugged by their friends. At the next table to us there were a group of eleven Korean ladies, with a male leader, and an elderly man. The women all had the latest gear on: ski glasses, trekking poles, knee guards, cycling gloves and colourful fashion items. They were members of a ladies mountaineering club. One of the women spoke excellent English, and she explained that once a week they go for a day trip for a trek in the Korean mountains. We had a few laughs with them and took several photos with them.

By 6:30pm the canteen was getting packed out with people and their rucksacks. Dinner finishes at 7pm, as they want everyone to rest early for the early morning wake up.

Three women from a different group of Koreans pushed themselves onto our table. Quite a different class of people from the mountaineering group, and to my eyes, with pretty unacceptable eating habits. One wanted to take my big soup bowl away before I had finished, and also to take our jug of hot water. But she did not succeed.

By 8pm we were back in our room. A woman had moved into the bunk above me, but the other bunk remained empty. Someone had not made it this far.

Laban Rata is a timber-framed structure, and so is very noisy. Being above the canteen we could hear a dozen languages, each trying to make themselves heard over the crescendo. Our room was next to the toilet and shower, and there seemed to be a continual stream of happy trekkers making there way there. They either had big clodhopper boots or sounded as if they were dragging along a sledge. It was nearly 9pm before any semblance of peace reigned.

Our alarm was set for 2:30am, and we agreed that we would only go on up if we really felt OK.

But when we woke, I still felt a bit off-colour, and suggested that as we had the guide, that Lian at least keep up the family honour. Actually, I was not looking forward to the torchlight parade with a hundred others.

The summit is just over 13,150ft (4,000m), and this was the height we had to trek to find the Mountain Gorillas in Rwanda. But I simply did not have the same desire to get to the top of Kinabalu.

So Lian went, but could not find Dimmy. When he arrived, he said he had been having tummy trouble, so they were about the last to leave. But, Lian being Lian, she said Dimmy helped pull her along in places, and they were the fourth to reach the peak.

And all the while I slept, awoken only by Lian's SMS message saying she had got there.

Yes—I did get up to take some dawn shots with my camera, and do some bird watching. One could very clearly see the lights of Kota Kinabalu about 60 miles (100km) away.

The canteen was open for the 2:30am breakfast, but then only re-opened about 8am. Just in time for Lian to arrive back. She was tired but obviously triumphant. Had breakfast, and allowed Lian a short rest.

Soon after 9am we set off down hill. I started out like a mountain goat. I was out ahead to take photos until Lian caught up, and then I was off again.

But the downhill trip proved to be even more difficult than the uphill one. Even though there was no longer a breathing problem, I found my knees going to jelly. Balancing was difficult, as the little muscles one automatically uses to push or pull the legs where on wants to go, did not seem to be working very well. Thank goodness we had our trekking poles. These really were a godsend.

Lian did not want to stop at all, as she was afraid she would stiffen up and not be able to move. I preferred short rests at each of the 'pondoks'. Just about everyone seemed to be passing us now.

The lady who shared our room passed us by, but she was having a piggy-back on a porters back.

Yes—I did consider it, but decided it looked too scary.

On our way up, a woman was being brought down on a stretcher, She was tightly tied in and wrapped with split bamboos. The four men carrying her were literally running and jumping down. That looked very hairy.

So it was 2pm when I reached the power station exit. Lian was already there waiting with a can of drink for me. At least I could drive the car alright, so we went to the HQ to drop Dimmy off, and then pick up our valuables and a Hill Lodge room key.

Time to take a wonderful hot shower, a coffee, and a rest. Then at 6pm out to our truckers shed for another excellent meal.

In August there is an annual international race up and down the mountain. The present record is only 2hours and 50 minutes for the 21km race. Now I have every admiration for all of them.

Next morning we had some early morning bird watching from the balcony, before packing and loading the car. I found it very difficult walking down any slope.

When we had checked out, we decided to take a more scenic route back to Kota Kinabalu. We drove down to Ranau, and from there on to Tambunan, before crossing the Crocker Range and dropping down to KK. On the way we stopped off at the Rafalasia Centre. They had some blooms open, but we did not have time for the trek to see them. I don't think my legs would have approved of this either.

By mid afternoon we dropped off the hire car at the airport, and took the early evening flight to Kuala Lumpur.

CHAPTER 16
East Malaysia. Sarawak: A trip to Ba' Kelalan in the Kelabit Highlands

The muddy track out of Ba' Kelalan.

The Kelabit Highlands are on the eastern side of Sarawak, parallel with the border to Kalimantan, Indonesia.

We had signed up to go with a Malaysian group of nine being led by Neal Nirmal Ariyapala. We were each responsible for booking and paying for all our flights, and Neal would book the accommodation, land transport and guides.

The plan was to take the Air Asia flight to Miri in Sarawak, and then fly northeast over Brunei to the coastal town of Lawas, which is quite close to the border with Sabah. From there we would take 4WDs to the village of Ba' Kelalan in the Kelabit Highlands. We would spend a few days here, including a trek across the border into Indonesia. We would then take a short flight to Bario, the major town in the Highlands, for some more trekking, before flying directly to Miri, and thence on to Kuala Lumpur.

But things do not always go to plan when taking such trips.

We usually travel on our own, and did not know any of the other participants, so only met them at the airport one Saturday morning at the end of November.

Neal, our trip leader, lives in Taiping, is involved with the Malaysian Nature Society, and runs adventure style trips.

Aneson (Annie) Au was the only other woman. She sells investment trusts, and soon got on well with Lian.

Andy Paul works in advertising, and proved to be an accomplished and avid photographer. It is obvious from his physique that he spends a lot of time in the gym, and he needs it when carrying the weight of all of his Nikon camera equipment.

There were two 'father and son' teams: Mr Ooi is a retired teacher, and his son Michael writes the software for games. Mr Lee is a lawyer, and brought his 17-year-old student son along to introduce him to some fresh air and tall trees. One senses however that Marcus is a somewhat reluctant participant, as he turned out to be continually late, and would rather watch whatever was on any TV, than socialise and chat with the others or any of the locals.

The 2.1/4 hour Air Asia flight was comfortable, landing at Miri. We then had a three-hour wait before taking a MasWings Twin Otter for the 45-minute flight to Lawas.

Here Borneo Jungle Safari's local manager, Rona, met us with a couple of 4WD vehicles for the short trip around the runway and into town, where we had bookings in the Perdana Hotel.

We all met again for a walk round town. Lawas is a quiet and pleasant riverside town with wide streets and plenty of parking. A giant ficus tree intrigued us, as the original host tree had long disappeared.

Small boats ferried locals across the 55-yard (50 meter) wide river to the residential side. We all boarded one boat, and the 15hp motor took us for a trip upstream. We stopped at the jetty of a Theological College, and decided to have a look around. Most of the single storey wooden buildings were in a pretty run-down and dilapidated state. They stood high above ground level on their timber piles, with rusty corrugated roofs and grey and splitting timber plank walls. There were also a few block-work buildings. We saw a few people about, so the site had not been abandoned.

The next morning we met at 7am for breakfast in a local coffee shop, but it was a bit disorganised.

The term 'coffee shop' here is not a Starbucks clone, but a small café selling various local foods from one or two individual stalls set up within the open fronted shop i.e. noodles, fried rice, chicken rice. Coffee and tea is available, together with a number of other drinks such as Milo, fresh barley water, ginger tea etc. The locally grown coffee and tea are likely to include spoonful's of condensed milk and lots of sugar, unless one can tell them to leave it out.

We then strolled along to the market and bought some snacks, as it was not clear whether or not we would find anywhere to eat during our forthcoming journey.

So it was nearly 9am before we had packed our bags into the back of two 4WD 'twin-cabs' and at last set of on our way. A 'twin-cab' is a 4-door vehicle with an open luggage area at the back. The front cab has two seats, and the rear seat is made for three. However, the nine of us plus two drivers had to be accommodated, so this meant that one vehicle had to squeeze four people on the back seat. They were not very happy passengers. Luckily I was allocated a front seat, as I obviously had the longest legs. Poor Lian was one of the 'four' on the back seat.

We were soon on a well maintained dirt logging road, and proceeding in a south-eastern direction.

Our driver, Leang Sakai, was good and stopped whenever we wanted to take any photos. After about an hour and a half we reached a logging camp, but had to wait nearly three quarters of an hour for the others to catch up, as they had been taking a lot more photos. We left them to rest, and set off again. At a smaller logging camp we came across a small café run by the camp security manager, and really enjoyed his coffee whilst we munched the curry puffs and doughnuts we had brought from Lawas.

An hour later and we left the good logging roads, and then came across the deeply rutted and in some places muddy dirt roads leading to the Highlands. The logging camps keep the roads in good condition with their dozers and graders, as without a good surface the big Mercedes trucks with their Doll trailers are unable to bring their 80-ton loads in from the forests at all times. Once the logs are unloaded, the Doll trailers are lifted up and stacked piggyback style on the back of the truck.

Luckily it had not rained and we climbed several hills of 5,000ft (1,500m), before dropping down into the 3,300ft (1,000m) high valleys.

At one point we stopped at a spot were people had been hand sawing some cut logs at the roadside. The timber was then stacked carefully to allow it to dry out. Leang, our driver, confessed that one of the larger collections was his own, as he intended to extend his house. He was paying the sawyers to cut his logs.

We pass a number of villages, each with the suffix 'Long', which means 'rivers meeting' in the local language. On the road we came across four separate gates across the road. These were erected to stop the water buffalo using the road to access rice fields. As I was the front passenger, I had the job of opening and closing the gates. Some were conventional gates, whilst some comprised a number of very long sliding bamboo poles.

It was mid-afternoon when we reached our destination of Apple Lodge in Ba' Kelalan.

The journey is only approximately 68 miles (110 km) as the crow flies, but had taken us close to seven hours.

We were the only visitors, so had a choice of bedrooms in this hostel. So we had a double bed and our own toilet. The shower, which sprays over everything, is solar powered, as are the lights. So plenty of hot water if the sun had been out, but very cool water and low wattage lights if it had been cloudy.

Coffee and tea are available freely 24 hours a day, with the hot water kept in thermos flasks. And a plate of bananas is always available if you need a quick snack.

The food was good, with the beautiful small-grained local hill rice. We were told that the famed Bario rice, actually comes from Ba'Kelalan and from across the border in Indonesia. Lots of vegetables are available, and every day we enjoyed chicken wings cooked in various ways. Mr Ooi had bought a lot of small fish and these were deep fried and crispy. So we were certainly not going to starve here.

The local inhabitants are from the Lun Bawang tribe, and Neal had advised us to talk with the locals and get to know how they lived and learn a little of their aspirations.

Next morning we had a leisurely breakfast of fried rice, and toast, before setting off for a walk to see a local salt spring. Walked back along the very muddy 'main road', and soon after crossing a steam, climbed over a bamboo gate and into a grassy field. Water buffalo stood watching us, with ears outstretched. White cattle egrets surround them, sometimes fluttering up to gain a vantage point on the buffalo's shoulder. As we walk past them the buffalo always seem to be facing straight on to us, but their movements seem imperceptible. One just had to make sure one doesn't fall into one of their muddy wallows as one returns their steady gaze.

Had three more stream crossing to go, and at the second, Paulus our guide, suggested I take off my boots and leave them there to be picked up on the way back. He was busy helping us over the clear but rocky streams.

The salt spring is in a small fenced compound to stop the local animals coming in, and comprised an open sided wooden shed housing the fireplaces, a wood shed for storing and drying the firewood, and the spring or well itself which is enclosed with a plastered brickwork surround about 3 feet (1m) high. The salt water overflows and runs down into a field, and it is then available for the local animals. The guide then demonstrated with a bamboo pole that the well is over 13ft (4m) deep.

In the shed are the fireplaces that house six open stainless steel barrels. The saltwater is poured into the barrels, and after two days and one night the heat from the fires will have evaporated the water away, leaving only the salt crystals.

As well as for cooking, it seems that the salt is in high demand in Chinese medicine shops, as it is said to have many therapeutic properties.

Andy had arranged for another guide to take him into the forest for a day's photography, and went on his way. The rest of us strolled back to town, remembering to pick up my walking boots, and went around the end of the runway and into the apple orchard.

On the way we saw a number of small motorbikes with 150cc engines, and simply loaded with goods. Bags of cement, floor tiles, 44 gallon drums, big sacks of other goods, motor oil, car batteries, cooking gas bottles etc. These are the barter traders who bring rice and other local goods in over the hills from Indonesia, and then exchange them for goods to take back into Indonesia on a daily basis. The bikes collect together in the late morning, forming a long queue at the Malaysian army post, and then drive together for the 6-mile (10 km) ride back into Indonesia. Not a single number plate in sight.

We also met a number of Indonesian women who had to walk all the way with their woven floor mats and other handicrafts for sale or barter.

It was not a large orchard. It seems that for several years they had no crop, so they brought in a specialist, who bent the branches down into big loops. Then they had a crop and the shape stays. Some trees had small apples growing the size of a date, whilst the majority were in blossom. This accounts for their claim of two crops a year. They also have some small oranges that we picked, and along the fence there were a number of passion fruit, and these were quite delicious.

Once a year the Ba' Kelalan Apple Festival is held, and the entire village can go in and eat as many apples as they like. But the crop is relatively small and hardly commercial when one accounts for the cost of sending the apples out by road or air.

Instead of walking around the runway on our way back for lunch at the Lodge, we climbed a fence and walked right down the middle of the runway. We childishly waved our arms around, pretending to be planes and hummed the tune from the 'Dam Busters'.

After lunch we went for a delightful walk through the rice fields to the next village of Long Langai. The path was narrow, but had been concreted so was wide enough for pedestrians or a motorbike. The path crossed a number of streams, and each crossing had a wooden bridge complete with a corrugated iron roof attached to a wooden framework. Just the place to rest if it starts to rain.

The rice was growing well, and the rice grains were now visible. Obviously there were a number of varieties planted, including some with dark brown grains, and some reddish ones.

As we entered the town, there was a surprisingly large school on our right hand side.

School holidays had started, so we all walked in. The buildings surrounded a large grassed playing field, with a grass running track. We peered into the classrooms of the 2-storey main block, and one had been labelled as the computer room.

Leaving the school we passed through a carved wooden entrance to the village. Surprisingly large wooden houses surround a large grass playing field. In the distance I could see a number of children, and suggested to Lian that she get her camera out ready.

But as we got closer, we could see that there were also a lot of women in mauve T shirts. This was none other than the village reception committee, and was a surprise to even Neal. So we lined up and started to shake hands with a line of children, men, and the women in the matching shirts. The women had dinner plate size black and white symbolic flowers, or were they hornbill feathers? They started to move and sway to a cassette recorder that had been turned on, and then performed a local song and dance for us. We gave them a good clap, and one of the older men introduced himself as the George Cigar Sultan. He was the Penghulu or village headman.

Then to our further amazement we were ushered into a room with a long table set out and laden with local delicacies. These comprised different methods of cooking the local rice: including steamed in pandan leaves and other local leaves, rolls like giant caterpillars, and banana crisps. This was washed down with vast quantities of tea. The women and children sat on rush mats around the edge of the room, talking, laughing and eating.

Penghulu George, told us all about his town, their staunch belief in Christianity and the Borneo Evangelical Mission, and how they want to keep their valley green and pristine.

He told a story of how some years ago, logging concessions had been given out to carry out logging on the valley sides. As the authorities would not heed the objections of the villagers, George said he personally kidnapped the loggers and refused to release them. A senior government minister and police officers were dispatched from Kuala Lumpur, but to no avail, until the villagers had written proof that the logging licences had been withdrawn and would not be re-issued in the future. Quite a coup for a few mountain people!

He told us of his early schooling and how one had a four-day walk to Lawas before the track could take 4WDs. He laughed, and said that he was practically running for all the four days, and it would probably take us ten days at a slow walk.

We were told that the thirteen villages in the valley do not allow alcohol, and smoking is frowned upon. Many years earlier, the men were drunk most of the time, so they would go out and collect a few heads. On their return it was time to celebrate, so they would get drunk again. The enemy would they counterattack and collect their own heads. So when the missionaries arrived, they stopped them drinking.

Only one Chinese shop in Ba'Kekalan sold beer, so the people boycotted the shop. But this turned out not to be a complete boycott, as their other goods are still generally cheaper, and beer is still available under the counter.

He told us that the people only want one rice crop a year, and do not use the pesticides or fertilisers they receive from the government. They prefer to do things naturally, using their own water buffaloes. Once the rice has been harvested, the buffaloes are used to till the fields, then left there to fertilise the ground naturally until it is time to replant. The buffalo are then sent on holiday and left to feed on the grassy fields.

Penghul George then gave us his official welcome speech in Bahasa Malaysia, and we got Mr Ooi, our ex teacher, to reply on our behalf. Not to be outdone, Mr Ooi got out his harmonica and our group got up to sing "You are my sunshine . . .", a tune we thought they would also know. It was all good fun, and we were sorry when it was time to leave after enjoying such uplifting hospitality,

On our way back into Ba'Kelalan, we stopped off at Leang's (our driver) house, before proceeding back for dinner. The wooden house is raised above the ground on stilts, and his wife and mother were cooking on their log fire. Neal has been there many times and often stays there if he has no group. He refers to the mother as his godmother. Woven rush mats and linoleum cover the floor, and there are few chairs, as everyone sits on the floor to chat or to eat.

We learnt that our hosts in Apple Lodge were the parents of Judson Sakai Tagal, who died in a helicopter crash in 2004. Judson was a deputy minister, and much of the development in the valley passed through his family. The house was full of pictures of their son.

The next morning we set off to clamber up the other side of the valley to a small covered viewing point. We crossed the rice fields, then in single file across a flimsy bamboo bridge, before starting our climb. From the viewpoint we could see Ba' Kelalan and the runway spread out before us, and the village of Long Langai in the distance. We all found lots of interest to photograph, be it landscape, plants and flowers, or even beetles.

And as we walked back we even met some children with a 3-week old long-tailed monkey. Its eyes were not properly open, and it had been suffering from some insect bites. One of the kids was holding a babies bottle, so they were intent on feeding it.

That afternoon, Lian, Angie and I walked back to the orchard to pick some fresh passion fruit, and got back just as it started to rain.

The pretty young cook had invited the group along to the church to watch the Christmas rehearsals for dancing and singing. So after dinner and a chat, we all walked up the hill to the main square and along to the church. The church is a timber structure with metal roofing. At 165ft (50m) wide, by 82ft (25m) deep, the church hall is simply huge.

Dance practise had already commenced, and was being choreographed by the pastor's wife. There were several rows of women, and a couple of rows of men at the back. Lian and Annie joined in at the end of a women's row. The women are very graceful, but this was not the word one would use to describe the dancing of one or two of the men. The words 'two left feet' come to mind—but there would have been even more had I the guts to join in myself.

Whilst this went on children were watching or running around without a care in the world.

Dancing practise complete for the evening, someone grabbed a guitar, and practise commenced for the new hymn or carol they were practising. This was melodic, and the words, in Bahasa Malaysia, were written up on a blackboard. But some had already transferred the words into their exercise book.

Sitting there watching the proceedings, one could not but ponder on the tranquillity of the place, and the sense of togetherness of these content and happy people. They are so open and friendly, and certainly have something that the city folk miss out on.

Its already Wednesday, and the day for our walk into Indonesia. We are about to trace the route taken by the barter traders. It is gone 8:30am when our group set out with a guide. At the Malaysia army post, I give them a photocopy of my passport, whilst the rest used copies of their identity cards.

The route is very hilly and extremely muddy. We meet the barter traders using sticks to clear the mud jamming the gap between tyre and mudguard, or gingerly riding down the deep muddy ruts with their legs out straight before them in order to balance or fend off rocky sections. Climbing the slopes needs careful throttle control to keep from suddenly skidding broadside to the intended direction of travel. I would certainly be petrified to be a pillion rider. And there was not a safety helmet in sight.

It's not easy walking, and after an hour or so I am ahead with an Indonesian businessman who has tagged along with us. But whereas we are soon all covered in mud, he seems to tip toe around, and his white shoes and dark trousers remain relatively pristine. And whereas I follow the track around a small valley, he makes a shortcut across the valley using a fallen tree. He must have been here before.

Mr Lee had been a policeman before taking up law. He had met the local police, and two young policemen put on civilian clothes and had joined us, as they had not made the journey before.

At last there was a long hill down into a wide valley, and at the bottom of the hill an archway announcing it as being Indonesia.

I sat down on some leaves and had a go at cleaning my boots. The others strolled in over the next 50 minutes. Some had taken an alternate route, but it had proved to be even muddier.

So it was nearly mid-day before we reached the Indonesian army post at Pos Pantas Long Midang. As we had the permit from the Malaysian army post, they were not interested in even seeing my passport.

A 4WD truck was waiting for us, and we all clambered aboard for the 6-mile (10 km) ride to our destination of Long Bawan, which due to the bad road conditions, took over an hour. This included a bridge crossing where half the foundations were hanging in mid air, and passing a number of villages.

At Long Bawan, arrangements had been made for us to have lunch at a restaurant, which turned out to belong to the businessman who had walked with us.

There was just time for a quick walk round town. All dirt roads, but drains were under construction to enable proper roads to be put in at some time. It appears that the only access to this town is by aircraft.

Knowing the time it took to get there, and that it would be dark soon after 6pm, Lian and I tried to get the group to get a move on. So at 2:30 pm we got back on our vehicle for the ride back to the border. But only a few minutes later, we had a puncture. The driver had a spare tyre, but no jack. So the driver's mate went off in search of one. But when he finally returned, the jack had insufficient travel, so the process was slow as a number of wooden planks had to be used as well. So it was a half hour later before we set off again. Light rain started, and those in the back were getting wet and muddy, especially when they had to walk past the really bad sections of the road.

At 4pm we started our walk back into Malaysia with our ponchos on, as the rain was now steady. Lian, Mr Ooi and I soon outstripped the others, even though the slopes were now extremely slippery. We passed a barter trader's abandoned motorbike, as he was quite unable to get any further.

It was 6pm when we reached the Lodge and we could enjoy a hot drink. The last of our group arrived over an hour later, with stories of having to walk in the dark, holding hands in single file, and nearly walking into a buffalo. At the end Marcus needed a piggyback from the guide.

That evening we had been invited to Leang's house for dinner. He had been away for two days in Lawas, and it was assumed that he was stuck somewhere on the way back due to the rains. So two of his brothers wives acted as co-hosts. What a spread they put on: local rice, lots of different local vegetables from the forest, heart of palm, and chicken cooked in several different ways. We all sat on the floor to eat our meal, and I find it quite difficult to know what to do with my long legs. The lotus position is quite uncomfortable for me after even a few minutes.

It's Thursday, and today we fly to Bario at 10:10am. We walk over the runway with our bags, and check in at the airport and have ourselves and our luggage weighed. But the cloud is quite low, and at 11am we are told that this weekly flight is cancelled due to bad weather. The control tower appealed on our behalf, and we were told that a rescue plane would arrive tomorrow.

So back to Apple Lodge and recheck-in. As no vehicles have been able to get through, the Lodge was still empty.

In the afternoon some of us wandered up the hill behind the Lodge to visit the abandoned chapel.

From there we strolled around town, and visited the 'longest kitchen in Sarawak'. Four family members have a block of four 2-storey terraced wooden houses. Then behind this is a single storey longhouse 165ft (50m) long by 16ft (5m) wide, with four separate kitchens attached to one side. The families cook separately, but join each other for their meals in the long open section. That morning they had cooked and fed four hundred people following a funeral. This was yet another example of their community spirit.

That evening the group had a B-B-Q in the Lodge garden.

Next morning the weather was no better, and at 9:30am we were informed that Mas Wings were unable to find a spare plane to collect us, and the plane to Lawas the following day was fully booked. We would now have no alternative but to abandon going to Bario, and try to return to Lawas by road.

Two 4WD's were soon sorted out and loaded up, and by mid-morning we were on our way. At one village we stopped and took on board a few sacks of rice. Our driver Galwat was very proficient, and we skidded our way through deep mud on many, many occasions. It was amazing how much the track had broken up after the rain. But luckily the rain was now holding off.

We reached a long hill as we started to leave the valley. It was a case of 'all out and walk to the top'. And the road seemed to go up forever. At each bend one thought one was at the top, but no, the road continued to snake its way upward. Lian and Annie had taken their shoes off and were squelching through the multi-coloured muds.

It was then that we heard the roar of heavy equipment, and puffing smoke from its exhaust stack was a large Caterpillar Dozer, its blade cutting a flat track through the mud and down the hill.

Soon after, we did reach the top and sat and waited and waited. Then we heard the roaring exhaust of the dozer, as it dragged the first two vehicles up the hill. It returned, and we prayed that our two vehicles would be next.

A small lorry had been abandoned trying to get down the hill to Ba'Kelalan. He had intended to take three buffalo back to Lawas, and so we saw two boys walking them up the hill to the lorry. By now he had unloaded chairs, cement and roofing sheets at the roadside, and was about to load the buffaloes.

Our prayers were answered when we saw our two vehicles being dragged sideways around the corner. It had taken nearly three hours since we started walking from the bottom of the hill.

Our driver, did not believe in wasting time, and soon left the others behind. So we stopped for hot drinks at the little logging camp, and waited for the others to catch up. The road was now much better as they had regular maintenance.

Then we saw some young Penans, a tribe of forest dwellers, walking towards us. One pointed to our front wheel and our driver realized we had a puncture. But the driver did have a spare and a jack, so not much time was lost.

It was past nine when we reached the Perdana Hotel, after or 11-hour journey.

All the flights from Lawas to Miri were fully booked, and we were unable to go by road, as the others did not have their passports to pass through Brunei. So we had a three-hour bus trip to Kota Kinabalu in Sabah, and then a flight back over the same route and on to Miri.

We stopped there over-night, before taking the evening flight back to Kuala Lumpur.

CHAPTER 17
China: Sichuan & the Tea Horse Route

Bronze figures commemorating the tea horse route in Kangding.

We may have all heard of the famed Silk Route, whereby silk and many other valuable items were sent westwards from China to Europe along a number of interconnecting routes.

Another, less known route was the one taking tea from the tea gardens of south-western China northwards, then turning westwards into the high plateaus of Tibet. Horses and furs were then brought back on the return journey. Although mules and horses were used for transporting the tea, in many places the country was so rough with it's gorges, cascading rivers and high passes, that the only way was to manhandle the tea on the backs of porters.

The fermented black tea was compressed into bricks, formed into slabs weighing 100 to 150kg, and carried on a wooden frame as a backpack. Just think of carrying two or three 50-kilogram bags of cement and staggering for even a few hundred metres. But these men had over a thousand miles to travel, at an average of 6 miles (10km) per day. They each had a stout walking stick, which could also be use to prop the underside of the backpack in order to take the weight off their legs when they needed to rest. On their feet they wore straw slippers. Spares were carried, as well as enough food to last the first week or so.

Chinese tea was traditionally 'green' tea, but the same leaf can be processed slightly differently to form the 'black' tea that is fermented and was to become so popular in Europe and Tibet.

At one time in history, the Emperor would accept green tea as a tax from the tea growing area of his southern provinces. The arduous journey would take over a year for the officials to make the delivery.

One story was that when the green tea arrived from the area of Pu Er, the officials unloaded their cargo, but to their horror, found that the tea had turned black. The heat and the sweat from the mules had spoilt the consignment.

But fearful for their lives, the men could not admit to this, and denied that anything was wrong. The Emperor was sceptical and demanded a sample, so hot water was provided and a pot of chai was made. The Emperor sipped it and passed it to an official. The men must have been weak at the knees, when the Emperor smiled and demanded that the Pu Er tea would all be kept in the palace and only he and his family would enjoy it.

So, until such time as the tea growers managed to duplicate the fermentation process at the estate, for several years the Pu Er tea sent to Beijing had to be allowed to ferment during the journey.

The Tibetans liked the black tea, and it soon became an essential part of their diet. They take it with a dab of yak butter and a pinch of salt. This may be an acquired flavour, but one that the Tibetans could not do without.

Beside the furs, the Tibetans also had something the Emperor needed even more, and that was the horses for his army. Thus a staple trade flow went on for centuries: tea to the west, and horses to the east.

And thus the Tea Horse Routes were formed and became the framework for trade in the area. Scholars, Buddhist monks, missionaries, traders, prostitutes, entertainers, soldiers and scoundrels all came to share these rocky roads and high passes.

But it was the men carrying the tea from the small estates who were the real heroes. These used the roughest tracks and the highest passes to deliver the tea. Even going south from Tibet and crossing the Himalayas into India, before India saw the importance and opened up their own tea estates.

We had previously visited the province of Yunnan with its tea estates around Pu Er, and had travelled about 900 miles (1,400km) on the windy roads going north from Kunming, Dali, Lijiang, Panzhihua, Emei Shan, Chengdu, to Jiuzhai Gou, on what was the start of the Tea Horse Route.

We were now interested on the start of the westward route from Chengdu to Llhasa in Tibet, a distance of approximately 750miles (1,200 kilometres) as the crow flies, but considerably more when following the twisting valleys and gorges. It would be here that the track would rise from about 1,600ft (500m) to the 12,000ft (3,700m) of the Tibetan plateau.

Chengdu.

So we flew in from Kuala Lumpur to the Chinese city of Chengdu, the capital of Sichuan province.

We had booked a room at the Bin Jiang Hotel, a modest hotel next to the Sofitel, and overlooking the river.

That afternoon we went to see the famed 'face changing' performance at Chengdu Jinli Street, a tourist area recently rebuilt in the old style into a few alleyways selling tourist goods, tea shops and restaurants. The show began with a tea pouring ceremony performed by a pretty girl who prepared the tea using exaggerated and rhythmic hand movements. Her fingers were long, and her wrists made of rubber as they bent and swayed and lingered as they went through the rigmarole of washing and warming the cups and teapot, and at last pouring the tea.

Then came a young man with a copper teapot with a 6-foot (2m) long spout. This was a very gymnastic performance with him leaping and twirling the teapot around his neck and back and every now and then stopping just long enough in a martial arts stance to pour the tea into a very small cup. Had he lost control of the teapot then someone would have come out with a very thick lip. And all the time he defied gravity by spilling no tea.

Then onto stage came a man in the full regalia of a Chinese opera villain, complete with a head-dress and a brightly coloured face mask, accompanied by the high screeching singing and the continuous clash of cymbals. He flashed his fan across his face, and one could see that the green background of the mask was now blue. Another twirl and it was pink, and then white. For the last couple of changes his face was thrust forward and the change happened in the blink of an eye. It was just too fast to see. Lian counted twelve different mask changes in the five-minute performance. So how does he do it, and what triggers the change? No idea, but perhaps they are on a spring that drops from the headgear. It was certainly a very impressive performance. He later told us he had taken several years to perfect his act.

Visit the Pandas.

The next day was my birthday, and we had agreed we would spend this with the pandas. So after breakfast we took a local bus' out to the 'Chengdu Research Base of Giant Panda Breeding'.

The research station is set in a large landscaped park area, with the buildings well spread apart. What a wonderful creature the Giant Panda is.

The first we saw were busy munching away at bunches of bamboo leaves and stalks. At times they would roll over on their backs and continue to enjoy their breakfast.

Lian wanted to see the youngest ones at the nursery. They would now be about 6-months old. We saw three who were being looked after by a keeper dressed in a greenish plastic long coat and hat and wearing a facemask. They would run around after her, and could not wait to get a hug and a cuddle from her. It was really delightful.

Once the older pandas had finished feeding they were inclined to climb a tree and wedge themselves onto a branch or into any bifurcation, where they would promptly go to sleep.

As well as the Giant Pandas, the centre has a number of the much smaller russet coloured Red Pandas.

We were reminded again of the difficulties of being a pedestrian in China. We had to remember that the traffic is supposed to keep to the right, instead of the left hand side that we are used to. We tried to use crossings with a traffic lights showing when it was safe for pedestrian to cross, but even then traffic filtering right seem to ignore the lights, as do cyclists and the ever-present electric motorbikes and scooters. The latter two also make use of the pavements whenever they feel it would be quicker for them.

When one considers how many new cars there are on the road now, it is a miracle that there are not a lot more accidents, as the majority of drivers have so little experience.

Ya'an.

The next day we walked to the main bus station, and boarded the 9:30am bus for the two-hour trip along the 3-lane highway to Ya'an. The land slowly rose from 1,440ft (440m) above sea level, and at 1,970ft (600m) we noticed a number of small tea plantations at Mingshan, before dropping to 1,575ft (480m) at Ya'an.

Lian had earlier used the Internet and set off to check out the Sage Hotel, whilst I sat sunning myself on a plastic chair and guarded our luggage.

The hotel was very pleasant, with a very modern bathroom and free Internet.

In the afternoon we had a walk alongside the wide river, and across the extraordinary bridge with it's 3-storey buildings built in the old Chinese style above the arched spans. The lower level is a pedestrian walkway with shops either side. Unfortunately the idea has not been a commercial success, and some of the shops are boarded up and the 2nd and 3rd levels are blocked off. However, the shops each side of the river are bustling, and full of restaurants and KTV karaoke joints. Karaoke seems to be the main entertainment of the younger set.

That evening we tried the local famed fish hotpot. We asked for one with reduced chilli, as the Sichuan food can be extremely hot, and they often use one type of chilli that leaves one with numb lips. A huge steaming metal bowl was brought to our table, and through the dark brown soup we could see chunks of fish. "Can we add some vegetable now?"

"No", said the waitress, "eat the fish first, or it will break up once we light the fire under the bowl".

The fish is a local variant of large catfish; soft and tasty, but full of small bones. And there was so much of it. When we had enough we took out the rest onto a plate, and it was embarrassing how much we would be wasting. Then we added quantities of different types of mushrooms, seaweeds, fresh green vegetables, lotus stalks, and bamboo shoots into the soup, and started up the fire. The vegetables were delicious, and the heat from the fire and the salty and chilli hot soup soon had me sweating. This semi open-air restaurant was crowded, and people were waiting for the noisy tables to clear. As the only white face around, we were obviously subjects of curiosity. The meal was finished with a sweet bowl of what was said to be bird's nest soup.

The next morning we set off for a side trip to another panda centre. We took a small minivan to Bifenxia. The minivan only starts up as soon as there are sufficient passengers. The trip took less than half an hour, and the narrow road rose through misty steep valleys following a rocky river from 1,800ft (550m) up to 3,300ft (1,000m), passing the Bifeng Gorge.

We had met two Chinese women tourists in the van, and set off with them to the reception to pay for our entrance fees. One pleasant surprise was that due to my great age, I paid considerably less for my entrance than Lian had to.

At one end of the entrance hall was a huge mural depicting Nu Wa, a Goddess, who collapsed whist trying to patch the sky with stones. Her body is said to have become the Bifeng Gorge, her hands became the 'patching' mountain, and her fingers became the Ya'an fish (which we had tried the previous evening). One stone she dropped became Hong Kong.

We started by taking a two-hour wander around a circular route along a steep sided valley with sides towering over 1,000ft (300m) high. A misty and mystic place, the path meandered along a rocky stream between huge rocks covered by mosses. A number of waterfalls cascaded along the main stream with such names as 'Dragon Flying Over the Clouds'. This romantic description sound improbable, until one looks up the waterfall to see the multi levels being the undulations of the dragon, and with its head disappearing into the mist above. Small falls dripped down from the heights above us.

In one section we saw a number of coffins clinging to the side of the high cliffs. These were the remains of one of the many Chinese minority tribes, but how and why had people placed the coffins in such a gravity defying location?

We had been slowly descending, and it was now time to join another stream for the 900 ft (275m) climb to our starting point.

We had not realised how long this diversion would take us, and were worried that we would not be able to see the pandas before they had stopped eating, so had left the two girls during the ascent.

The panda entrance closes during the lunch break, and Lian had to use her powers of persuasion with the entrance guards in order to let us in at the tail end of the morning session.

So we were in.

One panda was busy delicately peeling the bark from a thickish bamboo before chomping on it like he (or she) was eating a sugar cane. This was done just as well in a sitting position as it was rolling over onto it's back and then back to the sitting position. And where are the other pandas? They have all climbed high into trees.

The ground here is bare, and the panda's have their pristine white fur smeared with the colour of the earth.

We notice that the bamboo they are given may be a different variety to that given in Chengdu, with smaller leaves and thicker stems, but this may be just because it looks dry and shrivelled.

Time to go to the Panda Nursery and see the young ones. But when we got there, we could see nothing. Curtains had been pulled across the windows of the internal nursery. The local staff were not very tourist friendly, and only said that the youngsters may come out later in the afternoon.

It was really quite cold and damp now we had stopped moving.

It was as we were leaving the nursery area, we met a Dutch couple that had spent a couple of weeks as volunteers, having paid several hundred Euros for the privilege. They were due to leave the next day, and said they could not wait to do so, as they had not enjoyed their experience, as they were not allowed to handle the pandas at all, and were restricted solely to cleaning out empty cages. Their story about their reception, accommodation and food certainly does not make one wish to volunteer oneself. No cuddly pandas, but they were keen to show their photos taken from the same side of the fence as other tourists.

To Kangding.

Woken in the morning by the sound of cocks crowing even though we are in the town.

After breakfast we pulled our bags to the bus terminal, where we had bought our seats the previous day for the trip to Kangding.

Today we would be following the Tea Horse route westwards towards Tibet, climbing from the main plain up through the hills.

We had seats at the front, so should be able to enjoy the views. The bus was full, and we could not help but notice the difference in features of the majority of the passengers.

These had the darker and flatter features of the Tibetan stock. The bus pulled out on time just before 10am. A white prayer scarf dangles from the mirror, and the small plastic golden prayer wheel attached to the dashboard continues its spinning with the assistance of batteries. So with such religious artefacts in place, we felt reasonably safe.

The normal 2-lane road followed a river through a narrow valley with vertical red rock cliffs, before entering a wider valley with the sides covered in short trees and clumps of bamboo. The deciduous trees are bare and have yet to get their new leaves.

An hour later we took the bypass around the town of Tianquan, and traffic continues to be heavy.

We are soon back in a narrow steep valley with its sides covered with firs and bamboo. We are now at 2,700ft (840m).

The valley opens with 30-40% slopes, and we spot a flowering magnolia. At the end of the second hour we have passed 3,300ft (1,000m).

At 4,600ft (1,400m) we stop for diesel and a 20-minute tea break. The water tank for feeding the brake pads during long descents is topped up.

We have dropped off and picked up some passengers, but the driver is very strict not to have any passengers standing. And the bus is clean apart from the occasional spitting on the floor. But what a pleasant difference from the buses in India.

At 6,600ft (2,000m) we can see snow, and at 7,200ft (2,200m) we reach a 2.1/2mile (4km) long road tunnel through the mountain, thus avoiding the crossing of the Maan Shan Pass, which had necessitated the tea porters carrying their loads to a height of over 2,900m (9,500ft)

We then dropped rapidly, turning northwards to follow another river in a wide valley with mountainous sides. The landscape had changed, as this area was much drier. We saw cacti, grasses and shrubs, and the trees were gone.

At 4,500ft (1,365m) we reached the town of Luding, the site of a famed incident on Mao's 'Long March'. The story is that in 1935, the communists had to retreat across a chain suspension bridge that had been built in 1701, when the KTM (the other side) had removed most of the wooden walkway.

Proceeding northwards we passed a number of hydroelectric plants, either in operation or under construction.

At 4,900ft (1,500m) we turned westwards again into a narrow and steep valley, slowly climbing past another hydro scheme until we reached our day's destination of Kangding.

Kangding.

We now had to find some accommodation, and started to walk up to the main town area. It's a long town, squeezed in on both sides of a 100ft (30m) wide river. The mountains crowd in and there is little flat land, which must be the reason for most of the shops being six to eight storey's high.

The first few hotels we checked were not good value for money, so I performed my usual role of guardian of the bags, whilst

Lian went off hunting. This time I used the comfort of the lounge of the best hotel in town to wait in.

As usual, Lian had performed a little miracle, and we were soon installed in the Kangding Tian Ren Qi Hotel.

Actually we were delayed getting there when we came across a number of life size bronze statues depicting the old Tea Horse route. Men with tea bricks on their backs, Buddhist monks, a missionary, porters carrying other good, a wild looking horse and a number of other figures. So lots of photos were taken, as the sun had come out and the shadows were giving depth. But I find it not easy to reduce the effect of signs and backgrounds imposed by the 21st century.

Our bedroom was unusual, as it had the ultra modern gimmick of having an all glass wall between the bathroom and the main bedroom. Including having curved glass at the angle. But then they had to have an internal curtain, as however delightful it may be to watch ones partner soap and shower themselves, there are other bathroom uses better obscured from general view. Our room had the 'mountain view', where we had a vertical George Braque-like rock face only 40ft (10m) away.

After a hot coffee in our room, we went out to explore the town. The Tibetan influence here is very strong, both in the architectural details of the building, many of the peoples clothes, and the restaurants. Overlooking the town are a number of brightly coloured Buddhist paintings on the rock faces, and we can see prayer flags fluttering high up on the hillsides.

The town is at 8,200ft (2,500m), but the mountains either side rise to about 13,000ft (4,000m).

Blue and white taxis are parked everywhere, and there are also many brand new green ones that still have yet to be allocated number plates. Yet we saw few customers using them.

The guidebook warns that this is an area to be careful when moving around out of the town area. Robbers and wolves are mentioned, and I for one do not have to be told twice.

The weather is cold enough to add extra layers, pull down a woolly hat and find my gloves.

Lian had a headache, and she suspected from past experience that it was likely to be a touch of altitude sickness. So we found the local hospital, and arranged to have an hour's worth of additional oxygen fed through a face-mask. This usually clears the head and greatly assists the acclimatisation. The nurse in charge spoke good English and was very friendly and helpful. After she took Lian's blood pressure, Lian asked if she would also take mine. This turned out to be very high, even though I felt OK. Lian's headache did not go away.

Our next destination was to be the town of Litang, which would be at over 13,000ft (4,000m) with one 16,400ft (5,000m) pass on the way.

The nurse did not recommend that we went any further. Even assuming that my high blood pressure was altitude related, it would not be wise to take any risk and go higher until I had consulted my own doctor / cardiologist.

How disappointing, as Litang would have been one of the highlights of the trip.

But we would stay here in Kangding for a couple of nights before returning to Chengdu. It started to drizzle, but we were delighted when we reached our room to find that the radiator was on and the room toasty.

Our hotel was having some renovation works, and at exactly 8am the next morning we were woken by the noise of hacking and banging.

Today I put some long Lycra shorts on under my normal trousers, and it was certainly a lot warmer. But what a problem it is every time I wanted a simple pee. I suddenly appreciated how difficult it must be for women wearing tights, and why it seems to take them so long.

We discus possible alternative things to do now that the further exploration on Tea Horse route has to be postponed.

A trip to the grasslands is also out due to the altitude, so perhaps a Three Gorge cruise may be a possibility. At least we could go and check out Chongqing, the capital of the adjacent province to our east. This would depend upon the weather, as the forecast in this area was for rain.

So the next morning we set off, pulling our bags for the five-minute walk to the bus station. I saluted the statutes as we passed, and had a strange look from three passing monks.

During the loading of our bags into hold of the bus, one has to duck under the top-hinged doors. It was then that I felt a twinge in some of my lower back muscles, and it took a couple of weeks before the pulled muscles righted themselves.

Ya'an.

The return trip to Ya'an took just over five hours and it was interesting to backtrack on the notes I had taken during the earlier journey.

Our only surprise was when we finished up at a different bus station, and it took a while before we could orientate ourselves, and then make our way back to the Sage Hotel.

We took the opportunity of buying our bus tickets for the next morning.

On the way back we stopped at a small shop famous for it's 'Hit hit noodle' (Da Da Mien), and watched a young man roll out three long sausages of wheat flour dough, that he then flattened with his hand. After sprinkling them with flour, he doubled them over, and holding both ends he twirled them in the air round his head, and then really bashed them hard onto his table. He doubled the noodles over, and repeated the process many times. Each time the noodles became thinner and thinner, until he had a good quantity of fresh flat noodles.

They were very enjoyable with a chicken stock soup.

That night however I fell sick from 'both ends'. I could only assume that it was from chicken broth we had bought from a small place during our bus's lunch break. Such is life, and at least Lian was OK now we are at a lower altitude.

Still feeling delicate, we made our way to the bus station for the 9.30am bus to Chengdu, which we reached 2-hours later.

After a few days in Chengdu, we found that the weather to the east was still too unsettled, and Yunnan to our south had experienced an earthquake. (Just prior to the massive earthquake and tsunami suffered by Japan.)

Time to pack up and return to Kuala Lumpur.

We learnt that trips do not always go to plan. The important thing is to know when to cut ones losses. We may well get to Litang next year, but when the weather is a little kinder.

CHAPTER 18
East Malaysia. Sarawak: A trip to the Julan Falls on the Usan Apau Plateau

Fall feeding pool above Julan Fall.

The Usan Apau Plateau comprises an area of approximately two thousand square miles, in the highlands of central Sarawak, near to the border with Kalimantan on the island of Borneo.

It is a remote area once inhabited by the Kenyah tribe and the nomadic Penans. Now the Kenyahs may climb the steep

337

escarpment to collect 'damar' gum from some of the trees, as well as rattan. The Penans pass through on their hunting and gathering expeditions.

The area was visited by Tom Harrison, the curator of the Sarawak Museum, together with the Head of the Lands and Survey Department. Later, in 1954 and 1955 there were expeditions by the government and two men from Shell, but the earlier one was unable to reach the plateau.

A scientific and anthropological expedition from the UK's Oxford University passed over the plateau during their six-month expedition into the highlands of Sarawak. The leader of this 1955 four-man expedition, Guy Arnold, wrote an enthralling book called 'Longhouse & Jungle—and Expedition to Sarawak'. Prior to commencing, he had the chance to fly over his proposed route, and they 'circled the escarpment to the north where two magnificent waterfalls dropped eight hundred feet into the trees below'.

These waterfalls joined to form the Julan River, and climbing the steep escarpment to find the top of the falls was to be our destination.

Ashleigh Seow was the leader of our expedition, under the auspices of the Malaysian Nature Society. The group was originally set at twelve participants, but like Topsy it grew and grew until it reached twenty eight. This would obviously put a strain on the organisation and logistics.

We knew that our personal fitness would be an important consideration to our enjoyment of the trip, and joined the training walks set by the MNS, as well as walking up and down a minimum of twenty eight storeys in our condominium each morning for the previous ten weeks.

Some information on the Usan Apau plateau and the Julan Falls can be downloaded from the Internet, but it is interesting to note that the photo, with the said falls in the distance, is in fact a different waterfall.

So early mid August, we set off for the airport to take the two and a quarter hour AirAsia flight from Kuala Lumpur to Miri in Sarawak. Most of the group were staying at the Minda Guesthouse, so we joined them. Whilst most of the beds were bunk style in dormitories, we managed to have our own room. This was furnished with a double bed, a small round bar table and two bar stalls. We thought that the inconvenience of having no attached toilet facilities might even be good training for times to come.

The room had an air-conditioner, but it was set bone-chilling cold. We were told that it could not be adjusted as a guest had taken the controller. However, Lian persisted and another staff member found one and turned the setting from16deg C (60F) to a more comfortable 21deg C (70F).

That evening the group met together for a final briefing, before adjourning for dinner.

We had our breakfast in a local coffee shop. I was amused, as people kept changing their minds as what to have as soon as they heard what seemed to be a better suggestion. The poor waitress was crossing off orders as fast as she wrote them down. It was more like people changing their bids in a game of bridge.

A change of clean clothes and some other items we would not need for the trip were packed and left at the Mega Hotel, where we made a reservation for our return.

As some people could not get a flight the next morning, they left by 4WD vehicles, and we would all meet up later in the day. We had booked seats for a flight from Miri to the small airstrip of Long Akah, up in the highlands. Although some of our group could not get onto the flight as they were told that the flight was full, there were seven empty seats.

The nineteen-seater 'Twin Otter' was delayed and only took off at 11:30am for the forty-minute flight. The plane basically followed the main Baram River as it meandered over the plain, passing the small town of Marudi on the way. It was only on the last third of the flight that the ground level rose into the hill forests of the 'ulu', or upper Baram. We could clearly see the vast amount of rainforest that has been destroyed to an ochre colour to make way for palm oil plantations.

Long San.

On arrival we were picked up in 4WD vehicles for the short road trip to the village of Long San, where we were dropped off at the Keldong Restaurant. The owner, Anthony Lawai, is an ex-politician representing the Kenyah tribe. He and his family seem to own all the shops and any commercial interests. He is a bit of an Anglophile, and kept reeling off the names of various British police and army officers he knew in the old days. When he found we were both the same age, he insisted that on our return we would have some beer and rice wine to celebrate.

Lian was speaking to his wife, who had large holes in her ear lobes, and she showed the heavy brass earrings, which she then demonstrated by hooking them onto her open earlobes. The wife had spent the morning decorating local hats with coloured beadwork. The hats were shaped like mushrooms, with a 20inch (500mm) diameter convex woven top sitting on a shallow split cane 'topi'.

Lunch was served: stewed wild boar, rice, green fern tips and 'kang kong' another green vegetable.

To Julan Falls.

It was early afternoon when we all set off in three 4WDs, and in just over an hour we reached a logging camp that was to be our overnight base. Despite being unpaved, the logging road was in good condition, but was very dusty.

The roads are designed for the logging trucks carrying 40 tonnes of tropical hardwoods on their trailers. These guys are the 'Kings of the Road', and beware getting in their way, especially in the wet, when they are travelling at speed. Very often, they want and need to travel on 'the wrong side' of the road. Erecting wooden signs painted with one of three red arrows, and located at relevant intervals, surprisingly easily solved danger. If the arrows point right, then one stays on the right hand side of the road, and vice versa. The 'crossing' places are on straights, and in the case when you meet a larger vehicle crossing over, then self-preservation steps in, and one can come to a halt until the problem has driven past.

Our destination that day was a logging camp accommodation located at on offshoot of the main track, soon after crossing the Sungai Julan bridge.

A couple of charred wild boar heads were sitting on a wooden bench, and we were encouraged to rip it up and try it. The heads were thin with very elongated snouts.

Rain commenced soon after our arrival.

The residents had moved out into smaller rooms, leaving us to set out our bedrolls on the floor. Lian and I chose a section covered with some linoleum. We had decided to leave our sleeping bags behind and use our sleeping sheets (sheets sewn on 3 sides like a bag) set out on cheap blow-up plastic 'lillos'. These turned out to be quite comfortable.

The people had set up a tarpaulin-surrounded toilet comprising a 44-gallon drum set into the ground with a couple of wooden planks across. I think most people used alternative sites.

Some went for a bath in a rather dirty stream behind the huts. As the riverbank was covered in diapers, plastic waste and other rubbish, Lian decided to forego the pleasure of a bathe.

When everyone had arrived, we had a briefing for the next day.

Dinner was served in the other room and we squatted around on the floor. They served boiled rice and roast duck, which had been brought up from Miri, together with a vegetable soup. The residents sat watching us eat, but only tucked in themselves once we had finished.

We had ordered a porter to share, and found that he preferred to use his local collapsible backpack made of woven rattan circles. So we repacked our things into a soft dive-bag, and then covered it with a dustbin bag, leaving behind a few other items that might not be essential for our two nights on the plateau in our large backpack.

The camp had a portable generator, so visibility was no problem during our repacking.

Only one person seemed to be snoring, and he was lying next to me. Lian reached across and told him to lie on his side, which solved the problem until such time as he rolled back, when the process would be repeated. Apart from this, we slept quite well, despite the all-night rain.

The locals were very thankful for this, as it had been dry for many weeks, and water supply had become a problem.

In the morning Ngan, our Penan porter, stowed our items as well as his own and some general stores into his own backpack. It looked damn heavy, but proved no problem for him.

We had arranged for him to always keep close, as although we both carried a litre and a half of water in our daypacks, he was carrying the balance. We had taken the precaution of adding hydration powders to our water, as I am very susceptible to cramp, and this can be very uncomfortable. I also put some deep-heat cream on my knees and thighs.

We had a stand-up breakfast of glutinous rice, pineapple and a hardboiled egg, and were handed a lunch box each comprising rice and a chicken drumstick.

To save us time, we were to go as far as possible on the old logging road until the 4WDs reached a point where they could not cross the washed out areas. So at 7:30am we set off and half an hour later came to a wide washed out bridge. From here on it would be strictly 'shank's pony'.

The logging road was a gentle but energy sapping upward gradient under the hot sun, and after an hour and a quarter we left the track and descended to the Sungai Jiwan using ropes to lower ourselves down the slippery surface of a steep section.

It was time to wallow up the stream for some way before heading into the proper forest. I was using a lightweight pair of trekking shoes with perforated material, so had no problem walking through mud and water. Lian had chosen to use her old Brasher boots, so had a several changes into her 'Crocs' whenever we came to the water sections.

We had brought our adjustable trekking sticks, and these again proved a godsend. They could be shortened on uphill stretches and lengthened for the descents, thus taking considerable weight off the knees. We had been advised to bring gloves, and even my woven cotton ones proved very useful as a protection against cuts and scratches. They would however be of little help if one inadvertently caught hold of a rattan or a tree with a thorny bark.

The forest path rose for two hours, before we came to an extremely steep section that took us an hour to cover until we had reached the edge of the plateau. It was then time to walk through an area where the trees and trunks were covered with moss. Not quite a 'mossy forest' where the trees are stunted and knarled.

We then came to a descent into a river, where we had a half hour's walk along a rocky stream, before quite a steep ascent. Then the path dropped into another stream. Rain started and the group became more and more spread out as people tired.

We were apprehensive that we might miss the path if it left the valley and we waded past it.

In theory we should always be able to see someone ahead and someone behind. If not, one should call for the one in front to stop. With the rain pouring down this was not easy, especially as the stream was meandering down the steep valley and one had many small diversions due to rocks and dead trees blocking the bed of the stream.

During the whole days walk it had needed continual concentration to make sure one did not slip or fall. One's eyes had to be on where the next footfall should be. There was no opportunity to do any bird-watching, even at the hourly rest stop. We had heard the Great Argus several times, and even crossed over a 'dancing ground' that the bird had swept clean of dead leaves.

We came to a section of the stream covered with mossy black rock. This was very slippery, and I came down heavily on my hip, and narrowly avoided a split lip as I was turned over.

Then, a short time later, we saw some tarpaulins and were thankful that we had safely arrived at our base camp. It was just before 4:30pm. The GPS showed that we had only covered 7.3 miles (11.7 km).

The porters were already erecting the camp in the drizzle, and had completed the basic frame and set up the tarpaulin roof cover. They then made a row of 'stretcher' beds by threading two

3inch (70mm) diameter tree trunks through two polypropylene sugar / animal feed bags and laying them across larger diameter bearers. The poles were then lashed together with the bearers using jungle vines.

Some of the group had crossed to another campsite a short way away, and there was a problem as they had taken over excessive tarpaulins.

Due to the steepness of the valley, there was very little space around the sleeping area, and it took some time to set up the last five stretcher beds due to missing sugar bags and tarpaulins. We handed over our own tarp, which we had brought as a groundsheet, for them to use.

Ashleigh and two of the other experienced people had set up hammocks for themselves. These are very high tech and include built-in rain covers.

Others had brought tents, and the only location could be flat rocks on the stream base. Flat yes, but level no. The three girls laughingly said next morning that they had all finished huddled up in the lowest corner.

Lian had been suffering from a headache for the last couple of hours of the trip, but soon after she had an allocated bunk to lie on, she started to vomit. She could keep no pills or even a sip of water down. We were so cramped sleeping with our bags on the beds, and I was of little use in finding anything that Lian wanted from the bags, even using our newly purchased

LED head lights. Poor Lian had a miserable night and did not want any dinner as she would only have heaved it up. We did not know whether this was due to dehydration, exhaustion or a migraine.

The evening meal comprised over boiled rice and fatty pork. Not an appetising creation.

It rained for most of the night. It was cold and I was grateful I had brought a fleece top. Any 'walk in the night' had to be very short as the vegetation was thick and the ground very uneven. Patches of forest floor glowed in the dark.

We wore leech socks for the walk up, but saw only a few leeches. It was nice to get out of the trekking shoes and leech socks and put on slippers around the camp. However we found that the camp area was full of them, and soon had them on the hand, the neck and of course the toes. They were however quite small and chubby and did not bleed too much after feeding.

Woke at 6am, as the light filtered through the leafy canopy but we all stayed in quiet contemplation before rising at about 7am for a breakfast of tea or coffee and a biscuit. It was then light enough to see where we were. Lian and I strolled upstream over the slippery rocks, before clambering up the hillside to ablute behind a large tree.

The porters soon had a wood fire going and the clear stream water was boiling. They had used their sharp parangs to cut vertical slices of wood from some of the trees, and these long chips were stacked on a framework above the cooking fire to dry out.

The group would spend the morning at the pool above the waterfall, and then in the afternoon they would try to find some good views of the falling water.

Lian would rest in bed for the morning. I followed the group to find the way to the pool, and then returned to Lian.

The route to the pool only takes five minutes, but there are a couple of tricky sections. In fact we are very close to the main fall itself and this accounts for the loud background roar we heard all night.

The Sungai Julan falls about 33ft (10m) over the centre of an 80ft (25m) high horseshoe shaped cliff, into a large pool. The forest looms above, and giant ferns hang down the cliffside. The pool narrows back into a stream about 100ft (30m) wide and then plunges over rocks and out into space. Through the silhouetted trees leaning towards each other over the lip of the fall, one can see hills far in the distance.

It is a stunningly beautiful place.

Across the pool is a small hill with the other campsite.

After the mornings rest and a cup of steaming hot sweet coffee and some biscuits, Lian became her usual cheerful self. For lunch we had curried sardine and rice, and this went down well.

In the afternoon we joined a few others who had decided to stay around the camp area and go for a swim in the main pool.

We crossed over the Sungai Julan at the top of the fall to a low rocky area by the other camp. Around the edge of the pool we could see white froth like a giant bubble bath. Ashleigh explained that this was caused by 'saponins', a natural detergent found in some plants and the bark of some types of trees, These had fallen into the Sungai Julan, and the bubbles formed as the small fall plunged into the pool and became aerated.

So we all had fun swimming in the foam, and trying to wash ourselves in this cold water. Four of the young porters were also have a fine time diving and swimming across the strong current.

The sun was warm on our backs and caste streaks of dappled sunlight as it filtered through the forest trees and ferns. The trunk of one tree was a deep red where the bark had come away. The whole scene had a Disneyesque quality.

The hiking group had been unable to get a view of the falls as it plunged downwards, but had found a trail to a third small fall.

Dusk falls fast in the forest, and we all had to sort ourselves out before darkness fell and we would be reduced to using our torches. So we all enjoyed our stand up dinner of rice, corn-beef hash and heart of a Talong palm.

By 7:30pm it was dark and there was little option but to clamber up onto our stretcher beds.

It rained in the night and was quite cold. We were all up at 6:30am. It was time to collect our still damp washing from the clothes lines and start packing our bags prior to our scheduled 7:30am departure. We were standing around with cups of warm tea in hand, when above the roar of the falls one could make out the shrill sound of a whistle. This grabbed everyone's attention, and we waited until we heard the five clear whistles of a distress call. Some went off to the other campsite to investigate.

The reason for the call was that during the night the water level of the pool had risen, and instead of a knee-deep walk to cross the Sungai Julan, it would be a chest deep and with a strong current. The Penan porters did a great job in helping those stranded across the river, and bringing over their backpacks and tarpaulins. A potentially dangerous situation had been averted.

So it was 8:40am before the group started to wend it's way back up the small stream. We all walked with great care, as the paths were wet and slippery. The slower walkers were encouraged to keep near the front in an attempt to keep the group from spreading out to far along the track.

When we came to the very steep drop, we stopped for a rest and a lunch of well salted rice before going down. The group leaders and some Penans were then posted to the most difficult and dangerous sections of the steep descent, and the older members formed a queue to make the descent one at a time. The ropes and rattan that had been tied on proved to be very useful, but one still had to hold onto roots and small trees to avoid any rapid and uncontrolled descent. A few small rocks were dislodged, but luckily bounced around Lian who was in front of me.

Once we passed this point the path was much easier and we were pleased when at 12:45pm we reached the Sungai Jiwan. We could hardly wait to strip off the backpacks and sit in one of the rocky pools. Some even slipped off a large rock and fell in, but luckily the guardian angel was watching over us all, and people were unhurt.

Only then I remembered that my notebook was in my trouser pocket, but luckily did not get too soaked, as it was in a plastic bag.

It was time to make our way down stream until we reached the point where we had had to use a rope to assist our descent on the way up. It was much drier now, and we could clamber up with little assistance from the rope. By 3:45pm we had reached the logging track road, and within an hour we reached the convoy of 4WDs waiting for us. It was a long wait before all the others arrived, and we set off back to the logging camp to pick up the things we had left behind.

Before leaving, the local women came around and smeared our faces with the soot from the base of a kwali cooking pot. There was plenty of laughter as they chased those who had a chance to run away. This is the planting season and this ritual is carried out to ensure a good harvest, as well as being a traditional way of bidding farewell to visitors.

Long San.

We left the camp as dusk fell, and only reached the village of Long San after two and a quarter hours.

Here we had the luxury of beds, mattresses and our own room in the home-stay. We could also share the two toilet / bathrooms.

A cultural show had been organised, but was cancelled as a senior local Catholic priest had just passed away.

Dinner had been prepared, of 'sticky' rice wrapped in a leaf, stewed wild boar, and three green vegetables including green fern tips.

Anthony Lawai was there, and I bought a couple of bottles of Guinness and a Tiger beer each whilst we sang "Happy Birthday to You" to each other. Rice wine, known by the Kenyah people locally as 'burak', was served in coffee cups. Quite a pleasant taste, but Anthony kept insisting we downed each cupful in one gulp.

So Michael slept very well that night.

Breakfast, and the later lunch, comprised stewed wild boar and similar vegetables to those we had had for dinner.

We all went for a stroll around the town. Watched the junior schoolchildren having their outdoor assembly before forming crocodiles to their classrooms.

On the other side of the playing field opposite the school, is the Catholic Church set on a low hill. The high point of this church is that the carved Jesus on the cross is a Kenyah tribesman complete with local headdress, necklace and a short colourful sarong. He also sports a beard and a Hitler style moustache, which is unlike any Kenyah we saw around.

Some of our group were buying parangs. It turned out that our porter, Ngan Ah Boon, also makes very good ones. He had learnt the blacksmith trade from his father.

As well as a main parang, some also included a small knife. The blade is attached to a thumb thick wooden handle, which is made to measure for the owner. The end of the handle is put into the crook of the elbow, and the other end held firmly in the hand. Items to be cut or shaved are then pulled towards the sharp blade with the other hand, rather than the normal method of moving the blade across the item to be cut. This gives much better control. The blade itself is made with on side flat and the other slightly convex. Thus a stick can be cut so that the thinly shaved sections will curl and can be used as kindling to start a fire. It was also pointed out to me that this knife could thus be made for either right-handed or left-handed people.

Arrangements had been made for us to visit the old wooden fort at Long Akah. We had all just piled into three long canoes when the heavens opened and within seconds we were all drenched. It only took about five minutes for us to speed down the Baram, which was running full and fast. The fort is on the other side of the river, and is now abandoned. It was probably built in the late 1800's by Rajah Brooke as a way to keep the warring tribes apart, and later played its part during the 'Confrontation' with Indonesia.

This two-storey building is made with a Belian timber frame and outer walls. The upper floor overhangs and has a trellis opening to allow the defenders clear views and shots at any attackers.

We had only just started on our journey upstream, when the engine of one canoe packed up, so the occupants managed to clamber and transfer into the other two. The canoes were thus a little low in the water during our return trip.

Anthony Lawai also runs the local post office box. This comprises an open wooden pigeonhole cupboard fixed to the wall. This has a few letters awaiting collection by people from the outlying longhouses. Then I noticed a big cardboard box crammed with letters. Some looked old and stained: others had 'sulit'—secret or confidential—stamped on them. Anthony says he sorts them out sometimes for collection.

After lunch we brought out all our bags ready for our departure by 4WD down to Miri. We had to wait until all the vehicles had arrived before we departed in convoy. One vehicle was late, so it was 1:15pm before we set off.

Anthony had insisted that Lian and I be in his Ford Ranger, with his cousin as driver.

However the road out to the main logging road was steep and very slippery with a thin mud topping. We fishtailed all over the place, and soon came to a slope that we could not climb without a tow from a Toyota. The elderly driver did not help the situation by over revving the engine all the time, thus spinning the wheels. We had just reached the road junction with the main logging road, when the vehicle stalled and could not be re-started. Then, when they took off the radiator cap, they had to jump back quickly to avoid the scalding steam and water that blew out volcano style.

Luckily two of our other vehicles spotted that we had a problem and stopped with us. We were close enough to Long San to get someone to return and arrange for an alternative 4WD and driver to come to our rescue. But it was 3:30pm before a relatively new Ford Ranger arrived, and at long last we could get going again. The dirt road was in good condition even in the wet.

We had a brief stop for the young driver to pick up a clean shirt, and later at the Sky View Café, where we picked up enough diesel fuel to get us to Miri. The latter part of the journey was in rain, but we arrived safely at the Mega Hotel at just past 8pm.

What joy to have hot water, our own toilet and clean white sheets again, and after a seafood dinner we slept like logs.

Lian and I spent a couple of days relaxing in Miri and enjoying the local markets and food before flying back to Kuala Lumpur.

CHAPTER 19

Korea and the Cherry Blossom

Cherry blossom.

The huge earthquake and that devastating tsunami stuck Japan a couple of weeks before we were due to leave on a fortnight's trip to Korea. Then we heard of the radiation problem with the stricken nuclear power station. The prevailing winds were taking the polluted air into the Pacific, but the worry for us was that if this changed, then not only would Japan suffer even more, but the winds would be blowing over Korea and on to China.

Right up to a couple of days before our flight, we were debating whether or not to abort our trip.

The Air Asia flight time from Kuala Lumpur to Seoul was 6 hours.

Seoul.

On the flight we met up with a Korean soldier whom was very helpful in advising us to take the metro into town and showed us how to buy the tickets at an automated teller machine. The unusual thing is that one pays an additional amount for a deposit on the credit card size (or sometimes a coin sized) ticket, and after exiting the turnstile, one can claim back the deposit at another machine. Anyway, less than an hour later we were at Seoul's main station and ready to take another metro line for the few stops to our destination.

Lian had booked a room for our first night, and they had emailed us with instructions on how to find the hotel. By now it was nearly midnight, so just imagine our annoyance to be told they had let our room, and they had nothing available. This was despite Lian having phoned them from Malaysia before we left, to confirm our late arrival and the flight number.

He suggested he had a friend nearby, and so we set off pulling our luggage to find the Soo Eun Motel. We thought it a bit crumby, but what else to do at this time of night. Apart from being noisy from the traffic, it was quite comfortable and the price was acceptable.

So next morning we set off to find a more permanent place to stay, and finally found the Korean Guest House, a backpackers style place, but we did get a small room with a double bed and an en-suite bathroom. The vinyl covered floor is raised about 2" (5cm) and is heated, but this means the low ceiling is only 3" (8cm) above my head. The small windows are double-glazed.

Hot water to make tea and coffee is available in the reception area as are a couple of computers for Internet connection.

For us, it is important to stay in a central location close to the main tourist spots, and both the hotels fitted this requirement.

We had picked up a number of maps and tourist magazines. So it was time to explore Seoul.

Our first port of call was the Bukchon Hanok; an old housing area now enjoyed by the middle and upper class owners. The low rise houses, set on a hilly area, are surrounded by high fancy stone walls, and apart from the dark grey Korean roof tiles, one can see very little unless a garage door was open to show off an expensive foreign car.

From here we dropped down to the very trendy area of Samcheongdong, a street lined with restaurants and boutiques.

In the afternoon we visited Changdeokgung Palace, built in the 1400's, but destroyed by the Japanese in the late 1500's. Once restored, it became the main palace for nearly 300 years.

We joined an English speaking tour, and were delighted to meet an old friend from our Malaysian Scuba diving days over 30 years ago.

The palace architecture was typical of many other palaces and temples we were to visit in the next couple of weeks. Wooden frames, and multi-level tiled roofs with upward curving gables. The woodwork is mainly painted with a blue green colour, that reminds me of the hue and patina of a well-oxidised copper roof. This is unlike the similar Chinese temples, which would have a bright red as a major colour, or with a darker red if it were in Japan. The Korean buildings do have multi coloured and decorated roof timbers, but the predominant and calming blue green suffuses all this.

The palaces all have rather ugly figures lined down the gables of the sloping roofs. These figures represent the characters in the old Chinese story, 'The Journey to the West', and include amongst others, a monk, a monkey and a pig.

The local trees are bare, but one could enjoy the different intricate shapes of the bare branches for the various species.

The flowering cherry trees were everywhere, and the buds just about to open.

The next day we arranged to join a group from the Royal Asiatic Society for a guided trip to Mount Buga-san to climb the Seoul Fortress Hill. We did not know what to expect, and met up with the group at an adjacent metro station, where we promptly jumped on a bus through the exit door. The bus was very crowded and we were not sure what to do, but got off with our group without having paid for our tickets. Yes, you can just see the headlines in the next morning's national tabloids. 'Englishman and his Asian wife sentenced to 3 years hard labour on the border with north Korea, for avoiding payment on bus'.

The walk was interesting as it went up hill and down dale following the line of the ancient wall, which at one time surrounded the whole of the old city. Sometimes we were walking on the outside of the wall, and at other times along the wall's parapet.

We came to one gate, where we had to show our passports before receiving a numbered entrance pass, that we had to hang around our necks.

Security was tight and no photographs were allowed in many areas, and there were plain clothed guards to enforce this. These young guards were all like clones, with the same clothes, height, build and dark rimmed spectacles. It was a bit uncanny. We mentioned this to our guide, who laughed and said that for propaganda purposes, all the tall good-looking guards were sent to patrol the border with North Korea.

One of our party had to show a guard his camera to confirm that he had not taken some pictures he was accused of taking. Thank goodness for digital playback as in the old days they would probably have taken away his film roll.

We could see in places that there are two rows of chain link fencing, with razor wire concertinaed along the top. It appears that at one time the North Koreans had sent a killer squad to try to assassinate the South Korean President, and there was quite a gun battle right there on the wall, and only one North Korean survived.

We were show one pine tree next to the path, which had a number of bullet holes in it.

Visibility was rather poor, so the views over the city were not the greatest.

We then came to a very steep staircase that dropped down and down, and one had to take care as the treads and risers were not all equal, and the slats making up these treads gave a stroboscopic effect which was quite unsettling.

Our guide advised us of a local restaurant famous for their steamed dumplings. The place was very crowded, which is always a good sign, so we had to wait a while before getting a seat in the garden. The wait was worth it, and we had dumplings that were stuffed with minced chicken and vegetables and herbs. Or maybe it was pork? Anyway, although they were a little bland, the chilli hot kimchi (fermented cabbage and hot peppers) and pickled radish chunks certainly spiced things up.

On the bus back to town we did pay our fare.

That evening we wondered around an area called Insa Dong, full of trendy shops and restaurants. We were glad we had brought our scarves, as it was quite cold. In a narrow side alley, I watched a chef making huge stuffed dumplings through the restaurant window, so dragged Lian in. So once again we had a steamed dumplings, but this time in a soup and chased down with a local beer.

It was a Sunday morning when we took the metro to see the changing of the guard at the Deoksugung Palace. The guards look resplendent in their brightly coloured silk clothes, long black boots, and their wide brimmed black hats. They even have false wispy beards, and carry a bow and quiver over their shoulders. The band arrive in bright yellow long silk coats, blowing conch shells, bagpipe sounding reed instruments and local trumpets, and beating cymbals and drums. Lots of drums, and with clever ways of swinging their arms and the drumsticks. And some carry large embroidered flags.

It was all a very impressive spectacle.

From here we were back on the metro to find the famed 'flea market' by the Hongik University. But this was a big disappointment, as there were just a few stalls selling hand made jewellery and other items and a few paintings. The area itself was much more interesting and crowded with students soaking up the morning sun.

In the evening we returned to the dumpling shop, but this time also had a seafood pancake, which was like a giant omelette crammed with seafood. This was a meal for two in itself. We were really stuffed when we left the restaurant, only to find that it was drizzling and we had to walk back fast to our accommodation.

We have noted that just about anything you buy here goes up in increments of Won 1,000, which is near enough one US$.

The people are amazingly disciplined. Motorists accept zebra crossing and will actually stop for you. At major crossings, where there are traffic lights for pedestrians, the Koreans will wait for the green crossing light, even when the road is clear of cars for a hundred meters or so.

The queues to board the metro are amazing. People form a queue at 45 degrees on either side of where the train doors will open. They allow the disembarking passengers to exit in the middle, and then enter in single file on each side. It's quick and efficient.

The metro is always an interesting place to be and people-watch.

Often a salesman would arrive pulling a small trolley. He would then start his spiel and demonstrate what he was selling e.g. socks, plastic raincoats, or a set of spanners with a built-in torch.

People would leave their newspapers on the luggage rack, and there would be a number of sprightly old men who would continually walk from carriage to carriage collecting these discarded papers. We assume they would then sell these for scrap.

We had little language problem as the younger people had all taken English at school and usually knew enough to answer our simple questions.

The young people are very trendy and fashion conscious.

The girls and young women all have fancy phones that they clutch tightly where ever they walk or sit. They are all either sending SMS messages, listening to music, playing games or even talking into them. They use them as a young child would when holding onto a blanket or old stuffed toy, in order to cocoon themselves from other passengers, and so avoid having to make any eye contact.

The young men on the other hand, only use their phones when and if they make or receive a call. Even then it is short and sweet, and they soon get back to their daydreams.

We are amused to see one custom here that when a young man is out on a date, he will carry the girl's handbag for her.

The poorer elderly waddle around and look a bit lost.

The middle class elderly are very health conscious, and love to walk or trek. Everywhere one goes one sees small groups of them on the buses and the metro on their way to one of the many walking spots. They wear the latest trekking gear, boots and backpacks, complete with trekking sticks and gloves. The women wear co-ordinated colours matching their jackets, hats and boots.

Busan.

Seoul is on the west coast and we wanted to visit Busan, which is a big port city located in the southeast section of the country.

We went to the main railway station by metro, and booked seats for the fast train to Busan. As the 10am train was fully booked, we waited 30 minutes for the next one. We were then whisked away at 185mph (300kph) for the 2.1/2 hour journey on the KTX bullet train.

A couple of days earlier, Lian had booked us into the Busan Inn over the Internet as it was just around the corner from the station.

This again had the 'love hotel' logo outside. Our 4th floor room was larger than the ones lower down. Very comfortable, with it's own Internet connected computer, TV, and fridge.

We went off to find the Jagaichi Fish Market. Here they sell lots of fresh fish and other seafood, including octopus in many sizes, squid, crabs and many species of shellfish. Dried fish and different dried seaweeds are also specialities. On one side of a long alley are all the fish sellers, and on the other is a row of seafood restaurants, where you choose your fresh food and they cook them for you on a hot plate or a charcoal grill. My mouth was starting to water, when one of the cooks suggested we enter.

So we picked two different whole fish and went inside. Most people sat cross-legged on a raised platform, but they did have a few table and chairs on one side. One women customer took one look at me and suggested she would be happy to vacate a table and move to the raised platform with it's low tables. "Thank you Madame".

They then brought kimchi and a number of side dishes, and a beer, while we waited for our fish to cook. The plaice and the red snapper were so fresh and delicious.

In the evening we went for a walk around China Town, an area opposite the railway station. We were surprised to find how many Russian-run shops, seedy looking bars and restaurants there were. It's a bit of a red light area here.

As the hotel was comfortable, we decided to stay here and use it as a base for day trips to the surrounding towns we wanted to visit.

So next morning we took the metro to the out of town bus station, and from there took a bus for the one-hour trip westwards to Jin Hae. The bus was surprisingly comfortable, with two seats on one side of the isle, and a single seat the other. And with 1st class legroom. For the whole of the journey, on either side of the road were cherry blossom trees in full bloom.

We left the bus station and walked along the avenues of cherry blossom to a park where they have a watchtower overlooking the whole town. We had great views of the sea and the naval harbour and the hills behind. The hills are forested, but the leaves have yet to open from the already formed buds. Then, dispersed amongst the trees on the hillsides, are the white cherry trees. It's a sight to remember.

The next day we travelled in the other direction, along the coast to Gyeonju. This meant taking the metro to a different bus station for a nearly two-hour ride. We travelled along a wide valley about a kilometre wide.

It is a mix of agriculture and light industry. All the industrial buildings have either blue or orange coloured roofs, a mix that I have not noticed in other countries.

The hillsides either side are covered with bare trees and bushes and the occasional flowering cherry.

On arrival in Gyeonju we took a local bus to the Bulguksa Temple, about half an hours ride out of town. This UNESCO site had a simply amazing area of old mature cherry trees between the car park and the temple. The cherry blossoms are in stark contrast to the matt black of the trunk and branches. Sometimes a thin twig that had sprouted directly from the trunk would be laden with large white blooms.

The temple was typical of all the temples, but sited in beautifully landscaped gardens with some very old twisted pine trees. This will be even more splendid once the many types of trees come into full spring leaf.

That evening in Busan, we returned to the same restaurant we had enjoyed the previous evening and had another Korean beef barbeque.

One cuts the thin slices of beef into bite sized pieces and has the fun of cooking it on a small tabletop charcoal fired grill. Accompanied by vegetables and garlic, and plates of side dishes and kimchi. By now I had also learnt to appreciate 'soju', the local rice wine.

It was time to explore around Busan, so we bought day passes for the metro and the local buses, and set off.

Our first call was to the Beomeseosa Temple. This small but quaint temple complex is situated in a wooded area, and was made even more pleasant as we had a retiree as a guide. This volunteer service is free of charge, and he was able to explain the history of the temple as well as to explain the differences behind each area of prayer.

The main entrance path was covered from end to end with brightly coloured paper lanterns, and it was difficult to stop taking photographs. Then, further on, a courtyard was covered with white lanterns, which were slowly waving in the breeze and catching the bright sunlight.

Our next stop was to a shrine commemorating those killed by the Japanese sometime in the 1500's. The Chunghyeols Shrine was set in a landscaped garden, gently sloping up to the main shrine building. Women were trimming the bushes with small secateurs.

We had heard of a Fishing Village Museum, and found this only after great difficulty. People were very helpful, but several who lived within a stones throw away did not seem to be aware of its existence. Although a large building, it had little of interest to show, and all was in the Korean language.

Back on the metro, we set off for Haeundae Beach. Haeundae is famous for the casinos hotels that line the beach, but we did not bother to go in.

Although the beach was pleasant enough, there was a cold wind blowing. We pulled our scarves round our necks and sat on the sea wall to watch a lot of teenagers feeding the gulls and then screaming in fright when one tried to stand on their head or snatch food from their fingers. We had bought some snacks to munch, and were careful not to let the gulls have a view of them.

Jeonju.

It was time to leave Busan and start back in the general direction of Seoul. We decided to have a couple of days in Jeonju, and took an express bus there. We had just missed one, so waited till 10:30am before leaving. The dual carriage passed through hilly countryside, with many long tunnels connecting the various valleys. At about half way, the bus made a 15-minute pit stop, and we arrived at the bus station at 2pm.

A taxi took us to the old Jeonju Hanok village. This is a bit of a misnomer, as although there is one old palace here, the rest of the Hanok has simply been rebuilt in the old style. This is similar to what they have done so much in China.

Lian had made a reservation at the Hanok Guesthouse, but when we arrived the owner drove us a few hundred meters to a modern glass faced building where we had a room above a hat shop and a three-storey hat museum. We were given the choice, at the same price, of sleeping on a very thin mattress that one could unroll on a completely bare wooden floor, or a similar mattress on a bed. We chose the latter. But although the room was not very 'hanok' or old, it was very modern and comfortable with a great bathroom and all mod cons. These included a WC with a heated seat, and a choice of hot or cold douches, and a hot air drier. You need a PHD and very good eyesight to read all the instructions. There is an air-conditioner suspended in the ceiling, but this is not needed at this time if the year, and there is a heated floor. They had about 3 or 4 rooms, with a large common dining and kitchen area, and a huge patio with a number of umbrellas and seats. We seemed to be the only people staying up here.

We later found that the Guest House comprises mainly dorms and small rooms for back-packers, so our requirement for on-suite facilities could not be met.

Time to walk around the 'old' hanok, and admire the houses, shops, restaurants and a 500-year-old Ginkgo tree.

Although we did not need it, we were recommended a restaurant specializing in the town's speciality of a 'hangover' meal. This seemed to comprise steamed rice, a hot soup with a couple of raw eggs dropped in, and lots of fresh bean sprouts.

Next morning, after enjoying toast and coffee in the Hanok Guesthouse, we set off for a small hill beside the town in order to get some better views over the town and the roofs. Whilst there, we spotted what appeared to be a white Buddha figure set up high on a wooded hillside some way from town, and decided to go there.

We walked for some way by the dual carriageway, before striking off through a road tunnel, past an Ecological Museum and then beside a lake. We could no longer see the statue, as it was somewhere ahead and above us in the wooded hills. We did not know which road to take to get there, and when we reached a path going uphill, a woman stopped and indicated we should follow her. She had seen we were a bit lost and had guessed our destination.

Another half mile or so we reached an entrance gate saw a sign in English saying 'Martyrs Hill' and saw a life sized statue of Jesus looking down on us. This could not have been the statue we had seen in the distance.

We climbed up the steep path, which meandered around many 'Stations of the Cross', and were serenaded by classic and religious music from a number of small strategically placed speakers. The path was lined with flowering shrubs. It was well done, and not tacky.

Reaching a church, we went in and admired the stained glass and wall mosaics. Above the church was a levelled piece of ground with a large grass covered semi-circular mound. This is the grave of Yu Hang-geom, who was executed together with six of family members during the Catholic Persecutions of 1801. His head was displayed at one of the city gates as a warning to the citizens of the dire consequences of becoming a Catholic.

We continued upwards and had some superb views over the cherry blossom.

Spotting another path down, and we followed this and then came upon the white Buddha statue we had been seeking. There was a small temple building that was locked up, and a number of rough stone stuppas.

Continuing down we passed a pile of stones that were said to be the site of an old palace, and then a well laid out military cemetery. It had been a most interesting mornings stroll.

In the afternoon we visited the Wine Museum, but this most disappointing as it was devoid of any samples.

Next morning, after a casual toast and coffee, we took the 2hour 40minute journey by express bus back to Seoul. This included a 15-minute rest stop.

Seoul.

From the bus station we took the metro and were soon back in our little 'love hotel', the Soo Eum Motel.

Leaving our things in our room, we set off to join in the celebrations for the last day of the Cherry Blossom Festival. This is held on the island where the National Assembly Building is situated. The road by the river is lined with a couple of rows flowering cherry trees. Being a Sunday, the local citizens were taking full advantage and had come out in droves. We had to hold hands as we joined huge crowds surging across the wide dual carriageways as soon as the traffic lights turned in the pedestrian's favour.

It was quite a sight; the blossom was in full bloom, and the thousands of people were walking down the road that had been closed to traffic for the day. There must have been a billion photos being snapped. There were a number of dance groups in traditional costume, dancing and swaying to drums and bagpipe sounding wind instruments. Elderly women, still carrying their handbags, would jump in and join the dancers for a while before spinning out and joining the onlookers again. A brass band was knocking out local favourites—someone is off key?

There are rows of artists sketching kids and parents. We all crowd round them, admiring or criticising their accuracy and talent. Some artists certainly look the part, with beards and John Lennon spectacles.

A row of railings holds an exhibition of Korean photographs.

We had been 'blossomed out' over the last couple of weeks, and had not been expecting much. But this was very impressive, and it was great to see the many thousands appreciating it so much. However it was a bit scary trying to get on the metro, as the people forgot their normal good manners as they tried to cram into a carriage.

The only disadvantage of our 'love hotel' was lack of a Wi-Fi facility, and we had mentioned this to the owner when we left for our Busan trip. We were delighted when we heard that the owner's son had stepped in and arranged it, so now we could go on line with our laptop, without having to find a 'Wi-Fi friendly' restaurant.

Next day we took the metro for a daytrip to Suwon. The seats of our carriage are satin anodised metal instead of the usual cloth. Today is cold and the heaters are under the seats, so within the hour I felt I had a baked bum.

We took a bus to the tourist area, but overshot it and had to retrace our route on another bus. The summer palace, Hwaseong Haenggung, comprises a lot of small courtyards. Nothing new to see here, and the wind was so cold we had to put on our windcheaters. We seemed to be about their only visitors.

Time to walk up to the Bukseojeokoae entrance gate, which was the main entrance to the walled city.

We were cold and hungry, so enjoyed a huge plate of fried dumplings and kimchi in a small restaurant. It was raining when we got out, so we abandoned our planned walk on the city wall and made our way back to the big city.

Another day, and another trip. This time to Incheon, the site of the General Macarthur's famed landing in 1950 during the Korean War. This was once again an hours' journey on the metro.

Passing through the China Town we climbed steps to a park, where they have the Korea-USA Centennial Monument celebrating a Treaty of Peace signed between the countries in 1882.

The town has a number of old stone faced banks and houses of interest, and one well photographed house that is covered with coloured bottle tops forming patterns and mosaic scenes.

Walking though the local market, we saw a couple of stalls deep-frying chicken chunks, and pouring over a syrupy looking dark sauce. So we went into a crowded restaurant and ordered by sign language. It's not too difficult as this is the only thing on the menu. Anyway, the fried chicken was as good as I have ever had, and the sauce was sweet and hot rather than sweet and sour. The portion was large and it was quite delicious, and sustained us on our return journey.

The only slight hiccup was that the automatic ticket machine at Incheon Station was all in Korean, and we had no choice of English. But it only took a moment before someone stepped forward to help us.

Behind our motel is a narrow street full of small restaurants. So that evening we tried the barbeque pork with Kimchi, mushrooms and a bean sprout soup. These we cooked ourselves over a small charcoal fed table-top grill. The meat was a bit tough, but the rice wine made up for it.

In Korea we note that no hotel, guesthouse or motel have ever asked for our passport or identity card. This is quite unlike India or China where the lodging has to take a photocopy and pass this to the police.

Our 'love hotel' has not asked for any advance payment or payment on account.

For our last couple of days in Seoul, we checked the guidebook and walked around the main palaces and areas we had missed.

On our last day, the motel was quite happy to give us a 6:30pm late checkout, and we used the metro to get to the airport in time for the 11:30pm night flight back to Malaysia.

Air Asia X managed to cut the flight time to 6 hours, landing 30 minute earlier than scheduled.

CHAPTER 20

China: Sichuan, Hubei & Gangsu

Seven young inmates at the Panda Breeding Centre outside Chengdu.

The sole intention of this trip was to continue our journey on the ancient Tea-Horse route that we had started in March a year previously, but had given up in Kangding due to a combination of cold weather and my high blood pressure. So our plan was to take a bus from Chengdu directly to Kangding, where we had would spend a couple of days acclimatising at an altitude of

8,200ft (2,500m). We would then proceed to Litang, and then take a circular route taking us close to the Tibetan border.

Chengdu.

On flying in to Chengdu, we took the airport shuttle bus into town. As we intended to leave by bus to Kangding, we decided to stay at the Traffic Inn, ideally situated by the river, and adjacent to the bus station. The Inn is basically a backpackers place, but they have a few normal en-suite bedrooms on the 2nd floor of the Traffic Hotel. But whereas the Hotel has few English speaking staff, the Inn staff are very multilingual and are a great source of information.

The first inkling that things may not be to our liking was when we overheard an American complaining that he could not buy bus tickets to Kangding and the west of Sichuan province.

And when Lian went along to buy bus tickets for us, she was told at the counter that foreigners could not go to Kangding, and could go no further west than the town of Ya'an. It appears that there has been trouble with the Tibetans in the area, and the Chinese authorities want to ensure that no bad publicity gets out by way of photos on You-Tube.

We then considered going by taxi, and Lian found a driver who was willing to take us. Then we heard of a Russian group who had tried the same thing, but had been stopped at a police post, and then had to return to Chengdu. It would appear that the situation is more serious than we had at first assumed, and getting on the wrong side of the Chinese police is not very advisable. This was especially frustrating as we had listed out our proposed travel itinerary when applying for my visa at the Chinese Embassy in Kuala Lumpur, and it had obviously been approved at that time.

So we spent some time pouring over our maps and deciding what to do and where to go for the remaining two weeks.

One alternative was to take the train to Lhasa, but to do this the travel agents told us that for the travel visa they needed a minimum of four persons with the same nationality. So where were we going to get three other Malaysians and three British at short notice? So plan B was a non-goer.

In the afternoon the Inn had a session of dumpling making lessons for its guests. We each had to cut up and roll out very thin pastry skins about 3" diameter, and after putting a small dollop of meat and vegetable filling, we had to try to fold the pastry to make a small pasty shaped dumpling. The range of shapes produced was amazing, although one chap was doing it quite professionally and he admitted that his Shanghai girlfriend had shown him how to fold them.

Our concoctions were then taken away for a short while to be boiled or steamed, before they were brought back on plates for our delectation. That many were left on the plates clearly showed that such delicacies of 'dim sum' are best left to the chefs.

The Three Gorges.

Since a boy, the sound of The Three Gorges had always been somewhere I wanted to go. But from the prices quoted by a couple of travel agents, this would certainly blow our budget. Prices ranged from the international to the local, and so we chose the latter for a 3-day, 2-night cruise on a 'Chinese boat'—a 2-bedded cabin with en-suite toilet on the top deck. The price excluded food, which sounded unusual but later proved to be a better alternative. We would be picked up at our hotel, and the trip ended following a tour of The Three Gorges dam.

So a walk along the riverside to the local HSBC ATM was warranted. When we were here a year ago both sides of the riverside had hoardings up. But now the construction of tow paths each side of the river has been completed, and made for pleasant walks. In the evenings the locals were enjoying either a quiet stroll, or a more energetic jog. The river has also obviously been cleaned up, and as well as a few fishermen, there are a number of beautiful white Little Egrets gliding across the river to another vantage point to settle on the rivers edge and occasionally plunge their beaks into the water to spear an unlucky fish.

That evening we had dumplings and soup and a vegetable in one of the numerous Muslim restaurants. Sichuan food tends to be pepper hot and greasy, and this food was typical. But worst of all they like to put in a local chilli that has the effect of numbing the lips and tongue. This is called 'hua jiao' (flower pepper) locally, and it reminded Lian that she should ask to have this omitted whenever possible.

We were due to be picked up at the Inn at about 6:15am, but at 6am we had a call to say he was waiting. We were the first to be picked up, and were driven around picking up passengers until 7am when we were decanted into a larger bus. It was rather odd that no one asked for our names or any form of receipt for the trip.

Ten minutes later we left for Chongqing, the industrial hub of Sichuan and 2,400km upstream from Shanghai.

The countryside is pretty, with many small valleys, and the green hillsides are studded with scattered houses. The rice is ready for harvest. The tops of many hills are lined with fir trees. We pass through a couple of very long tunnels, and come to a flatter industrialised area before reaching Chongqin at 11:45am.

We are then all squeezed into a much smaller bus, together with our luggage, for a tour of Chongqin. A guide was provided who spoke only Mandarin. The first stop was to a restaurant, and we were asked to pay a set sum for our lunch. The restaurant was really crowed and noisy, but we were led into a private room, and the 13 of us took our places around a large round table. Twelve dishes were brought in as well as a huge dish of rice. Although the food was a little cold, everyone tucked in. and it seemed only minutes before the others had finished and walked out, and we were the only two still eating.

Had a visit to the old Guildhall. The temple here specialised in reading your palm for sickness, and then sending you round the back to pick up a prescription of herbs and animal parts that would put right whatever the palm reader decided was wrong with you. There was no point in our joining the queue for a reading when we would not understand what was said to be wrong with us.

The next stop had a sign in English saying it was a 'Healthy Living Centre'. It seemed to be a shop selling face towels and shampoo etc. We made use of their toilet facilities and waited in the bus for the others.

Chongqing had been a centre for the Guomindang government and only fell to Mao's communist forces in 1949. We made a visit to a mansion up in the forested hills, which had at one time had a coalmine. The mansion had been used as a prison for the anti-Kuomintang. Rather a depressing place with lots of photos of the prisoners who had been incarcerated and died there. Much is supposition, as little information was available in English.

Then, yet another shopping stop at an emporium selling jade. Certainly I could not understand a word of what was going on, but the salesmanship was enthralling. Our group were herded into a room and the door closed. A young lady then started a spiel by talking into her headset attached to a small amplifier. This went on for some time before the door opened and two more senior salespersons walked in. The original girl gave the impression that she had won the lottery, bowing and backing away into a corner so that we could all hear what the two were saying and be delighted that a discount was being offered. Then after some time the door opened again and a well-dressed man walked in—all very smooth with a gold watch and sleeked down hair. This had to be the manager or owner, and he was offering a very extra special discount, as it was his birthday. The two salespersons looked on with awe, clearly showing how lucky and privileged we all were to actually meet their hero. When he had finished, there was a rush to get out of the room and we went back to the bus. But then we had a quarter of an hour to wait for a couple that had been hooked. The wife came back to the bus smiling, with two necklaces that she had not been wearing earlier, and the husband simply looked glum.

This delay meant that we only had ten minutes at the Great Hall, so no time to explore inside. After a rather miserable and wet day, the sun was breaking through, so we enjoyed our short time in the gardens.

Chongqin is spread along both banks of the Yangzi River as well as the Jialing River, which joins it. It is a city of bridges, and the interesting thing is that each bridge seems to have a different form of construction, as though they were experimenting with different types to see which was the better value.

The last visit was to a small supermarket, and this gave us the chance to pick up water, beer, nuts and noodles.

By 6:30pm we were back at the tour office and checked in. When we arrived in Chengdu, one of the first things Lian did was to buy a local Chinese SIM card for her telephone, She could then call hotels etc. and make enquiries. This telephone number was given to the travel agent when making our booking, and we were surprised to find that the last five digits of the number was being used by the staff as their reference for everyone on the tour, rather than using their names. This also had the advantage that if someone were late or lost, then the guide would simply telephone him or her. But of course we had problems remembering the new telephone number in Mandarin, so the guide simply referred to us as 'Michael'. So any roll call comprised a long list of numbers with a Michael thrown in somewhere along the way. It certainly worked well.

In the tour office we were all pestered by a number of porters, each with a long pole and with ropes tied at each end. They would tie a bag at each end and sling the pole across their shoulder. We took advantage of some muscle, as we did not know how far we would have to walk or what the conditions would do to our baggage wheels.

It was past 7:30pm when we formed a crocodile to walk down the road to the Port Office. It was here that our porter announce that he would not be carrying our bags to our cabin, so we simply only paid him half the agreed fee. Had to pass our bags through a scanner, and then enter a large cabin, which would ran down steep sloping rails to a floating jetty.

Our boat, 'No 6', was docked here and we clambered up the steep narrow companionway (stairs for you landlubbers) to the top deck where we had been allocated cabin number 411. This had two bunks, and the smallest 'bathroom' I have seen. A squat toilet filled most of the space, but there was a basin and a shower that rained down over all. In lieu of the traditional porthole, we had an openable window.

No towels or toilet paper were provided, and certainly no soap, toothbrush, shampoo, or comb, as there would not have been anywhere to put them.

There was a knock on the door, and a housekeeper suggested we might like to upgrade for a double bed and a small suite on Level 1. We had a look, but decided that the extra cost was not justified and retired to our squirrel hole.

The shower was cold, but washed away the day's grime and sweat. So we were soon in deep sleep as we started the 600km trip to the dam.

It was drizzling when we woke, so when we all left for the day's excursion, it was a long walk along floating pontoons and up the slope. All one could see before and aft (yep—another nautical term) was a line of colourful bobbing umbrellas. We then were loaded onto giant electric golf trolleys for the short ride to the Fengdu Ghost Town. I'm still not sure what it represents. I do remember lots of steps up to temples full of giant demons. And many demonic figures graphically depicting the tortures that would occur to all who had not followed the paths of righteousness. The buildings are all new apart from one at the highest point, and this had some memorable painted walls.

Another stop was made at the Zhongxian World Resort to see where Bai Juyi, a famous poet, was said to have lived. Not a memorable visit.

The drive was through two lane roads winding through wooded and hilly countryside. There were several rock falls from the shale red soft rock. We pass a spectacular bridge.

Another stop was made where we walked up even more steps to a house. Outside there was a carved column that was a Qing dynasty 'sobering-up post'. A drunk was chained to this to ensure he or she would not harm themselves or others until such time as they were sober. What a great idea.

At this point we were put onto smaller buses. What is happening? No idea—it is like a magical mystery tour, as being the only foreigners we have little idea of where we have been, and even less of where we are being taken.

The road leads eastwards along a hillside overlooking a wide valley. The houses here are very pretty and dotted over the landscape. They are all white, with a 10cm (4") wide brown band painted at each floor level, and around the windows and doors, as well as at the gable ends, as a representation of a timber framed house.

Stops were made at Shi Boazhai to see a 'shopping street' and the opportunity to buy some lunch. There was one young boy, Peter, on the trip with his parents, and we joined them for lunch. I first met him when he had marched up to me and said, "My name is Peter". That was the limit of our conversation, but he often came up to wave or say "Hello" before skipping away.

Shi Boazhi is a rocky fortress with a couple of temples. Access is by way of a shaky pedestrian suspension bridge. Unfortunately it started to drizzle as we arrived. However it was an interesting place.

We then walked down to the docks and clambered back onto boat 'No. 6'. An 'international' boat was also docked and we had a chance to compare boats. We could see a fancy restaurant and cabins with floor to ceiling windows and each with a narrow balcony.

Our top deck had a full width lounge and then a long viewing deck with about 10m (30ft) being covered. In this covered area most of the passengers gathered. Small tables and plastic stools were set out and they were full of card players. Some were playing what looked like poker, and others had long cards that seemed to be a form of dominoes. All had little piles of bank notes in front of them.

A couple of tables were crowded with noisy and laughing women. Their tables were piled high with plastic bags of food and sunflower seeds, with hardly enough room to throw down their cards. It did not take long for the deck to be covered with cigarette butts and sunflower seed shells.

Being the only white person around, I was obviously a centre of discussion and the Chinese are very inquisitive.

By mid afternoon we set sail again downstream. The wind has come up, and many gamblers have taken their games into the lounge.

The hillside is scattered with houses, and rice terraces. As we pass towns we see many huge multi-storey apartments under construction, and wonder who will occupy them.

Some cargo boats ply the river, and we see some small container ships.

By late afternoon we reached the big town of Wanzhou.

Young Peter comes over with a can of beer for me, and I join his father for a couple of drinks. We cannot correspond with each other, but it's surprising how one can get on with a few nods and smiles.

We had noodles in our cabin for dinner. We passed several towns in the night and were woken by the loud ships horn as we approached the jetties for brief stops. One town had especially well lighted apartment blocks with coloured neon lights running up and down the buildings. All a bit weird in the middle of nowhere, and one wonders who they were trying to impress.

By 5:15am we are stopping by a number of other cruise boats. Women are selling noodles from small boats. It is overcast and cloudy, and we will pass under a red painted bow bridge. We are about to enter the 'real' gorges.

By 6:30am the guide has everyone out on the open deck and is giving a running commentary on everything we pass. Everyone has their digital camera out, and the girls and grandmas have put on their finery for the photo opportunities that would occur. Some people want their photos with me.

The scenery is good, but must have been spectacular before the river level rose an additional 400ft (130m) when the dam was completed.

The guide speaks English, and had been trying to get us train tickets so we could return to Chengdu once we had finished the tour. But to no avail. We have little alternative but to stay on board for an extra night when the boat returns upstream until we reach Wanzhou, and from there to take a bus to Chengdu.

We pass the town of Badong, the site of a beautiful suspension bridge. Many of the older buildings near the riverbank seem to be abandoned. Coal barges are loading from very primitive but practical coal handling facilities. The coal is tipped into a brickwork bunker at the top and falls via gravity into a chute made of blue plastic barrels cut in half and with the top and bottom discarded. The lower end of this chute is upturned and the coal dust flies up and out, falling in an arc and down into the bottom of the barge.

We reach our destination of Maopong Port in Yichang, and again I am in demand for final last minute photos with other passengers. Lian finds it all quite amusing. We leave our luggage on board and join the others on a bus for our tour of the dam.

Security is tight, and we go through airport style scans and checks.

We are taken to see a model of the dam, and then views of the dam from both banks. It is certainly large; being 2.3km wide, but it is not as visually impressive as compared to say the Hoover Dam in the USA. Although there were plenty of instructive signboards, none appeared to be in English.

We visited a temple and then a supermarket, and only got back to the dock at 5:50pm, and by 6:15pm the 'No. 6' cast off and proceeded westwards. Slightly surprised that there were quite a few passengers on their way back to Wanzhou.

Heard our foghorn sound several times in the night as we made brief stops. The morning was overcast, and I spent much of my time on the small bow deck.

Return to Chengdu.

We docked at Wanzhou at 10:20am, and caught a taxi to the main bus terminal. Bought tickets on mid-day bus for the 7 hour ride to Chengdu.

Interesting scenery, including couple of 3km long tunnels, and before we knew it we were in a bus station outside of Chengdu. But it was no problem to take a bus into the part of town we knew. This time, instead of staying in the Traffic Inn, we tried the Traffic Hotel as we had surprisingly got a better deal that included a breakfast.

After a wonderful hot shower, a shave, and the opportunity of getting some washing done, we walk along the riverside to the 'High Fly' restaurant. This is an old favourite and serve a good pizza and a cool Tsing Tao beer.

The free breakfast next morning was very sparse: a fried egg and 2 slices of toasted bread, some strawberry jam, and a glass of orange water.

Bought an adapter to charge Lian's iPad, and also a detailed map of Sichuan province. We investigated various ways of travelling to the west, but it appears they are all still closed.

So we made Plan C or is it D? We would travel north, staying in SongPan, then on to LangMuSi and finally to Xining, where we would take a train back to Chengdu. Prepared a new budget to cover this remaining 9 days, and decided that another walk along to the HSBC ATM would be a wise move, as there is no certainty that cash would be available in the small towns.

In the afternoon we went to sit on one of the benches provided by the riverside, and continue with Charles Dickens 'Martin Chuzzlewit'. The print is small and faded on my copy, and reading is slow if one wants to enjoy the English and the humour. Where does he get all those strange surnames? I am sitting deeply involved with Mr. Pecksniff and his family, when a big boisterous Labrador comes lolloping out of nowhere and jumps all over me. A Chinese lady explained that the owner was a European, and that 'Cocobean' loves all foreigners.

SongPan.

The bus station for buses travelling to the north is situated on the north-western outskirts of town. We had booked the 6:30am bus, so had to order a taxi for 5:30am as the town buses had yet to start at that time. The roads were empty, and we reached the terminal before it opened its doors at 6am. Crowds were milling about outside, and there was a crush as they all tried to get in at the same time, but they soon disappeared into the 20 or 30 buses waiting to take them to their different destinations.

Our bus finally got away ten minutes late, onto a highway through flattish agricultural land before reaching the foothills and started climbing. We passed through a number of very long tunnels, some 2 to 2.1/2 miles (3 or 4km) in length. Some had little or no lights inside.

We were stopped at a police checkpoint, but there was no objection from them. After two hours we had our first 'pee stop', and it was much cooler at 3,750ft (1,150m). In the narrow valleys we could still see evidence of the 2008 earthquake, where sections of the old elevated highway had collapsed. A number of hydroelectric schemes are under construction as well as the re-routing of the elevated highway.

After 4 hours we reached 5,250ft (1,600m) and an area where there was little new construction going on. Another 45 minutes and the road started to switchback upwards, reaching a 1.1/4 mile (2km) long tunnel at 7,200ft (2,200m) and the chance of a15-minute break to stretch our legs.

At 1:30pm we reached the bus station at our destination, the walled town of SongPan.

Walked out of the compound and down the street, when we saw the Old House Hotel, a 3-storey wood framed building. It was decorated in Tibetan style, with rooms around a central covered atrium. The floor of our room was finished with linoleum over a thick felt underlay—so thick and spongy that one felt a little unsteady when walking on it. Can only assume this is a noise deadener, as we could see from our ceiling that the floors were of pinewood on pine joists. The room had twin beds, and a bathroom with a shower and a big hot water cylinder. Three of the walls were painted a bright orange and the other a sunshine yellow.

We were quite hungry after our early morning start, so walked down to 'Emma's Restaurant' for an egg and bacon sandwich and a beer.

Walked down to the town and through the walled north gate. The local residents are a mixture of Hui Chinese Muslims, Tibetans and ethnic Chinese.

All the 2, 3 and 4 storey shops on the main streets both inside and outside of the wall are new, but built in the old style. It is only on the side streets that one finds the old 2-storey wood framed building that had withstood the shock of the earthquake.

There was much to photograph with so many shops selling yak meat hanging up to dry, and wolf furs, and Tibetan artefacts.

At an altitude of 9.200ft (2,800m), we notice the lack of oxygen whenever we walked up steps.

Wi-Fi was available in the hotel room, but the reception was better in the small restaurant section. So Lian had no problem with the iPad.

In the evening we had dinner at 'Sarah's'. My Spanish omelette was fine, but Lian's big bowl of tofu and vegetable soup was well laced with the dreaded Sichuan 'numbing chilli', of which she is not fond.

Returning to the hotel, we were surprised to find that each bed had an electric blanket. I put mine on for a while whilst I had a shower, but perhaps I should have kept it on, as in the night I had to get up and put on some socks as my feet were frozen. I had noticed that the wooden windows could not be opened as Sellotape had been used to cover all the gaps to keep out the drafts and the weather.

Enjoyed the breakfast, before setting off on a walk to find the oldest parts of the town. What appeared to be an old Chinese temple was actually a mosque. We were welcomed into the outer-courtyard by the Hui men wearing their scull-caps. The women, wearing their typical black lacy headdresses, were cooking in a central kitchen, and kindly offered us food. They were all very curious as to where we had come from.

We continued our stroll southwards along the main road, keeping outside of the outer wall, stopping for a while at a shop selling coal fired cooking stoves complete with built in ovens. Next-door was a coal merchant. The shopkeeper was lazing on the grass with some friends on the other side of the road, and waved at us. Many more shops were selling dried yak meat, and the long stringy things hanging there may well have been the male animal's sexual organs.

On the southern outskirts of the town we turned westwards and made a circular tour alongside a small stream until we reached our starting point. At one shop in town we bought Lian a spare battery for her little Sony camera, as it was very competitively priced.

In the afternoon we thought we would climb up to what looked like a temple, sited on a hill overlooking the town. This is the old West Gate and was under reconstruction. It was then that we also noticed the remains of the old wall snaking up the steep hillside. We were not sure of the access road and were standing looking up when a young man walked over and asked if we remembered him. "Why yes, you are the young man we met and talked to on the bus, and who works for the Agricultural Bank". It was his lunch break, and he insisted on showing us the shortcut, and accompanying us up the hill until he had us on the right path. He was keen to practise his English, and whilst he kept talking we had a chance to gulp in enough oxygen to keep us going. He was quite disappointed when he had to return to his bank.

We got a bit lost about halfway up when we reached a local cemetery, but soon found the steep dirt track again. The views we very impressive when we looked down on the old town, and tried to follow the route we had taken in the morning. We spotted our hotel, and with our binoculars even recognised our window by the hanging clothes.

Across the valley we could see mountains in the distance, with snow on the summits. The huge numbers of black dots on the lower green hillsides were yaks.

Returning to the town, we sat down for some yak beef noodles, and more of the deep fried dough pancakes that we had so enjoyed for lunch. After deep-frying, the 6" (15cm) diameter bread was dried off by stacking them around the flame of the charcoal cooker.

The next morning, after breakfast, we had looked at some of the shops to the north of our hotel. Most were selling the usual dried yak meat, but one had a very good selection of furs, including white, silver and brown fox, and wolf with dark coats. Some of the furs had stripes and spots, but somehow the stripes or spots look artificial so we thought that instead of being members of the cat family, they were probably treated wolf skins.

The bus going north was due to leave at 10am, so we said our goodbyes at the hotel, before we walked over to the bus station.

LangMuSi

The road slowly rose along the steep sided valleys and an hour later passed a sign showing an altitude of 11,500ft (3,500m), and the view slowly changed to a wide grass covered valley with rolling hills all around. This is the area of the 'Grasslands National Park'. We see huge herds of yaks and also herds of sheep grazing on the hillsides like maggots on green baize.

Some sheep are crossing the road, and we see they have brown heads and the males have delicate little spiral horns.

It was nearly 1pm when we reach the town of Zoige—also know as Ruo Er Gai.

Here we had to buy tickets for another bus in order to reach our destination of LongMuSi.

The next one leaves at 2:30pm, so we had time to explore the town. All new and drab buildings. The people are predominantly Tibetan. The men all seem to have Honda motorcycles, but have customised them as they would their horses. A small carpet covers the seat and petrol tank, and carpeting saddlebags straddle the seat.

A dust storm passes by and visibility drops dramatically.

Three young Hui girls have their heads wrapped with scarves, leaving only their eyes are showing. They want their photograph taken.

We go into the covered market selling chickens and meat and vegetables. The chickens are slaughtered and de-feathered for sale. The feathers and guts and blood overflow from a barrel that partially blocks access to a public toilet. The inside of the toilet was no cleaner as it comprised holes in a slab, and no available water, so I ignore a man who tries to extort payments for it's use.

The bus was surprisingly empty when it left. We continue across the grasslands, sometimes crossing low passes into the next wide grasslands valley. About 1.1/2 hours later the bus took a side turning for a few kilometres, and stopped at the main crossroads in LangMuSi.

I sat with the luggage, whilst Lian set off to find some accommodation, which she found at the LangMuSi Yuen Hotel. It was quite a modern building, with an impressive reception area. Our room was comfortable with its double-glazing, electric blankets, TV, and an electric kettle. We seemed to be about their only guests.

The town is surrounded by mountains, which in some directions look very 'alpine with fir trees and stark white mountains, whereas other directions seem to be of a different geological formation.

We took the high street and walked up to the Dac Ang Lang Mo Monastery, one of the two main lamaseries in town. We did not pay the entrance fee, as it was late in the afternoon, and we would return the next day. The stupa and buildings looked very impressive in the setting sun, and I was surprised when the gatekeeper kept saying "No photos", and even wanted me to delete a couple I had taken. We were not impressed by this attitude. Was this going to be a problem tomorrow?

The sky was blue, and there were a few big eagles soaring above us. We became very excited when we saw the shape of some of the rapture's wedge shaped tails. These were Lammergeiers, also known as Bearded Vultures. The other raptors we spotted were mainly Black Kites, with a few Himalayan Vultures. And whereas we had never seen more than a pair of Lammergeiers together, here we could see three or four pairs at a time, and later we noted that they were flying low over a sandstone mountain range know locally as the canyon. On the sides of the canyon, one could clearly see through the binoculars, the white smudges below ledges or caves, where these huge birds had had their nests.

Walked into the Hui village and admired their mosque with its Chinese pagoda shaped tower.

The next morning we decided to visit the other monastery, as the light conditions might be better in the morning. After paying out entrance fee, we walked up the hill towards a pile of wooden spears decorated with prayer flags. The ground around it was covered in small squares of white paper on which was stamped a prayer horse. It had been raining in the night and the grass looked as if it had been covered by snow. We watched as a man threw handfuls of the small squares of paper up into the air. Some were caught by the breeze and sailed high into the sky spreading their prayer wishes across the valley, whilst the majority joined the soggy mass on the ground.

We could hear a crowd of workers chanting as they rammed in unison the damp soil to compact it between stones set against wooden formwork. They were building a tradition wall around a temple platform.

Not a cloud in the sky, and an unbelievable clarity. Had a pleasant wander through the streets of this old lamasery and it's numerous small temples. Saw people prostrating on the street and also on their sliding boards in the temples. The people were very friendly and would stand nodding and smiling at you, which gave a feeling of peace and contentment.

Leaving the monastery, Lian bought some handicraft and trinkets from a small jeweller.

In the afternoon we visited the other monastery. No problem this time with taking photos. The construction was quite new, and some golden roofed temples were yet to be finished internally.

We walked to the wooded hill behind the monastery and had great views of both the monasteries and also the town. A few cheeky young monks joined us, and wanted to have their photos taken and to look through our binoculars.

We sat up there on the hilltop for an hour or so enjoying the panoramas and also counting the probable nesting sites of the Bearded Vultures. The black Red-billed Choughs also enthralled us, as without their red bill and legs, one would assume they were local crows.

In the evening we returned to the 'Black Tent' for dinner of pizzas. At least they had Wi-Fi so we could catch up on our emails.

Xiahe and Labrang Monastery

Next morning we were up early to catch the bus to Hezuozhan, where we would change to another bus to Xiahe and the Labrang Monastery.

A big bus was already waiting, and we bought and nibbled at a small round of freshly baked local bread before boarding. The bus was away by 7:30am and 5 minutes later we were at the junction to take the main road north.

The road kept very straight across the high plain, stopping to pick up passengers who flag us down. The majority of traffic comprises heavy lorries, and in places their tire grooves are deep into the tarmac surface. We have to slow a couple of times due to sheep or yaks crossing the road.

We pull into the bus station at Hezuozhan at 9:50am, but find that the bus to Xiahe leaves from another bus station right on the other side of town, a six-minute taxi ride away.

Our small bus left 15 minutes later. We notice that the distance signs have changed from Chinese and English, to Chinese and Tibetan. We are leaving the 9,900 ft (3,000m) high plateau and slowly descending, and the new leaves are just breaking out on the trees.

After about 50 minutes the bus turns westwards off the main road, and 30 minutes later we reach the bus station in Xiahe. The monastery at Labrang is at the other end of town, so we jump in a taxi.

Time to find some accommodation. I wait with the luggage whilst Lian has a look at a number of hotel rooms. Just somewhere clean and with Wi-Fi was needed. The White Stupa Hotel answered these requirements and we were soon settled in. The room even had it's own computer.

It was at this time that we find that I had managed to misplace a plastic bag containing our food. Probably serves me right for not giving alms to a number of beggars who approached me whilst I was waiting around.

We had visited Labrang some years ago whilst on the Silk Route. It is a large monastery with 1,400 monks. Although the walled monastery has little changed, the main street and the shops adjacent had changed considerably. The little boot maker was no longer there, but they still sell coloured ropes from a stall.

Lian had heard that they had an English-speaking guide at 3pm every day, so we wandered along to the ticket office and sat in the shade to wait.

The guide was a jolly faced young monk who never stopped chuckling and smiling. We were the only ones on the tour. I didn't understand everything he said, but this did not seem to matter. He took us into a number of prayer rooms and temples. Several had to be unlocked before we were let in. It was so cool and serene inside. Unfortunately he was quite strict on the 'no-photos inside' rule. The only room I could take pictures was the store-room for the amazing figures made from coloured flour.

We were rather surprised to see some pictures of the Dalai Lama in some temples, and to hear that the Dalai Lama was our guide's idol, and that he had met him a number of times, as we had understood that the Chinese authorities would not find this acceptable.

We were told that there would be prayers in the main hall at 11am on the following morning, and we could sit in with the monks sitting in the courtyard in front of the main prayer hall.

Had a little trouble getting into room's computer as it was all set up in Chinese, but managed in the end to get into Lian's old emails and find the notes I wrote during our Silk Route trip. I was especially curious about the town of Xining, as this was Lian's preferred next destination. As we found in my write-up that the town was a bit crumby, we decided to go straight to Langzhou by bus, and get a train from there. This would save both time and expense.

We would spend an extra night here, and leave in the afternoon after the prayers.

We find the toilet cistern is broken, and it runs continually. The porter cannot mend it, and neither could I. The hotel said they have no spare room. So the answer was to use the stopcock to stop the running water—problem solved. The shower was deliciously hot, so all is forgiven.

Had a pizza in the 'Snowy Mountain Café'. Met an English girl and a Portuguese man who seemed to be helping out there.

It was drizzling when we awoke, and the dull grey sky did not look as if it was going to stop for some time. Would the monks sit in the rain? Or did we want to sit in the rain?

Lanzhou.

So yet another change of plan. Just take a taxi straight to the bus station and leave town on the 8:30am bus.

On board we met a young couple who had asked to have a photo with me yesterday, and a Chinese man who we had met a few days ago and seemed to be on the same route as ourselves.

Overflowing streams had caused a few rock and mud slides and this slowed us down a few times.

The scenery had changed, and we are often in narrow valleys with any flat areas put under cultivation.

As we pass the houses we see that many have solar powered kettle boilers, but they were not working today. The inside of a mesh satellite shaped dish was covered with small glass mosaics, and a hook is used to keep the kettle body at the focal centre-point. Such a simple and cheap way of getting boiling water for the tea.

The valleys get wider and there is yet more cultivation. We pass a number of brickworks, some of which are making black roof tiles and dark grey bricks. The people here are mainly Hui.

At 11am we have a brief stop in a wide valley that seems to have a large mosque every kilometre. And in just over an hour we reach the Lanzhou bus station.

Where is the railway station? "Follow us" say the young couple, and 15 of us cram into a minibus together with the driver and all our luggage. It's like how many can people can you cram in a Mini?

We recognised the station when we got there 20 minutes later. A huge place, with very long queues at the ticket counters. We had already agreed that we would try to get a 'soft sleeper' and enjoy a little comfort. But would any be available today or would we have to wait until tomorrow? Again people were very helpful and Lian managed to make the booking clerk understand her Mandarin.

Big smiles when she came back with tickets for the 5pm afternoon train. And both were lower berth.

We made use of the KFC at the station until it was time to go onto the platform.

Return to Chengdu.

We found coach 10, and our cabin. At present we have no other passengers, but perhaps they will join us some time during the 20-hour journey? The distance is only 728 miles (1,172km), so the average speed of about 35mph (60kph) is pretty slow. We understand that by 2016 the time for the journey will be cut to only 4 hours. But perhaps a little of the romance of rail travel will be lost.

The first thing to do was to get out the coffee mugs and the coffee before stowing our gear under the seats. Then locate the hot water boiler and make the coffee.

Soon after, along came a woman selling fresh fruit—"No thanks". Then came a man selling beer. "Yes—a large one please".

We set off on time. The train stops many times at both stations and out in the back of nowhere. By 9:30pm we had made up our beds and pulled shut the sliding door. The altitude then slowly dropped from 4,850 ft (1,480m) to 1,970 ft (600m) by 6:30am. We were in a steep valley, following a river. We have left Gansu Province where we started, and are now in Shanxi Province. Soon we would reach Sichuan Province. As we pass roads, we see we are travelling only at the speed of the lorries.

The countryside gets flatter and flatter, and the visibility gets poorer and worse.

We pull into the railway station at 1:50pm and shortly after are on a no. 55 bus for the Traffic Hotel.

The next day was to be a relaxed day with a trip to the Panda Breeding Centre. A bus leaves from just outside the hotel, and we arrived just in time to enjoy the feeding time for seven of the juveniles, so there were heaps of good photo opportunities.

We then walked over to see the Red Pandas. They are also very cute, looking more like a russet-coloured racoons. It seems that these were originally called Pandas, but when a French monk 'discovered' the black and white panda, they were quickly re-named the 'Red Panda', and the new star became 'The Panda'.

In the afternoon we made a trip to the 'Large and Small Alleys', only to confirm that we had been here on a previous trip. It still comprises lots of fancy shops and restaurants serving a thriving local and international tourist market. It is however a good example of how the Chinese can make what appears to be an old and established area from the piles of broken bricks and rubble that we had seen many years earlier.

That evening we had dinner in the main Traffic Hotel restaurant. It was very full; with of couple of company dinners taking place, and it was fascinating to watch the main company players with their macho drinking. One minute chatting up the girls and trying to get them drunk, and then the next minute with their arm round a fellow workers shoulders. Is that a pep talk, or a stab in the back? Most of the men looked a little the worst for wear by the time they staggered out.

And our meal of Sichuan traditional dishes? Large portions, but rather chilli hot and oily, and with more than a hint of that lip-numbing ingredient.

Next morning we took a bus out to Huang Long Xi, one of the 'ancient towns', just outside of Chengdu. The driver cuts through the traffic like a hot knife through butter. It is drizzling, and he does not slow down. Might is right, and a bus is bigger than a car and a lot bigger than motorcycles or bikes! Several times I close my eyes a fraction of a second before a crash, but perhaps divine providence stepped in, or a fairy appeared and snatches a bicycle out of the buses' clutches. I don't know, as my eyes were still closed. A red traffic light means little to the ever increasing number of electric motorbikes, as they just swerve around and cross at will.

Huang Long Xi is now purely a town for tourists—local Chinese tourists, with only a handful of obvious foreigners. But it is so well done that even Disney would have trouble bettering it. The entrance way follows a delightful little stream with stone frogs and toads in it and cute little bridges. This opens into the 'town square' comprising a huge water feature, before crossing a bridge with a stone dragon on the left hand side overlooking the main river. It is on the other side of the bridge that the slightly older part of the town shows with cobbled streets and single storey shops and restaurants.

Old women have made head garlands of fresh flowers, and sales are brisk. Lian buys one, and it certainly suits her.

There has been a slight drizzle, and the cobblestones sparkle.

We stop at a noodle shop where a TV programme is being shot. The 'throwing' noodles have been made as a single string carefully coiled on the top of an old barrel. This stands about 2 meters (6ft) from a huge pot of boiling water. The chef is being interviewed, and then gives a demonstration of how he picks up the end of the noddle coil and then tosses it through the air in a number of snake like movements, so it feeds continually into the boiling water without breaking. It is very skilful. Later the interviewer has a go to everyone's amusement.

Later we went back to the noodle shop and sampled a bowl. The 'throw' beef noodles were quite delicious, even though I did not suck them up as a single strand.

Found only a few wooden houses that may have been original.

The mid afternoon traffic is much easier, and it took only 1.1/4 hours to return to town.

The next day was our last day. In the morning we went to have a look around the Tibetan quarter. Just a lot of shops selling Tibetan items such as beads, prayer wheels, 'tankas', and Buddha figures. Some had very rare and expensive items, and all in all this was the best selection we had seen during our travels. Nearby we found a number of travel shops and finished up buying a few items.

The hotel would not give us a late check out after 2pm, and so we spent the rest of our time in the lounge / dining area of the Inn. It was comfortable, and we could order food and drinks as we needed them.

Before 9pm we slowly made our way alongside the river to the airport bus shuttle stop. Our Air Asia flight was on time, taking off just after mid-night for the 4-hour flight.

CHAPTER 21

Sarawak—Bario Highlands & up the Baram River

Huts in the Penan village outside Bario.

This would be our third attempt to reach Bario, the small yet major town on the plateau area in Sarawak's Kelabit Highlands, close to the border with Indonesia's Kalimantan.

At our first try, the aircraft was due to fly us from Ba' Kelanlan, but did not arrive due to bad weather. At our second try we got as far as the departure lounge in Miri airport when the airline closed down for some months due to restructuring.

Miri.

So it was with some trepidation that we flew into Miri from Kuala Lumpur. We stayed at the Walk Inn, a new budget hotel. This was clean, and Wi-Fi was available in the room.

Walked down to the information centre and found the staff very helpful. Then found a stall that we had visited before and was well know for its 'ABC'. The 'Air Batu Cacang' comprises a bowl heaped with shaved ice and filled with spoonful's of various sweet beans, green noodle like 'worms', little jelly chunks, coconut milk, brown and red syrups, etc. Very Malaysian, and very tasty.

Having a couple of spare days before our flight into the interior, we took a taxi out to the Lambir Hills National Park, about 30 km south of Miri, where we spent one night. The accommodation we stayed in was quite new, but provided no hot water, soap or towels. The bathroom soon flooded, as the drain outlet seemed to be situated at the highest point. They did however provide brooms and a mop to assist one to push the water up hill.

The park itself was well maintained and kept clean. Most visitors were there to visit the main waterfall, which had a section roped off for swimming.

We spent our time walking the trails and doing a spot of bird watching. The heavy afternoon deluge was a good excuse to rest in the room for a couple of hours.

At noon the next day we telephoned our taxi driver to come and pick us up. Although the taxi was pretty old and decrepit with its split seats, the Chinese driver was fat and jolly and tried very hard.

So we arranged for him to come and pick us next morning for the run to the airport. At check in, as well as weighing our bags, we were each weighed together with our backpacks.

Bario.

We boarded the 'Twin Otter' for the 45-minute flight to Bario. I took a front seat, but had to suffer a small fan that blasted air onto my head until I put on my cap. However I had a good view of the plane's instrument panel, the captain and his first officer through the ever-open doorway.

Thereafter I was glued to the window, camera in hand. The plane took off using very little of the runway. For some time all we could see below were oil palm estates: the flat areas set out in square grids, and any hilly areas had a jigsaw of access roads dependent upon the contours.

We reached our cruising height of about 10,000 ft (3,000m) in the unpressurised cabin.

Below one had clear views of the Baram River, and a big oxbow lake.

After 25-minutes we could see the airstrip of Mulu National Park, and then the ground seemed to rise below us as we reached a mountain range.

Against a backdrop of low cloud we had views of a finger and a thumb of limestone outcrop pointing into the sky. This is known as Batu Lawah, and is one of the trekking destinations.

Soon after, we dropped down over the edge of the forested hills and could see a flattish plateau ahead. The ground below was a patchwork of flooded padi fields, the home of the famed 'Bario rice'. We could see settlements and then a small town, and soon after landed at the new Bario airport.

We did not have long to wait for our luggage. Luckily there are few maps of Bario on the airport noticeboards, and we took photos of these, as we could find little in the guidebooks or the Internet. Now we could at least have a feel of our orientation.

We had made a reservation at 'Nancy & Harriss Homestay' for three nights. Harriss appeared in a newish Land Rover Defender pick-up, and I sat in the back with our luggage for the less than10-minute trip to the Homestay, passing the town centre on the way. It was a good concrete road, apart from a track for the last couple of hundred yards. The house was next to the now abandoned old airstrip.

The double room we were allocated was quite confortable, and the toilet facilities were along a corridor and down some steps.

We were sharing the homestay with a group of 16 English students from a school in Bristol, together with their 4 teachers. They were away a month with 'Global Venture Expedition 2012'. Having just completed a few days jungle trek, they were about to carry out some 'good works', before going on for more sightseeing in Sabah. The good works were about to start by their repainting a Forestry Department wooden bungalow, and putting down a cement screed in a storeroom. The management of their project was left to the students, with a new leader appointed each day. The teachers were there to advise only. We hoped they had plenty of the green oil paint, as they had so much on themselves when they came back.

I am sure they would all have a holiday they would always remember.

Talking to Nancy, Lian heard that there was a hornbill bird that someone kept, but was allowed to fly freely. So after coffee and some peanut butter and bread, we set off walking northwards towards Bario Asal—the old town. Harriss caught us up and gave us a lift as he was going to meet his mother who lives in the big wooden longhouse. Once there we asked around, and heard that the hornbill owner lived in the end room of the same block.

So this is how we met James and Mary Maga. He told us he found the baby hornbill, 'Toroo', when he was out near a mini-hydro project. He did not know what the English name was for the species.

"Where is it now?"

"Maybe at the school, or maybe the airport. She comes back later in the afternoon."

The wooden longhouse is on stilts. The Maga's use wood to cook, and the fireplace is in the main long common hall. Over the fireplace is a blacked kettle and a large cooking pot and lid. Above the fire is a shelf with chopped wood left to dry out. We did not visit their sleeping and private area, but James took us through to the meeting room, that runs parallel to the main hall. I paced this room out, and it is nearly 400 ft (120m) long by 13 ft (4m) wide. Along the walls are many old photos of the resident's parents and grandparents, as well as many showing diplomas being presented at convocations.

After James left the army, he worked for a short while with Tom Harrisson, who was then the curator of the Sarawak Museum in Kuching. Harrisson was an explorer and anthropologist, and had retired in Bario. James said there was a commemorative plaque a short way away on a hillside.

Lian and I set off to find it, and were soon overtaken by James on his motorcycle. He took us to the brass-faced tribute. Major Harrisson had parachuted in with a group of British and Australian commandoes in March 1945. They would fight the Japanese occupation forces with the help of the local tribal warriors.

It was whilst enjoying the views, that we realised we were late for lunch, and had a 30-minute fast walk back.

Nancy had cooked us a delicious meal on her wood fire comprising: pineapple curry, omelette, green vegetables, bamboo shuts and Bario rice. This was finished off with sweet Sarawak pineapple, and coffee. Although the students ate in the dining area, we chose to sit out on the big covered verandah area.

We walked off the lunch with a return to Bario Asam, but by a more circular route, passing through quite a large school, where the students were holding their sports day.

We then took a muddy track north for a visit to Arul Dalam. The track was very muddy in parts, and we hitched a ride on the back of a tractor in order to pass a bad patch.

The small village was very quiet and we saw virtually no one around, but one could sense that we were being watched. It was a little bit creepy. The village have four windmills that were installed in order to provide electricity, but for some reason were never commissioned.

So we picked our way back to Bario Asal, washing off the bulk of the mud from our shoes in a small stream.

There, outside Jame's room was a Wreathed Hornbill sitting on a perch. It was a female, generally with black and white feathers, but with a female's bright blue skin sack under her bill, and bare red skin surrounding her eyes.

James called us up. 'Toroo' seemed very tame, and kept demanding that James to scratch her bill. If he stopped she would gently nip at his fingers. Perhaps being a female made her wary of Lian. I however was allowed to stroke and scratch her beak for a while as she gently nipped a finger. Then the nip got a little too hard, and being a coward, I withdrew whilst I was in one piece.

Got back at 5pm, and had a cold shower and washed some clothes. Yes, the water was quite cold. We are at 3,400ft (1,000m) here, so it is pleasantly cool, and we do not suffer the high humidity and temperature of the coastal plains. Time for tea and a freshly baked cake.

Once again the food was plentiful and excellent. If we stay here too long I will certainly put on weight.

Our Plan A was to fly back to Miri, and then the next day to take a boat up the Baram River to Marudi, before proceeding further up river. We hear that twice a week there is a flight from here to Miri via Marudi. This would save us time as well as some money. So for Plan B we ask Nancy to check if they have seats for two days time, and if so to make reservations, and we would forego the Marudi to Miri sector.

Had pancakes and coffee for breakfast.

It had rained most of the night, so was quite pleasantly cool when we set off at 7am in a southerly direction to find the village of Pa Umur. Cheated a bit by cadging a lift in a pick-up truck part of the way.

The village was very small, but had a small wooden church with a rusty iron steeple. The room was full of plastic chairs, with a drum kit and two electric guitars by the lectern. We sat at the covered entrance and opened some biscuits that we shared with a mangy looking dog and a number of scrawny yet highly sexed cockerels.

It was a long walk back, so we stopped at another Homestay. The owner was an ex head mistress and invited us in for tea. She was busy getting her place ready for some guests due to arrive in a day or so. She had an interesting set of photographs on the wall, including two that she said were of Tom Harrisson's Kelabit wife. In one she was playing a bamboo stringed musical instrument and had a cat on her lap, and in the other she was bare breasted.

On our walks we had passed quite a few Homestays. But they were either closed, or did not seem to have any guests. So how did Nancy and Harriss keep so busy? Probably it simply comes down to excellent and friendly service, and good food.

As we passed by town we popped into the Forestry Dept to see how the school kids were getting on. They were actually doing quite well.

Greeted by the Forestry Department man who was supervising the works. He comes from Pa Umur, and we had met him earlier in the day when he had stopped for a quick chat during our walk. Also met another man, named Lian, who would be supervising another English group, whose task would involve some re-forestation, by planting Meranti hardwood saplings on a cleared hillside.

He mentioned that there was a small Penan settlement in the foothills, so we made this our afternoon's destination. The Penan are the nomadic people of the forest.

Back at the Homestay by mid-day, in time to watch yet another group of young Bristol scholars with the 'Global Venture Expedition 2012', arriving after their 3-day trek. Muddy boots, huge rucksack and wide grins.

Lian and I looked at each other—where are they going to sleep? But Nancy had it all worked out with plenty more beds at the back of the house.

Nancy had arranged for our change of itinerary, and we had seats the next day on the MasWings flight to Marudi.

The Penan settlement was past Arul Dalam, and we crossed by some buffalo wallows, a field, and alongside a narrow rocky stream. We first saw the smoke from a fire filtering through the trees. There were about ten shacks built on stilts. Some had rusty corrugated roofing, and some had blue tarpaulin as a roof cover. Walls were of bamboo, rough timber planks, or matting.

We wandered in saying "Hello", and keeping big smiles.

Saw no men in the encampment, but there were a couple of women with two young children and two babes in arms.

On the way back we were disappointed that 'Toroo' was not outside Jame's longhouse. But halfway back we saw her perched on a power line and being dive-bombed by a pair of small Wood Swallows in a 'mobbing' routine. They probably have a nest nearby, and they were unsuccessfully trying to get the hornbill to fly away.

Woke early the next morning and sat chatting with the teachers before breakfast was served.

Watched a small chocolate brown Dusky Munia building a nest in a tree. At first I thought I was seeing an Asian Paradise Flycatcher with its long streaming tail. But no, this endemic Munia was carrying long pieces of raffia like weed that it was weaving into its nest. In total we had spotted or heard 27 species of bird during our time in Bario.

Then at just past 8am, Harriss drove us to the airport. We checked in, after having ourselves and our baggage weighed.

Told that the plane would be late, as it was not scheduled to leave Miri until nearly 1pm. Seems that the flights were delayed yesterday due to bad weather, and they had to catch up with the stranded passengers. So we returned to the Homestay to wait in the comfort of the verandah and endless cups of hot drinks.

After a fried rice lunch we returned to the airport, and were relieved when the 19-seater 'Twin Otter' touched down before 2:15pm. Fifteen minutes later we were in the air with only three other passengers.

In order to clear the surrounding hills, the plane does a spiral climb over the plateau in order to get sufficient altitude before heading westwards.

Had some clear views of logging roads built along the mountain ridges, with steep falls either side? Then the clouds rolled in.

Marudi.

Marudi was another very small airport. No taxis outside, so we had a 10-minute walk down a hill and into the town.

I sat in a coffee shop, whilst Lian went in search of accommodation.

The Marudi Hotel was a good choice for us, facing the main square and adjacent to the boat jetty.

We had a recently redecorated room at the front—very Japanese décor: raised floor, mattresses on the floor, airconditioning, flat-screen TV, and 3 tall slim windows from ceiling to floor. The bathroom had one wall of red tiles.

Good to have a hot shower and hair wash before setting out to explore the small town.

The hotel has Wi-Fi, but not very good reception. But at least we could check up on emails.

Got the schedule for the next morning's up river express boat, before visiting a Chinese temple, and walking around the shops.

Next morning Lian had a touch of migraine, so we decided to stay an extra night in comfort whilst Lian rested.

I took the opportunity of further exploring this small town, and visited the old wooden Fort Hose. This had been completed in November 1901, but burned down in 1994. Each of the various tribal communities donated a Belian (a very tough hardwood) pole to use in the reconstruction.

It is now a very interesting museum, with many old photos. The fort is named after Charles Hose, who was an administrator and a Resident of Baram. He presided over the Baram Peace Making Ceremony. He is now known for his book 'The Pagan Tribes of Borneo'.

Lian had some fruit for lunch and was feeling a little better. It rained all afternoon, so was a good excuse for a rest. Later we both went for a walk to the fort, but by now it had closed.

Next morning, Lian felt much better and we would take an express boat upstream for a 3-hour river trip to the town of Long Lama. The boat was due to leave at noon, but might be late arriving at its destination as the Baram River was flowing fast.

On the way to the fort, we passed a crowd around a man cutting up three catfish. One was a giant, and over 4 foot (120cm) long. He was chopping it into 6" (15cm) thick steaks after taking out all the guts. The heart was only 2" (5cm) long and still throbbing.

Long Lama.

At 11:30am we wandered over to the jetty and boarded our boat. The Sarawak river express boats are long and thin, just like an aircraft's body and air-conditioned. They have a central corridor with a pair of seats either side.

We took the front seats so I had a little legroom, although this seat had no side window. It is all a little claustrophobic. Luggage and cardboard boxes filled the curved roof and along the external walkways each side.

Everyone was very friendly and we spoke with a Penan headman who was on his way to a logging camp.

At mid-day we set off, and a conductor came to collect payment. As the weather was fine, the entrance doors were kept open and we enjoyed the breeze and some view.

We stopped a number of times on the way at various longhouses, schools and logging camps. The jetties usually comprised a few floating logs, and one would need plenty of confidence or luck to avoid taking a swim. This was the only access for many communities, so all their supplies would have to be delivered via the express boat.

They had a toilet on board. One walked down past the boat's 74 seats, and through a very noisy engine room. A man was sitting here with a small monkey that was being teased by a boy. Then a door opened onto a squat toilet that was on a platform about knee-high above the deck level. The roof was low and curved, so anyone my height would need to be a contortionist to climb up and squat down.

Passed a few logging camps, but the diameter of the logs was not large. We had seen some large barges filled with crushed stone, and we passed a large quarry set-up.

Surprised to see a ferry boat taking lorries and vehicles across the river.

Soon after we reached the town of Long Lama, and it was 4pm when we walked onto the floating jetty. We reached land, and I sat with the bags whilst Lian went off to find accommodation.

The Zia Bin Hotel, was very basic and not very clean even if it was the same price as our much better hotel in Marudi. But this was a small town, and Lian found other places to be smaller or dirtier. The air-conditioner worked, but the old TV had only one channel, and there was no Wi-Fi.

But we were told that the waterfront had Wi-Fi. Yes it did, and the iPad had strong reception—but there was no onward connection.

Had noodles in a coffee shop on the waterfront, with some smuggled Dutch beer. I have to assume it was smuggled, as it was relatively cheap. So I had another one.

Lian wanted to visit a longhouse at Long Belian, but was told by a women from there, that there would be no-one there as everyone in the area would be attending a festival the next day at Long Laput, a village a little upstream. All are invited.

We walked the waterfront and enjoyed a spectacular Sarawak sunset over the river.

This was somewhat spoilt by a number of single-seater speedboats powered by small motorcycle engines. This seems to be the main hobby for the youth of the town. They race up and down the waterfront at full throttle with no silencers.

Those who have no boat just cruise around town on their motorcycles. Often whole families with 5 or 6 people crammed like sardines in the back of one machine.

This is a very Chinese town, and even the main street has a Chinese name with Mandarin writing below. The population is about 10,000.

Slept well on a surprisingly comfortable mattress. For breakfast we had a choice of only noodles. I ordered mine with an egg on top. No bread, the excuse being that bread has to come from Miri.

Long Laput.

We arranged for a 4WD to take us direct to Miri the next morning, and were back in the room when there was a knock on the door. There was a woman who said she would take us by boat to Long Laput.

"Isn't it too early."

"No. Come now".

So against our better judgment we set off in her boat, just the 2 of us, for the 15-minute trip.

The landing was a bit muddy, but the jetty and roadway into the Kayan settlement was well decorated.

It was only 10:45am, and the VIP's would only arrive by helicopter at about 4pm.

There are three longhouses in the village, with a total of 140 'doors' and a population of 1,800 people.

We wandered along to the main empty VIP area.

The reason for the celebration is that a woman from the village, Elizabeth Deng, has a major appointment in the capital, Kuching, and the deputy Sarawak Chief Minister was coming to celebrate.

A small group of women are hammering out a series of rhythms on lengths of bamboo. They ask me to join them, so I whack away and it still sounds OK.

Men are stringing up brass gongs for an 'ang klong' orchestra that will provide the main music for the celebrations.

The walls of the covered open area have many of the wide local hats hung up, and decorated with patterns of coloured beads.

We wander along to the older of the longhouses. Even this is not an old longhouse on stilts, but at least it has a wooden frame. A man tells us that the longhouse at Long Bedian is very similar to this one. Lian and I exchange glances—not much point in visiting there now.

The village has recently formed its own home guard, known here as RELA. So many are walking around in new khaki coloured uniforms, with yellow berets and shiny boots which just look too large.

The RELA people are having a packed lunch, and insist that we join them: chicken, pork, bamboo shoot, and steamed rice wrapped in a banana leaf.

We move on to the 3rd and longest longhouse. We meet up again with the leader of the bamboo gong group. So we take photos with her and her family, including an old woman with stretched ear lobes. We note that her left foot only is covered with tattoos, as well as some fingers.

We move back to the central longhouse. Lian keeps some children entertained with her iPad. It starts to rain, and we are offered accommodation for the night if the boats do not go back to Long Lama.

Women are appearing in their Kayan traditional dress, with coloured bead-covered traditional designs on a black background. They have in their hands 'pom-poms' made of finely shaved wood strips. They are all a little middle-aged, and I wonder where all the young maidens are.

A few elderly men walk around, their only traditional dress being a finely woven cane hat with a couple of hornbill feathers at the back. We note that most are Rhinoceros Hornbill feathers (white with a black band), but some are Wrinkled (black with a white end)

I have been busy writing notes, and a little boy has been watching me. He comes over and very gently turns page after page and is in deep concentration. This is the same boy who earlier was trying to knock the iPad screen off its edge. He gently took the notebook from me and studied an upside down page.

I took his cuddly soft toy, so at least I would have something to bargain with if things got nasty and he refused to hand back my precious notes!

A helicopter appears overhead, and there are a few ripples of excitement as the crowd was encouraged to stand along the roadside.

A Kayan warrior appears in full regalia, complete with a long carved shield and sword. His beaded headdress is adorned with Rhinoceros and Helmeted Hornbill feathers; he wears a long beaded loincloth, and a deer-fur cape with about 40 more Rhinoceros Hornbill feathers covering the whole back.

It was past 5pm when the Guest of Honour finally made his way down the road, surrounded by his political allies, and the ladies and the warrior were about to perform for him to the music from the gongs.

We watch all this, but before they sat down for a meal and the long speeches began, we found a boatman, said our goodbyes, and set off back to Long Lama.

Long Lama to Miri.

Woke the next morning at 6am, and packed our things. We were due to meet Ah Seng at 9am at a coffee shop. Although he was a bit late, he still sat down chatting with us and the owner of our hotel and his wife. Time is quite elastic here.

We loaded up his Toyota Hilux twin-cab, and then went off to pick up his son and another passenger from the main school.

It was 9:45am when we eventually left, and only a short while later we were at the ferry. There was quite a long queue of lorries and other 4WDs waiting to cross. Ah Seng drove right to the front, and to our surprise, no one seemed to complain.

The ferry is self-propelled and not on any kind of rope or rail. It therefore takes some skill by the captain to maneuver his way across the fast flowing water.

The paved road is in bad condition and we were told that it had broken up in under a year due to poor construction. Much of it is under widening and renewal.

It took 2.1/2 hours before we reached the junction with the main Bintulu to Miri coastal road, and 45 minutes later we were dropped off at Miri Airport.

We had come this time without any return ticket, but 4 hours later were on a plane back to Kuala Lumpur, albeit having to pay way over the price of our initial journey for the privilege.

CHAPTER 22

An Arctic adventure—camping on Baffin Island

Our camp site in Tremblay Sound.

When the first Narwhal tusks reached Europe it was assumed as proof that the unicorn was a fact and alive. Where else could a six to eight foot long spiral tusk have come from?

A whale? Don't be stupid! Not possible!

So someone must have been embarrassed when a small whale called a Narwhal was found and accepted by the scientific community.

The easy way of seeing one is to turn on National Geographic, and the most difficult is to travel up to the arctic region of Canada or Greenland.

So as often happens, we decided to take the latter.

We agreed to join a small expedition arranged by Keith Jones of Baja Jones Adventure Travel, who was arranging his last visit to see this toothed whale. Pond Inlet, at the northern end of Baffin Island was to be the starting point, and we were to find our own way there by 15th August.

The two of us arranged to meet up with old friends in Canada, and this part is subject to another story.

It was hard for us to appreciate exactly how big Canada is on it's north south axis. The 2,000-mile journey would take about 5 hours flying time.

Our Canada North flight was from Ottawa to Iqaluit, the capital of Nunavat Province, situated on the southern end of Baffin Island.

This sector was late departing, as we had to wait for a replacement stewardess as the original one called in sick. Time was regained as we flew north direct to Pond Inlet, having bypassed Clyde

River due to the weather conditions, and landed on the dirt runway. We noted that on both sectors of the flight, the majority of the aircraft's fuselage was taken over by goods and cargo.

Pond Inlet.

Picking up our bags, we were bundled into the Sauniq Hotel bus and taken to the hotel. As Lian and I were the only couple in our group, we were taken to the Black Point Lodge Hotel and given one of the four rooms, but would have to walk up to the Sauniq Hotel for all our meals. This suited us very well, as the bedroom had full height windows with a magnificent view over Eclipse Sound to Bylot Island. Although over 14 miles (22 km) away, we could see high mountains and two glaciers flowing to the shoreline.

We also found it an excellent place for bird-watching.

Pond Inlet is very much an Inuit settlement with a population of about 1,600. (Inuit means 'the people' and is now the word used instead of the word Eskimo)

The housing generally comprises small single-storey prefabricated buildings, and are raised from the sandy ground. Roads are all dirt /sand, but kept in good condition by frequent use of a grader.

Plenty of 4WD pick-ups about. But most of the locals are using small 4WD ATVs (all terrain vehicles), and we often see a couple of small children sitting on the back with the mother picking them up from school. There are also a number of 'snow cats' in various states of disrepair. These will take over or supplement the ATVs when the winter comes, and then they can be used to drive over the sea ice to Bylot Island and other settlements.

The hotel's mealtimes are at set times, and it pays to follow them; breakfast 8am, lunch at 12mid-day, and dinner at 6pm

After dumping our bags in the room, we took a brisk 5-minute walk up too the inn for the buffet dinner. Good solid, no-nonsense food. This evening it is roast beef, and plenty of it.

No beer or wine available, as Pond inlet is dry. This is to protect the Inuit, who have problems with any alcohol.

After dinner we had a walk around to familiarize ourselves with the place. Visited one of the two shops, The Co-op Supermarket. This sells everything from clothing, to vegetables and meats, to ammunition.

The Inuit were very friendly and quickly responded to a smile.

A small group of women were huddled together outside a house, so we went over to say hello and see what they were doing. They were gambling.

One woman had a big bundle of cut lengths of coloured wool. Attached to only three or four lengths were small prizes. The other women were paying a dollar to choose one piece from the bundle and to pull it. If they were lucky and it was attached to one of the prizes, they would win. They kept paying for another chance, but the odds were very poor.

The sunset was said to be at 11pm, and sunrise at 3am. However, the dusk is so long that we found we could read at any time during the 'night'.

Bylot Island looks magical. The black rock of the mountains have a dusting of fresh snow. The sea takes on a number of hues of grey and sea green. A thin layer of mist sits just above the sea on the far shore. Dark grey ominous clouds hang over the mountains. It is difficult to believe this is 14 miles (22km) away.

We slept well, and Lian was up by 5am making tea and checking the iPad, as Wi-Fi was available in our room.

So what is a Narwhal? It is a small toothed whale about 12 to 13 feet long (3.7 to 4m). *Monodon mononceros* can live to about 60 years old. The females calve every 3 years, and the 5 foot (1.5m) long baby matures in 5 to 7 years. The males grow a tusk that protrudes through their upper left lip and can grow to well over 6-foot (2m) in length.

Occasionally a female can also have a tusk. The tusk grows slowly in a twisting manner, thus ensuring that it keeps straight.

The weather here is unpredictable and so Keith Jones had planned for spare days at both the start and the end of our camping session to allow for untoward happenings.

This foresight proved effective for one of the participants who had left her USA home without her passport, thus having to take the next days flight from Ottawa.

After a full fried breakfast, we sat around and waited to meet our Inuit guide, Narman. We hear that instead of camping near Bruce Head, we would be going to the adjacent Tremblay Sound, as the Narwhals had been keeping out of Kolktoo Bay due to disturbance caused by the commencement of a large iron ore mine being set up to the south by the Baffinland Iron Mines Corporation.

A camp site would be picked only once we arrive, as we would have to keep away from the Inuit hunters camps, as they consider tourists to be bad luck for their hunting. We should be ready to leave our hotel at 10am the following morning for the 100-mile (160km) boat trip.

Nayman's father, Charlie, dropped in to say hello. He is a short stocky man with a huge grin, and is just as one would imagine an Inuit should look like.

Most evenings around dinner-time, a few of the local artists would be around selling their handicraft to the visitors. Usually of Narwhal or Polar Bear, carved from stone or Caribou bone.

We go back to the room and do some sorting out of our luggage in order that we can leave one of our three pieces of luggage at our hotel.

Went for a walk in a slight drizzle to the west of the town, passing the quaint little white and red Catholic Church. Called in at the National Parks office and admired their small exhibition including Narwhal tusks and picked up some local maps and literature.

The library was now open, and had an interesting hour or so looking at their exhibition.

A couple of large icebergs are slowly drifting by.

The plane arrives with our missing expedition member, and Keith is delighted that his lost luggage has also arrived.

The next morning we see that a large cruise boat has arrived for a days visit. The 'Le Boreal' has 250 passengers, mostly French.

After a full breakfast we are told that due to the weather conditions, our departure has been delayed until after lunch.

Children are playing outside the Junior School during their morning break. Lian has brought a bundle of plastic golf pencils, and passes them out to some excited kids. We get chatting to one of the teachers, who explains that her class is for children at only their second day at school. We are invited into the classroom, and the teacher, Carmen, explains to the children that we come from the other side of the world.

Carmen explains that most of the kids speak English at home, so she has to teach them to speak, read and write their Inuit language. The written language is fairly recent, and is based on the signs and lettering that USA linguists invented for some American Indian tribes. Carmen put both our names up on the blackboard in Inuit script, and the children had no problem reading it.

Camping on Tremblay Sound.

After lunch we hear our boat had been blown up into a stream somewhere, and we will have 2 boats, so we should be at the beach by 3pm. The Hotel bus took us down, but the trip was slow as we were held up a big aluminum boat that was being towed down the road by a Caterpillar tractor.

It was only later that we found this was to be our own boat, as it was backed into the water and floated off the trailer.

Charlie arrived on an ATV towing a small trailer with all the camping equipment and foodstuffs. This was loaded onto a slightly smaller and more open boat that Charlie was to skipper.

Our boat had an inflatable and we used this to ferry ourselves and our luggage on board.

It was nearly 4:15pm when the twin 150HP outboards opened up and we soon left Pond Inlet and set off after Charlie. Passed a few icebergs.

As well as ourselves and our leader, Keith, the group comprised: Bill—a marine biologist, Stacy—an administrator, Louise—worked for an airline, Karin—an anesthetist nurse, Eleanor—75years old and this was her 15th Arctic trip.

By 6:30pm we were about to enter the top end of Tremblay Sound, which is about 34 miles (55km) long x 2.1/2 miles (4km) wide.

We passed two hunters camps, and it was gone 7:30pm when we started to unload all our gear on a black sand beach adjacent to a stream that would supply our fresh water for the next five nights camping. The black slaty sand had a lot of big stones in it, and these proved useful to put in the corners of the tents to keep them from blowing away in the strong north wind.

Lian and I shared a 'Eureka' tent, and also put up a smaller one to store any unused items in. Needed some help from the Inuits (Narman, Charlie and 3 others) to show us how some of flexible rods fitted, and to put on the flysheet. Tied the guy ropes to big stones, as the fixing skewers just pulled out of the sand too easily.

By 9:45pm we were comfortable, and had installed our sleeping bags atop insulated sheets to keep the sleeping bags off the sand, and stowed our bags.

Time to help the others now.

Narman had set up the kitchen and dining tents, by combining 2 larger semi-circular tents that just gave me headroom in the center.

And by about 11pm, and Narman and his helper had served up some delicious salami sandwiches and noodle soup.

It was midnight when we crawled into our tent with its small outer porch, and zipped up the circular main entrance. It was still light enough to read, and we pushed the large stones into the 4 corners of the tent to reduce the flapping in the strong wind.

Lian had a down sleeping bag, and mine seemed to be based on a number of thick woolen blankets. The side zip did not work, so I simply pulled it over myself and lay in its envelope. I slept well.

At 7:30am, Lian called out that there were Narwhals in the Sound. I pulled my clothes on as soon as I could. Yes, there they were, passing close to the shore. The dorsal ridges were showing as the whales glided past us—mostly underwater, but their backs showing as they surfaced for air. Occasionally, one saw the mist from a small spout. The youngsters have grey or black backs, The older ones have a white background with grey blotches. I go back to get my video camera. Is that a tusk? It is hard to say. There are at least 100 coming past us in a number of pods.

We note that Charlie's boat is no longer with us. He has returned to Pond Inlet with one assistant.

The hunters come past fast in their small speedboat.

Further down the sound we can see quite a large group of tents, and are told that this is the Research Station.

So we are all excited and have plenty to talk about over our sausage and fried potato breakfast. Bill has a photo with his small camera showing a tusk just out of the water. Both Karen and Stacy have been popping away with their telephoto SLRs. At least we have now all seen the Narwhals.

At 11:30am we used the inflatable to get on our boat, and set off south to follow the Narwhals. The sun is shining, the water is calm, and the scenery magnificent with high hills and cliffs closing in on the Sound. But where are the Narwhals? Not a sign of them.

We stop off at a narrow beach of slaty black stone. As well as Narman, we have an Inuit, Daniel, with his rifle.

We walk along and I am surprised at the number of small ground hugging plants we see, as well as the multi-colored patterns on the pieces of rock caused by various lichens. Lots to photograph.

After reaching to southern end of the Sound without spotting any Narwhals, we headed north and passed our camp where we saw a few some way away, then returned to our base camp for some more watching from the beach.

We had been in our tent for a couple of hours, when we heard Nayman call out "Polar Bear across the river". Put our clothes on as fast as we could, and through our binoculars we could clearly see a polar bear and two cubs walking along the beach towards the Research Station. They are walking fast. One cub runs ahead to the waters edge, but soon joins back with the mother. Would the guards shoot at them? But before that could happen, all three walk into the water and start swimming across the Sound.

We then realize that we have an Inuit night-guard with another rifle to guard us during the 'night'. His name is also Daniel, so we refer to him as 'Night Daniel' and he spends the official day sleeping in his tent.

The wind is now much stronger, and we tighten up the guy ropes in an effort to reduce the flapping the tent is making.

We wake to find that an iceberg has been blown past us by the northern wind, and has grounded near the Research Station.

See Narwhals, but it is too rough to get good views. During the night Narman and a Daniel have had to move the boat into a more protected spot.

Later in the morning Narman took some of us on a walk towards a waterfall. This time we walked inland across the tundra. Often uneven and spongy, with many species of plant and lichen, it was fascinating. We passed passages or 'runs' used by the lemmings everywhere. Then spotted a number of pale pellets that had been regurgitated by the Snowy Owls, who cough up the bits of fur and bones they cannot digest. Tiny bones are clearly seen and are probably from the lemmings.

Then we hear the call of a raptor, and spot a pair of Gyrfalcons soaring and calling each other across the valley. A wide river is cascading through a narrow gap below us.

Narman starts kicking at and pulling up a small shrub with small parsnip type roots. This is 'i-ra'. We clean the dirt off the root and chew it. Then he spots a heart shaped and slightly succulent wild sorrel leaf. This is very tasty and we have a number as we make our way back to the camp, together with a few blueberries.

That night the wind was strong, and the tent flapped all night.

When Lian woke and trained her binoculars along the beach, she saw two pink blobs on the beach some way away. Were these kayaks, or Narwhals? She is told that the hunters had killed four Narwhal during the night, and they had left two on the beach.

She called me and sets off at a good pace. By the time I had myself dressed, she was a long way ahead, so I set off in the bright sunshine to catch her up. I was a little disturbed to see polar bear tracks on the beach sand, as well as those for arctic fox.

There were two Narwhals, and both had been skinned, and had the tail and fins cut off, and the internal organs cut out. Neither were males with tusks, but we had good views of the head, and eyes and mouth. Then Daniel arrived puffing, with rifle in hand. We apologized profusely for setting off without informing him.

The skin, or 'muctaaq', is a delicacy, and after breakfast some of us tried a 2 foot square that the hunters had given us. It is eaten raw and tastes very like raw squid.

That morning I was relieved to find my knitted woolly cap, which had gone AWOL on the night the polar bears came by, and had been hiding in the full sleeve of a fleece jacket. I had assumed that I had dropped it and it had been blown away by the strong winds into the stream and then the Sound.

Narman had put out feelers to the Research Station, and they had agreed to entertain us and brief us on what they were doing. Keith explained that on previous occasions other Research Stations had said they were too busy.

So we set off across the tundra for the camp. On the way found the ruins of an old Thule (early Inuit tribe) 'sod house.' A shallow pit is dug and a low stonewall is built around it. They then use the rib bones from a Bowhead Whale to form a domed roof that is covered with furs, and earth. The skull and vertebra of the Bowhead lies nearby.

Then we spot an Arctic Fox, still with his white coat on.

The senior man at the Research Station, Jack Orr, introduced some of his staff and explained some of the things they were doing. They have a vetinary dentist who is trying to find more about the tusk and its use as a sensory organ. A vetinary woman had been taking blood tests to check stress levels during the period of captivity. A senior man from the WWF is in attendance, and a photojournalist has been putting all on film.

The few Narwhals were caught in nets, and recorders have been attached to the dorsal area to record GPS positions, depths and times under water. These recorders will fall off after 400 days.

The work at this station was all but complete, and they would be flying out by Twin Otter on the same day as we were going to leave. They would take their tents and equipment, leaving only the wooden research laboratory, which would be left unlocked for the use of anyone who wanted it.

When asked, Jack Orr confirmed that their count for the day we had estimated 100, to be over 1,000 individuals.

He confirmed that the Narwhals eat mostly bottom dwelling flatfish such a halibut, as well as squid and cod. He did not think they ate the Arctic Char. Nayman smiled, as he had told us that they did, as they had found them in the stomachs of slaughtered animals.

The Narwhal can swim to 650 feet (200m) depth and stay underwater for up to 20 minutes.

As we left, the team offered us an Arctic Char, and Narman slung this over his shoulder in a plastic bag. This would be for dinner tonight.

We had some raw as sashimi, and the rest fried. Both were delicious ways of eating this 25lb salmon like fish.

That night a male polar bear came in front of our tent before 'night Daniel' managed to shoo it away.

Nayman then followed it down the beach, where it tucked into the dead Narwhals. I slept through the excitement.

By midday the wind had reduced enough for us to go out on the boat and up the sound for a few hours. A pleasant excursion, but no Narwhals spotted.

So what of the toilet facilities? Well, they set up a tent about the size of a British telephone box. Inside was a plastic pail, on top of which sat a plastic toilet seat. The ground was not particularly flat, and I had fears of being the one who managed to topple it all over. Once a day or so, the pail was emptied. So if it was only for a pee, then I usually walked over to the stream.

For our last dinner, Nayman did us proud with excellent succulent T-bone steaks. The meat must have been good, as Eleanor ate hers raw.

It was 10:45pm when the call "Polar Bear" reached my brain. By the time I got dressed the animal was in the water and swimming strongly. I went back for the video camera, but by then I could no longer see him until he emerged near the Narwhal carcasses.

Next morning, we were all just finishing our sausage and fried potato breakfast when again the call "Polar Bears" rang out. So binoculars and cameras were at the ready to see the mother bear and two cubs striding towards us from the direction of the Research Station. She obviously wanted to walk along the beach through our camp on the way for their breakfast at the remains of the two carcasses. But we were in the way. She sniffed us, and the cubs followed suit sitting on their haunches and peeping over the embankment, with black paws lifted up. One had a sore bottom and was rubbing it on the coarse ground. Perhaps it has worms? The mother decided to walk in a semicircle around us, but then thought better of it and returned to her starting point. Then doubts set in, and she decided that skirting round us was the best and sensible option. By this time my pulse was returning to normal, and I sat on the ground using my knees and elbows as a tripod to get some acceptable video of the mother and her two following cubs all the way as far as the carcasses. But it took a while for the adrenalin levels to subside.

It was now time to take down our tents and pack them, and do the same with our sleeping bags and underlays.

As Nayman would be returning in a few days with a client, he was leaving 'Night Daniel' with a couple of small tents and half of the dining / kitchen tent.

The rest was loaded on our boat, and by 12:30pm we were on our way back to Pond Inlet. Luckily the wind had dropped and the water was not rough.

Soon after leaving Tremblay Sound we pulled into a beautiful secluded bay by Cape Hatt where we had our packed lunch. Here we saw a flock of Snow Geese.

Pond Inlet.

We reached Pond Inlet safely by 5:45pm, and the bus took us back to our accommodation. As dinner was delayed to 7pm, we had a chance to enjoy a shower and myself a shave in beautiful hot water.

The dinner comprised thick slices of roast beef, and a lobster tail each.

That night we slept very soundly. We have a spare day today, and used it to revisit the school, the Visitors Center and Library, and the check out the other store. Then at dinner we heard that the afternoon plane did not arrive due to bad weather, and so there was no plane to fly out on the next day.

Those on this flight handed our passports and e-tickets to Keith, in an attempt to get on FirstAir, the other airline serving Pond Inlet.

So we were up and packed and ready to go to the airport by 7am. We then heard that the FirstAir flight had not landed yesterday, but overflew to Resolute, and would be unlikely to arrive before 10am.

So by 9am we were at the airport, and those who already had tickets checked in. We sat with our fingers crossed.

At the airport we saw the following on a hand written note in regards to our Canada North flight.:-

> August 23rd 2012
> Canadian North has
> Been Cancelled today
> Will Arrive Friday
> Around 5:40 No Mornings
> Flight.
> Re booked on Saturday
> THX

We then saw that our bags were being weighted, and at 10:45am the FirstAir turbo jet landed, and an hour later we took off with it. We were lucky that the people from the Research Station had still not arrived, so there were a few spare seats.

Due to the weather conditions, we overflew Clyde River, where 4 of the passengers had hoped to get off. Our flight was only as far as Iqaluit, where we would have to wait for the Ottawa flight, but by the time we arrived, our flight had left, so the airline agreed to give us a night's accommodation at the Frobisher Inn.

Iqaluit.

Although this would mean that we would be a day late reaching Ottawa, where our friends were due to pick us up, it did give us a chance to see Nunavat Province's capital. The first thing that struck us looking out over Frobisher Bay was the large number of small icebergs. Many bus-sized blocks were grounded on the shore of the bay as the receding tide had left them. Once again, the housing seemed to be prefabricated, but 2 or 3 storey high. We were able to contact our friends in Toronto before leaving the airport, so at least they knew what was happening.

We had plenty of time that afternoon and morning to look around the town and the main shops.

We noticed that here it actually got dark at night.

On the way to the airport we had mistakenly given the taxi driver a food voucher instead of the transport voucher. I can only hope that it was the more valuable of the two.

Three hours later the Canada North flight landed safely in Ottawa, and our arctic escapade was over.